The Comparative Analysis
of Human Societies

The Comparative Analysis of Human Societies

Toward Common Standards for Data Collection and Reporting

edited by
Emilio F. Moran

LYNNE
RIENNER
PUBLISHERS

BOULDER
LONDON

Published in the United States of America in 1995 by
Lynne Rienner Publishers, Inc.
1800 30th Street, Boulder, Colorado 80301

and in the United Kingdom by
Lynne Rienner Publishers, Inc.
3 Henrietta Street, Covent Garden, London WC2E 8LU

Library of Congress Cataloging-in-Publication Data
Moran, Emilio F.
    The comparative analysis of human societies : toward common
    standards for data collection and reporting / edited by Emilio F.
    Moran.
        p. cm.
    Includes bibliographical references and index.
    ISBN 1-55587-514-9 (alk. paper)
        1. Ethnology—Methodology. 2. Social sciences—Methodology.
3. Ethnology—Field work. 4. Social sciences—Field work.
I. Title.
GN345.M66 1994
300'.723—dc20   94-3601
                                                                              CIP

British Cataloguing in Publication Data
A Cataloguing in Publication record for this book
is available from the British Library.

Printed and bound in the United States of America

    The paper used in this publication meets the requirements
∞   of the American National Standard for Permanence of
    Paper for Printed Library Materials Z39.48-1984.

To my father, Emilio F. Moran, M.D.,
and my mother, Caridad C. Moran,
with love

Contents

Illustrations

Tables

Figures

Map

Preface

Ethnographic, geographic, and agricultural studies rarely present quantitative data in a form that allows one to compare data from a number of independent studies. For example, one study reports monthly temperature means, another reports annual means, and still another reports monthly or daily maximum and minimum temperatures. Is one of these types of data possibly more informative than the other? Studies reporting on soils in a certain area vary even more. Not only are there confusing differences in soil taxonomy among the U.S. Department of Agriculture; the Food and Agriculture Organization; and French, Brazilian, Belgian, and other systems, but the manner of reporting soil analyses also varies significantly. Is soil color important? Is soil texture more important than chemical composition?

Reports on social processes also vary significantly. Agricultural calendars, which were often used in reports before 1950 and gave a snapshot view of labor allocation on different tasks, have become a rarity. Studies on population may report density per square kilometer at national scale or state scale but not necessarily at the scale of the study. Some discuss data for young people using a 0–18 years age interval, others use a 0–15 interval, and still others 0–5, 6–10, and so on. The flood of studies of the past twenty years has made it more rather than less difficult to understand and compare fundamental social processes, such as the division of labor or the interaction between people and their physical environment, as a result of the lack of agreement on a core of research instruments (Guarnaccia et al. 1988).

Reporting on agricultural production, consumption, and distribution has often been idiosyncratic (Loker 1988; C&A 1986, 1988). Sometimes prices are reported in local currency, often unadjusted to rates of inflation and with unstated base years. Other times they are reported in U.S. dollars based upon an average exchange rate over the period of fieldwork (which may be two years or more). Yields may be reported in pounds, kilos, bushels, sacks, or some other local measure. Rarely are they consistently reported in the international metric standard (Système International d'Unités, or SI) of kilograms per hectare or in kilograms per man-day of labor. The reported data may or may not be discounted for consumption or rent. Yields may be averaged between rain-fed and irrigated areas, thereby confounding the relative role of these distinct areas of an agroecosystem and differences in tenure, male/female domains, crop yield variability, and other factors.

What units are most useful in explaining a system's structure and function? How does a particular study relate to other village studies in a given region or nation or within a given mode of production or ecosystem? Is there a way to discover regional patterns and processes and to locate specific community studies in those meso-levels of analysis?

It is the goal of this volume to work toward the development of such canons or standards for fieldwork data collection and, more important still, for data reporting. This exercise should not be taken as entirely new. All disciplines have at one time or another, explicitly or implicitly, followed "traditions" and "styles" of field research that provided guidance and a measure of standardization to research procedures. Bronislaw Malinowski's model of prolonged field stays relying heavily on participant observation came to be emulated and unintentionally contributed to the development of the ethnographic method. This was followed by later efforts to systematize the data observed through manuals such as *Notes and Queries on Anthropology* (RAI 1951) and the *Outline of Cultural Materials* (Murdock et al. 1971). As these standards grew dated and new interests developed in the various social sciences, a cacophony of ways of presenting the data has emerged, enriching the scope of social science but making it increasingly difficult to carry out comparative studies. In the past twenty years, no evident canon has risen to guide the fieldwork of the growing number of researchers. This lack of structure stands at present as a major obstacle to the development of social science theory and to the participation of the social sciences in the global analysis of human impact on the earth. It is now accepted by the global-change community (that is, social scientists, biological scientists, and physical scientists who study global environmental change) that studies by earth scientists must be informed by a sophisticated understanding of the human dimensions of major global changes (Miller 1994; Turner et al. 1994). Human populations have brought about many of these changes (deforestation, carbon release, and pollution, among others), and people may or may not respond to the evidence of such change. However, it has proven difficult for social scientists to give priority to the development of standards that can be universally applied in data collection to inform global and regional comparisons of human interactions with their physical environment.

The chapters in this book have been written in response to this need.

The authors propose standards of measurement and data to be reported. They do not claim the minima proposed to be the best data that can be collected today, or the most sophisticated—choosing such standards may put them beyond the reach of most field-workers. Rather, the authors aimed at those data and measures that would be most informative to colleagues in the various disciplines that study human (and particularly rural) populations and that would also meet the criteria of collectibility and relative worldwide accessibility. This is a difficult and challenging task, one that will not end with this book. Indeed, each author hopes that the book will initiate a process of rethinking among researchers about the standards and measures currently in use—and that researchers will discuss and improve on the ones suggested herein. As Sutti Ortiz reminded me once, "We have to be careful when designing methodologies that we not just pay attention to recording techniques, but also that we devise ways of standardizing the significance of the measurements" (personal communication, 1988). Such uniformity is increasingly important if data sets are to be publicly available and distributed. Global-change studies and funding sources, such as the National Science Foundation and the Social Science Research Council, urge researchers to deposit their data in archives for distribution. In what form should those data be presented? Data accessibility is becoming part of a researcher's accountability to those who fund studies. The need to arrive at some commonly agreed standards for data collection and distribution will increase, as well it should.

A first effort at addressing these issues took place in a symposium I organized for the 1988 meeting of the American Association for the Advancement of Science and in a symposium at the Ninth Congress of the International Union of Anthropological and Ethnological Sciences that same year. Several of the papers presented at those symposia did not address the issue of standardized minima, and those authors' participation in the project ended. Other authors were invited to prepare papers that would address the effort to develop standards and that would round off the coverage of major topics. This incremental process of constructing the volume added several years to the project. Although the chapters herein focus on measures relevant to agrarian and rural societies, most of the minima proposed would be equally relevant to the study of hunting-gathering, pastoral, fishing, and, with some modification, even urban societies. We have focused on data of a baseline nature that permits the characterization of the physical and social environment (climate, soils, crops, social organization, economy, health, nutrition, and demography).

The authors have circulated their chapters widely among colleagues in an effort to obtain reactions and critiques of the proposed standards. Our goal has been to propose standards that are feasible to the great majority of researchers on a worldwide basis. We hope these minima are parsimonious, easily collected and reported, and hierarchical—so that the minima fit broad questions of theoretical importance to the comparative study of societies and the study of the human impact on the physical environment.

I wish to thank Jan Smith, Debbie Templeton, and Martha Zuppann for their assistance in preparing the chapters for publication and ensuring consistency and completeness. I am grateful to Martha Peacock and others at Lynne Rienner Publishers for their support in making this subject available to the scholarly community. The authors thank Indiana University for a grant-in-aid that helped defray the costs of copying, illustrations, and the index.

I also wish to thank the authors. They quickly recognized the need for this volume when the idea was proposed to them, and they recognized that the standards would not please everyone. It will be hard for many readers to accept some of these minima—but no harder than it was for the authors to put aside their less-than-minimal list of topics that *they* would have liked to have seen listed as minima. They had the fortitude to recognize in most cases that personal research interests often intrude upon efforts at comparison. In the end, we tried to balance our specialized interests with our obligation to generate data that others can use and build on.

We hope this volume will be useful in training a new generation of social scientists and as a resource to colleagues in other disciplines. This is not a cookbook or primer; we hope it helps guide the tough choices that must be made in the field—and that it encourages social scientists to opt for those measures that can best lead to comparison and data sharing. We seek to promote a dialogue among the various disciplines that are concerned with human activities in a physical landscape. Will you join us in this effort?

Emilio F. Moran

References

C&A (Culture and Agriculture Bulletin), 1986. No. 29.
———, 1988. Special Methods Issue, no. 35.
Guarnaccia, P., P. Pelto, G. Pelto, L. Allen, L. Meneses, and A. Chavez, 1988. Measuring socio-economic status: Assessing intra-community diversity. *C&A* 35:1–8.
Loker, W., 1988. "Weight and measures" revisited: Methodological issues in the estimation of agricultural productivity. *C&A* 35:13–17.
Miller, R. B., 1994. Interactions and collaboration in global change across the social and natural sciences. *Ambio* 23:19–24.
Murdock, G. P., et al., 1971. *Outline of Cultural Materials.* 4th revised edition. New Haven: Human Relations Area Files.
RAI (Royal Anthropological Institute), 1951. *Notes and Queries on Anthropology.* 6th edition. London: Routledge and Kegan Paul.
Turner, B. L., W. Meyer, and D. Skole, 1994. Global land-use/land-cover change: Towards an integrated study. *Ambio* 23:91–97.

1

Introduction:
Norms for Ethnographic Reporting

EMILIO F. MORAN

Any effort at suggesting a set of standards—whether for language, sports, ecology, or anthropology—is likely to meet with the resistance of practitioners. Standards evoke images of rigidity, lack of creativity, and loss of individuality. Although we can live without standards, we also need them to ensure consistency in quality (for example, acceptable percentage of natural juice in fruit drinks), to ensure fairness in competition (weight categories in boxing, boat classes in racing), and to allow comparisons over time (consistent size in the playing field or in size or weight of the ball). Standards do not prevent innovation. Gifted individuals have challenged the canons of the most rigid literary academies—and won. In sports, as in music or science, standards exist—and they are changed over time. In fact, it can be argued that standards *promote* change by setting up a clear canon against which to match the gifts of individuals, who are challenged to best the current standard.

A standard is a measure, or set of measures and procedures, that practitioners of a given art, language, sport, or scientific discipline agree to follow to facilitate communication, competition, or comparison. Without a willingness to abide by those standards, there is no capacity to effectively share results or means by which to be judged fairly; there is no "evenness in the playing field." Judgments of quality are intrinsic to human affairs. Human beings always use their experience, and values, to make such judgments.[1] Standards, when they are put into place and followed, bring some order to "unmapped territory"—that is, situations otherwise lacking in agreed-upon referents. Classical ballet, for example, has its obligatory leaps and pirouettes (Royce 1977) that establish competency—but that perform-

1

ers routinely exceed both physically and emotionally in order to be judged brilliant or superb. The obligatory movements, though not the best moments in a ballet, tell us what to expect: a pedestrian performance, or one that promises to excite.

Standards in Anthropology

Anthropology has had both implicit and explicit standards in the past.[2] The monumentally thorough ethnographic practice of Bronislaw Malinowski served as a normative model—another term for a "standard"—that aspiring anthropologists tried to emulate, down to the categories or chapters into which an ethnographic report fell. Not everyone abided by this implicit model, but most practitioners tried to and in so doing contributed to the development of a science of humankind. If there had been no imitation of Malinowski's model of ethnographic writing and research, it is doubtful that anthropology could have contributed the ethnographic method of participant-observation to the repertoire of the human sciences. This procedure has been, in the opinion of most, anthropology's most lasting and important methodological contribution to date (cf. Ellen 1984; Kuper 1983). Educators, demographers, sociologists, agricultural economists, and urban planners today do ethnographic studies to gain the kind of "insiders' view" that has been associated with Malinowski and anthropology for almost a century. Has this been one of the rare cases where canons of ethnographic practice were followed?

A more explicit effort at developing a "canon" is represented by the field manual known as *Notes and Queries on Anthropology* (Royal Anthropological Institute [RAI] 1874, 1892, 1899, 1912, 1929, 1951). It was written to assist British social anthropologists in the field.[3] This fine little book, often derided or ignored today in European and U.S. academic departments, provided thoughtful reminders of things to ask—some obvious,[4] others counterintuitive and profound. Such is the nature of a primer or field manual. After all, there is very little that can be said unambiguously to be common sense. Things become common sense when they are shared by a community that has encoded in everyday language and behavior a given set of standards. Much of the standard of Malinowski became implicit in the socialization of that small community of British practitioners. It is with diversity in language and practice that we begin to feel the need for explicit canons to ensure evenness and fair assessment of quality.

Notes and Queries in Anthropology advised social anthropologists to distinguish clearly between observation and interpretation. It recognized that theory and working hypotheses guided fieldwork and influenced observation, wisely noting that "the observer who wishes to give a theoretical construction to his material should consider this separately *after* recording the facts" (1951:27). This manual noted the need to be scientifically trained in observation and the danger of overlooking the familiar or judging some kinds of data as unworthy of being recorded (see beginning of Chapter 4, this volume): "It is in order to overcome these obstacles that the notes and questions in this volume have been framed, as well as to indicate lines of inquiry worthy of investigation and the method of obtaining and recording relevant facts" (1951:27–28). *Notes and Queries* also advised that "no sociological study of a community can be undertaken without an understanding of the natural environment within which it exists. . . . The investigator should make himself familiar, therefore, with the geographical, geological and meteorological features of the district . . . some knowledge of the flora and fauna . . . demography . . . technology . . . economic life . . . and material culture . . . must seek information from those who are [competent on all these subjects]" (1951:35).

This volume has a different objective from that of *Notes and Queries:* to help readers reflect on alternatives to data collection and reporting so that research is more productive and comparable. Contributors to this book still believe in the possibility of objective, verifiable, replicable social science, unlike many contemporary cultural anthropologists. The range of comparison is left to the investigator. It can be comparison of systems of agrarian production across the world or the more workable comparison of farming systems within a given region. The latter have proven most satisfying over the years, as it is possible to know the historical context of communities within a region better than across regions, in which cases the role of historical contingency must perforce be reduced (Kuper 1983: 200).

By the time *Notes and Queries* began to be prepared for its sixth edition, in 1936,[5] another effort was taking place on this side of the Atlantic. *The Outline of Cultural Materials*[6] was designed for the organization of "available information on a large and representative sample of known cultures with the object of testing cross-cultural generalizations" (Murdock et al. 1945: v). It also sought by this method to discover deficiencies in the literature and direct corrective fieldwork. Its origins go back to the efforts of G. P. Murdock and the Human Relations Area Files project to code ethnographic information to facilitate searches and quantitative cross-cultural or holocultural studies (Lagace 1974; Narroll and Narroll 1976). In practice, the *Outline* was used in two ways—by cross-cultural analysts to arrive at theoretical generalizations and by others as a list of topics of potential ethnographic importance while in the field—and modified as needed to conform with one's ethnographic situation. Most of us who were put into contact with the *Outline* found it curious and somewhat archaic—but almost inevitably we used it in the field and appreciated it for reminding us of certain things to ask that were tangential to our focused topic. It made available to others information that otherwise would have never been recorded and reported. Unfortunately, all too often the information collected was not reported in publications and ended up lost along with the researchers' raw data. Does it matter if we do not tell readers what the rainfall is in the area we studied? If we are engaged in the development of a science of humankind and want to be part of a community of scholars who share data, it is of great importance that we collect "baseline data" that establishes the biophysical characteristics within which people exist.

Standards come and go, but the challenge of teamwork and comparison of data has tended to galvanize the demand for and implementation of standards. The challenge of the International Biological Program (1964–1974) to study human adaptation across the world using common data measures led to the creation of a section concerned with human adaptability. This section, made up of physical anthropologists to a large extent, found it necessary to agree on a set of measurement standards (Weiner and Lourie 1969). Their work proved to be a major step in standardizing methods of data collection in physical anthropology and facilitated dialogue with human biologists in other disciplines. The results of this international effort were substantial (e.g., Baker and Little 1976; Jamison et al. 1978; Baker 1978, among others) and enhanced sharing of data not only among biological anthropologists but also with scientists in many other fields. Some of the standards have been improved on since that time, whereas others have stood (Frisancho 1990). Efforts in the early 1960s to include cultural anthropology in this international effort failed because of the apparent unwillingness or unreadiness of cultural anthropologists to select and follow clear and unambiguous data-collection procedures. The entire effort to understand the "ecology of mankind" was weakened by the absence of this important information (Worthington 1975). Anthropologists working in other disciplines on a daily basis experience regular pressure to abide by predictable canons of data collection and reporting (e.g., van Willigen and Finan 1991; Epstein 1988), resulting in several such efforts at application-specific standards.

It is striking that despite the return of a post-Boasian historical approach to anthropology (e.g., Wolf 1982; Smith 1984; Mintz 1985, among others), so little has been done to ensure the comparability of time-dependent data. Though quantitative and social historians have increasingly adopted the more rigorous canons of the social sciences, much of contemporary historical analysis in anthropology seems to follow a humanities model of history—idiosyncratic and literary rather than analytical and deductive.[7] Moreover, agreement on data sets facilitates collaboration on research, permitting an efficient and effective division of labor among collaborating colleagues. As early as 1967, Epstein noted that "as anthropological analysis becomes more refined, it becomes increasingly important that students in the field should at least be aware of the need to collect certain basic kinds of data and know how to set about this" (vii). In this regard, this volume follows in the steps of that earlier effort, aimed at giving guidance rather than producing a "cookbook." However, it relies less than Epstein's did on a set of colleagues from a particular "school"—a "roll-call of the Manchester school," as Kuper has suggested (1983:129). This volume's contributors hope to suggest fruitful ways of making choices among alternatives.

Comparative research is important to anthropology, as to any field of science, because of its potential contribution to the development of robust theory. Much anthropological research and "theorizing" has fallen victim to myopia.[8] All too often, investigators have constructed theory based on a single case or upon a set of noncomparable cases and claimed broad significance for such "theory." The very fact of human biological, linguistic, social, and cultural variation makes comparative studies necessary, though no less difficult, to the development of theory. Reluctance to produce broadly useful and reproducible data sets gradually marginalizes anthropologists from social science and scientific discourse, ensuring the impoverishment of the discipline both academically and in its policy significance.

To advance our current state of knowledge and to enhance our capacity to participate in joint scientific research with colleagues in other disciplines, we must make some progress in defining fundamental variables, agreeing upon the form in which they should be collected and reported, and deciding how to share such data with other researchers. There is a growing movement across disciplines to share data. To do so, such data must be in standard formats and must be integrable in normative models based on accumulated and testable knowledge across disciplines. Though anthropology often highlights what is unique in a culture, not everything in it is idiosyncratic and noncomparable. As Edgerton (1970) noted, East African pastoralists were more alike across ethnic groups than were pastoral and agricultural members within a single ethnic group. This conclusion was defensible only because Edgerton and his colleagues applied standardized research procedures from ecology, economics, psychology, and other disciplines to a carefully sampled cross-section of the four ethnic groups.

The tradition of the lone researcher needs to be balanced with a greater acceptance of team research—just as the twelve- to eighteen-month-field-stay "standard" may not always be *the* appropriate time frame for research. There are various ways to organize field research from an operational standpoint. The classic method of prolonged field residence with heavy emphasis on participation and observation is most effective when applied to small, relatively homogenous populations whose system of meanings is widely shared and who have relatively low degrees of economic differentiation. How many communities like that can we find today? Key informant interviewing, for all its merits of providing in-depth knowledge, cannot make claims to representativeness or account for intracultural variation (van Willigen and Finan 1991:2). To deal with most communities today, it is necessary to address internal variation by means of survey research and standardized schedules or questionnaires. This method permits the results, if the sample was appropriately drawn, to be offered with a certain level of confidence as representative of internal variation. For surveys to be useful, they must be carefully designed to meet objectives, follow standard procedures and scales to ensure comparability, and distinguish between fundamental variables and exploratory ones.

When time is severely constrained (as it often is in development consulting) or is exploratory in nature, neither participant-observation nor survey research may be the method of choice. For time-constrained studies, interactive methods such as focus groups (Merton 1989) and rapid appraisal procedures (Hildebrand 1981) may be more appropriate. They more effectively get at local idiom and at general patterns of variation than unsystematic surveys or key informant interviewing in a six-week time frame (a common length for predissertation field visits and development consulting). Increasingly mentioned in the literature is the development of projects in which the research subjects become partners in the research process (McCracken et al. 1988; van Willigen and Finan 1991:8).

This book is firmly within the canons of social science—to which a number of contemporary anthropologists do not seem to want to belong.[9] It assumes that claims to knowledge must be ultimately testable and that explanations are tested in due time through comparison (see also Hunt, Chapter 9, this volume). The rapid growth of the discipline of anthropology in the late 1960s and early 1970s brought about a cacophony of standards and measures from a variety of sources.[10] This proliferation was not necessarily all bad, as it was a part of the effort to question standards and set new priorities. Many productive approaches emerged from this period that constituted advances in measurement. Unfortunately, since that era passed there has been no comparable effort to return to agreed-upon standards for ethnographic research and reporting. Is it because we do not need them? Anyone systematically reading a large number of studies would conclude that ethnographic information, even among well-intended social science–oriented practitioners, is not often reported in formats that make comparison of findings easy or likely. The subjects of study allow unbridled relativity. The perception of culture as a "text" to be interpreted denies the possibility of comparability and measurement. The idiosyncratic reigns supreme—and though this must surely please those who deny that anthropology is a social science, it should give pause to those who aspire to a dialogue with other social and natural sciences. Noncomparable data is the surest way to guarantee irrelevancy and loss of theoretical significance.

In the rest of this book, the authors propose sets of standards for anthropologists and other social scientists working on agrarian, agropastoral, and hunter-gatherer societies. Many components may also apply to urban groups and other ethnographic settings. Although changes and refinements in these settings may be required, the selection of topics is not complete. Priority is given to behavioral data over cultural data; readers will not find minimum levels proposed for the latter. By its very nature, culture is idiosyncratic, or, as is commonly stated today, "constructed." The authors in this volume do not examine meanings and symbols, nor is our work interpretation. Because each person constructs his or her own conception of culture, such a variable, though useful in exploring what it means to be human, is not amenable to comparative analysis—one of the goals of anthropology and one toward which we hope to contribute. Behavior, though no less structured and no less a product of people's experience than culture, has the advantage of being observable, measurable, and comparable across populations (see also Hunt, Chapter 9).

The authors do not claim that all the data they discuss need to be collected by everyone without regard for orientation. In this sense, this book differs in scope from earlier field manuals such as *Notes and Queries* or the *Outline of Cultural Materials*. The authors hope to engage the reader in a thoughtful dialogue about data collection. In this dialogue, they explore different *levels of intensity* of data collection. They hope to provide some useful resources and ideas about how to think through the choices made in the field and about what to include or exclude in a written report. Most readers will be interested in things other than the whole agrarian system; for them, the first level of intensity constitutes what we might call a *minimum data set* for an ethnographic report. This minimum data constitutes a baseline for understanding fundamental questions that keep appearing in the social sciences and to which we ultimately contribute (as discussed in Chapter 9). They also serve to locate geographically, environmentally, socially, demographically, and economically the people who are the subjects of study. To be widely useful, the data need to be standardized. This is our obligatory bow or pirouette to our colleagues in the social sciences who will be grateful for our thoughtfulness.[11] To gain their admiration, however, we will need to go much further analytically and theoretically than these minima, probing deeper into those variables most relevant to the basic objectives of the study. The authors in this volume propose other levels of data collection beyond the minima but also try to abide by the most useful standards available in the social, physical, and biological sciences.

Purpose and Scale

Before setting out to discuss what data are (or should be) minimal or standard, it is important to relate data issues to the purpose for which the study is being conducted and to the scale appropriate to that objective. These two dimensions, purpose and scale, are closely interrelated, and discussion of one inevitably will have the other as contingent.

For studies that are broadly ethnographic in purpose and village-scaled, the proposed minimum data are likely to be the appropriate level of intensity. Only in some variables (for example, social organization) would a broadly defined study need to go into greater data intensification. It is more appropriate here to take advantage of the luxury of time and resources to engage in prolonged participation and observation and in-depth inter-viewing. This is the kind of study that yields detailed kinship analyses, intricate linkages between symbolic systems and practice, and precise microecological adjustments between people and local resources. Surveys and censuses are not uncommonly done; the second level of intensity pro-vides suggestions for what to include in such household-level surveys to enhance data comparability.

More typical are studies focusing on a specific problem—e.g., pas-toral adjustment to drought, adaptive responses to population growth, and shifts in household structure with declining supplies of labor. For these kinds of studies, investigators may wish to go to the second or even third level of data intensification when the variables proposed are central to the problem under study. Three of the most often neglected variables in classic anthropological writings and in contemporary training are demography, health, and nutrition. They have been included in this volume as substantial chapters not only because of their fundamental importance but also because of their past neglect. Ideally, the detail of these chapters will be taken not simply as a representation of their relative importance but rather as a resource to help readers understand how to integrate these variables into traditional approaches and strengths.[12] Further, these are variables that per-mit our findings to articulate with the work of social scientists, nutrition-ists, epidemiologists, and others who contribute to these areas of knowl-edge.

The problem-specific study can be executed at a number of scales, from the village level to the cross-national level. The larger the scale, the more reliant the investigator becomes on existing data sets. Several of the chapters in this volume address the kinds of caveats that use of such aggre-gate data require. All too often, anthropologists' awareness of the problems present in regional and national data lead them uncritically to dismiss their usefulness. Particularly in exploratory and time-limited research, these data offer a "window" into variables that may be worthy of attention and that may be overlooked unless we get familiar with these large-scale data sets. Climatic data, as per the minimum data set proposed by Wilken in Chapter 2, relies on the collection of rainfall and temperature figures over at least twenty years. Even if collected imperfectly or with a limited number of col-lection stations, such long-term data may be more precise than one-year rainfall and temperature data collected in one village at one collecting point (often near the investigator's home) to predict trends over time. Depending on the range of variability present from place to place and from year to year, one-place-one-year data may be either useful or worthless. It is an excellent source as a complement to longitudinal data but not as a reliable measure of climate (an inherently statistical phenomenon).

A third category, one we have alluded to before and that is of growing significance, comprises studies concerned with development assistance, target population analysis, and social impact analysis. Commonly, such studies are of extremely limited time duration and aim to recommend certain kinds of interventions—whether to increase yields or how to increase income, reduce parasitism in humans or domestic animals, or decrease infant mortality. This kind of study is rarely village-level but is more commonly regional, sometimes even national in scale. It may focus not on all people in a region but on groups within the total population—the poorest of the poor, farmers without access to irrigation land, or women-headed households. Under these circumstances, the approach will surely not be that of participant-observation or key informant interviewing, although these may be used as complements to more systematic procedures. Such studies should rely on available statistics, informal group interviews (Rhoades 1985), focus-group interaction (Merton 1989), or "culturally adapted market research" (Epstein 1988). It is remarkable that, in a discipline that prides itself on always putting people first (Cernea 1988), anthropologists have been so slow in formalizing methods for training local people to generate their own data by making them partners in the research effort. The advantages of such a procedure become quickly obvious— people not only increase their capacity to control valuable information and use it for their own purposes but also increase both sample size and confidence in the responses when they understand the value of such research. Though it may not work in all cases, such participation has greater possibilities than most investigators have been willing to admit. The minimum data level is appropriate here; further data intensification may be appropriate depending on basic purpose and scale or investigator or local community needs.

In a recent publication, Epstein (1988) set out a list of "key cultural variables" that refer largely to social variables, most of which can be found within our minimum data set across the various chapters. As in time-limited research or comparable research, Epstein's key variables address basic considerations in human behavior, such as the culturally relevant unit of decisionmaking, how status is allocated, the structure of kinship, patterns of residence, rights to tenure in land, and dominant gender relationships. Unlike the minimum data proposed here, which have both academic and applied research in mind, Epstein's key variables are fine-tuned for development assistance using the insights of market-research and anthropology. The standards proposed herein are consistent with the key variables proposed by Epstein but are more comprehensive in that they include such factors as climate, soils, crops, health, and nutrition, which are not included in Epstein's set. However, they may be less detailed on social variables than Epstein's, given that the objective is a minimal standard rather than comprehensive treatment of variables relevant to development studies per se.

Unlike the "rapid and reliable research methods for practicing anthropologists" proposed by van Willigen and Finan (1991), the standards offered here conceive of research as taking place along a continuum from time-constrained to prolonged field stays, from broadly ethnographic to highly specific and purposive research, from village-level to cross-national studies. Whatever the purpose, scale, or time availability, the standards proposed herein are graded from low intensity (minimum data sets) to medium intensity (second level of data collection) as a function of the above variables. The baseline is the minimum data set, viewed as a professional obligation to make basic information available to others. These data have been chosen for their broad availability, basic usefulness to comparison and theory, and potential to be combined with other data to generate indices of analytical value. The authors had to make some hard choices in making these recommendations, and they were not always happy to have to make such decisions. Readers may not be happy, either. Following standards is tough, and trying to get down to minima is even harder. Hopefully, readers will take them as a "first approximation," a step toward the emergence in the not-distant future of better standards. At this stage we can only hope they serve to initiate a constructive dialogue among researchers over the value and/or level of difficulty in collecting these data. It is wise to remember that any single data set may be easier to collect in one location than another and that any single minimum data set need not be central to a particular investigation. As Hunt makes clear in Chapter 9, there are an infinite number of questions to ask, but some have been of persistent significance in the analysis of human societies. We hope these minimum data get at fundamental variables in human behavior and propose levels of data collection to be implemented as appropriate. We leave it to others to fill in the outline we have provided and to propose improved standards for the comparative study of agrarian and other social systems.

The Minimum Data Set

The length of this volume might discourage some with the thought that what is proposed herein is hardly minimal. There is, fortunately, considerable overlap in the measures proposed by various authors, so that their collection does in fact serve multiple analytical purposes. Some of the minimum data are qualitative in nature and obtainable by simple observation or informal interviews; others can be derived from quantitative national aggregate data or a quick village census. This difference is not surprising given the disparity between, say, variables such as climate and diet. Whereas climate is a statistical expression of weather potential over time, diet is a product of food habits, agricultural productivity, local distribution systems, and access to tradable foods in particular populations. Aggregate diet statistics serve little purpose other than to justify food aid. Even then, a particular local measurement such as weight-for-age (to establish the percentage of children with acute malnutrition) may be a better measure than total caloric deficit, which fails to identify at-risk individuals.

We begin our data sets with climate. Climate is one of the most determinant variables in hunter-gatherer and agropastoral systems. Farmers and hunters devote considerable effort and cultural attention to mollifying its effects on plants and animals through various degrees of intervention (e.g., crop varietal selection, irrigation, fertilization, wind rows, and mobility). Though farmers cannot change climate, they can modify the microclimate at the level of the plant or animal, thereby reducing the impact of drought, wind, sheet erosion, and frost. As with all other variables that will be discussed, there is an infinite variety of climatic data that could be collected, but only some are available on a worldwide basis.

The tendency in most studies has been to cite total annual rainfall and average annual temperature, two widely available and often reported statistics. These constituted an earlier implicit standard, before we understood as clearly as we do now that annual averages make it difficult to assess agricultural potential and the impact of temperature and rainfall on crop development and seasonality. Annualized data swamps variability—which, we have come to appreciate, can be quite high. Wilken proposes in this volume a new standard that is not much more onerous to obtain but is more useful than the earlier one. He proposes collecting and reporting daily maximum and minimum temperature and daily precipitation based on a twenty-year cycle.[13] These two minima can be combined and aggregated to produce useful indices such as potential evapotranspiration, drought probabilities, heating degree days, continuous days of rain, number of continuous rainless days, monthly rainfall, seasonal patterns of precipitation, and, of course, the old standard of annual temperature and precipitation. What these new minima do is enhance our analytical capabilities and link the data to all sorts of processes relevant to crop and animal growth—and the strategies humans use to address these climatic contingencies. The value of this more disaggregated data is to increase substantially our ability to understand farmer decisions—which presumably is one of the things we are trying to understand in agrarian studies. This data is no more time consuming to obtain than the annual means: If one exists, so does the other. However, anthropologists may have to specifically request the new minima because statistical offices assume that nonclimatologists only want to know the annualized data. Even purely ethnographic studies may be (or should be) concerned with drought or frost probabilities—an impossible task without the daily data.

These minima, as well as others in this volume, could change in ten to twenty years. Considerable advances are promised in the not-distant future that may permit the use of satellite imagery and georeferenced information systems to estimate climate's influence on biomass, net primary production, rates of secondary growth, leaf moisture indices, yields, and other consequences of climate. If this occurs, many new possibilities will come up. However, the minima proposed will continue to be useful whether these advances occur or not—and are more likely to be broadly useful than more precise but technically demanding information.

It is difficult to evaluate any agrarian system without recognizing the difference that variation in available soils and crops makes in the returns farmers can get from their fields. These data are not always reported by social scientists, who seem to believe they are purely agronomic variables. However, if we take the time to talk to farmers about their soils and crops, we quickly discover that every farmer is a folk agronomist capable of making remarkable associations between soils and plants. They can predict crop response under variable conditions, and in some cases they can build up soil fertility on otherwise poor soils (e.g., by using green manures, mulching, and applying village garbage). Soils data should be available from local, regional, or national agriculture departments or extension services. Given the difference that scale can make, this information should be sought, preferably for the village or region of interest to the study. Given that soil classification taxonomies vary a great deal from country to country, it is useful to report "typical" soil analyses for each major soil type present to permit assessment of chemical and textural characteristics. In Chapter 3, Nicholaides and Moran also propose the use of the Fertility Capability Classification (FCC) as a useful shorthand to bring out the most limiting factors in the "plow layer" (0–20 cm surface layer), which is the effective rooting area of most crops. Reporting soil taxonomies may be less useful, as most classification schemes ignore the plow layer and concentrate on the subsurface layer. Of particular importance are pH, nitrogen, phosphorus, potassium, cation exchange capacity, organic matter, calcium, magnesium, and carbon. Soil maps are widely available, and reproducing these on a report makes the data readily usable as long as the scale of the map is reported. A world soil map at 1:1,000,000 scale is in preparation and constitutes an improvement over the 1:5,000,000 scale of the current Food and Agriculture Organization map.

Crops are another matter. It is very easy to lapse from minimal to complete data on crops. As Netting et al. and Hunt point out in Chapters 4 and 9, respectively, minima should include a list of crops planted, with indication of both local and scientific name. This is not a difficult requirement; a conversation with a knowledgeable agronomist can ensure that local terms are scientifically precise. To list crops unaided is to invite error unless one's training includes considerable botany. In getting the list of crops, it is helpful to discuss informally what is planted when, permitting the production of an agricultural calendar, which is also a minima under social organization of labor. Asking what is planted when and by whom further permits collection of minima about the relation of gender, age-grade labor responsibilities, economic stratification, and food habits to the agricultural system. Further asking what crops are planted where allows exploration of tenure arrangement, sexual division of labor, use of irrigation or terracing, crop use after harvest, and land fragmentation.

The list of crops should also differentiate between crops planted and consumed, on the one hand, and those strictly or largely sold, on the other. Moreover, it should distinguish between staples and supplementary foods and give an assessment or estimate of yields (per man-hour or man-day and per unit of land). These are useful not only as economic minima but also as nutritional minima. Data should be reported in metric (Système International d'Unités, or SI) equivalents as well as in local measures. These must be explicit in the report to ensure equivalencies and avoid errors arising, say, because of differences between British and U.S. pints, gallons, and bushels (as Hunt points out in Chapter 9). Using metric standards avoids these sorts of errors in the use of colleagues' data.

This is no trivial matter, and its pursuit could yield interesting findings. For example, the system of weights and measures used in Bolivia has three layers.[14] At the core is the indigenous system, still the most important. Mixed with this is the traditional Iberian system of weights and measures imposed by the Spanish; finally, there is the metric system. The indigenous system is not uniform; it varies by ethnic group, each occupying distinct agricultural and ecological niches. Trans-Andean trade led to the emergence of some widely shared measures, such as the *costal,* a volume measure. As a general rule, the volume of the costal varies with altitude, which reflects the ability of the beast of burden to carry a given unit of weight, or *carga.* Local people distrust the metric system because they fear that intermediaries rig the scales against the seller. Intermediaries in fact exploit both producers and consumers by manipulating the meaning of "standard measures": In the countryside the intermediary may buy a carga weighing the local standard of 250 pounds, whereas in the city they can sell a carga that has a standard weight of 216 pounds. Thus, they could make a profit even if there were no difference in price paid—which, of course, there is. The weight of a standard volume may vary by season and by the quality of the harvest that year. Commerce is rarely a cut-and-dried affair, and thus it is preferable to report harvest weights. A given weight must be understood as a function of complex negotiations and understandings between buyers and sellers. Lack of attention to these differences impoverishes a report and makes comparison impossible without provision for equivalencies.

In Chapter 4, Netting, Stone, and Stone make the task of studying the social organization of labor and agrarian production clear, if not simple. The three levels of intensity of data collection are most clearly explicated in this chapter. They note that the minima are names for things (the ethnoecology, if you will) and the list of activities in space and time (as noted earlier in discussing crop minima). Basically, it is a matter of reporting who does what, when, and how. It is remarkable that this requirement needs to be explicitly stated, but ethnographic reports often fail to take note of these baseline (if mundane) aspects of agrarian life.[15] It is worthwhile to note local people's perception of the constraints they face. They are far more keenly aware of what most limits their achievement of production goals (i.e., land, labor, pests, soil fertility, slope, or exploitation by others) than is any visiting scientist. This information alerts readers to particular variables that may be worth pursuing or may help interpret the behaviors reported elsewhere.

After being produced, goods are either consumed or traded.[16] The minima for understanding the distribution of what is produced is to report what is distributed by whom, and when and where it is distributed. How is it organized? Are trade and distribution largely local/regional processes, or are local producers linked to external national and international markets? On the consumption side, reports should minimally take note of what is eaten (again, local and scientific names), whether it is a staple food or a supplementary food, how it is obtained and prepared by households, when in the year it is available, and by whom it is consumed. It is basic to annotate differences in the age/sex distribution of food consumed should important differences be present. Informal interviews are probably the best way of getting at this data.

Perhaps no information is more basic than demographic data, yet probably no other kind is so often overlooked or improperly reported. As Hern notes, we must begin by reporting the *total* population. As Netting et al., Dufour and Teufel, and others in this volume point out, a population must be reported in relation to some explicit territory that encompasses it. Without this information, it is impossible to calculate (in persons per square kilometer) demographic density, density per unit of agricultural land, density per unit of irrigated land, and other basic indices relevant to the analysis of agrarian systems. Demographic data is best acquired via a household census in small villages and from statistical offices in larger, more dispersed settlements.[17] Whether taken from local census or aggregate statistics, the minima should include not only total population but also its age and sex distribution in the standard five-year intervals.[18] Without standard intervals it is not possible to construct age-sex pyramids—one of the most useful data sets that can be reported in any study. The number of deaths and births in the past year is rarely reported and is recommended here as minima, as is the recording of who came and left the population in the past year.[19]

With this information, one can generate a number of important indices, including age-sex distribution, dependency ratios, infant mortality rate, crude birth rate, crude death rate, and rate of natural increase. In Chapter 8, these minima are confirmed by Fleming-Moran as being equally important in constructing indices of the health of a population. The percentage of newborns under 2,500 grams born per year is a particularly good proxy in assessing the health of both mother and child and is at least as informative as infant mortality rate. Other useful health minima are total days lost from work due to illness in the past two weeks and leading causes of death for infants (0–4 years old), children (5–15 years old), adults (16–44 years old) and seniors (45+ years old).

Finally, Hunt notes some very basic minima that all too often are overlooked: the latitude, longitude, and altitude of the study site(s); the availability of basic infrastructure such as roads, drainage canals, bridges, terraces; the level of technology that is commonly found (such as animal traction, mechanical traction, dibble-stick, pesticides, herbicides, fertilizers); and the general characteristics of the year in which the field data were collected (was it wetter than average? drier? or just average? were crops affected to the normal extent by pests, or more severely?). This may seem like quite a list, but in fact most ethnographic reports provide at least this much "general information." However, it is often chosen without explicit objectives. The minima proposed here offer broadly useful data that relate to major questions in the social sciences, that can generate other data and indices commonly used in analysis, and that argue for standardization of units to enhance data sharing and comparison.

Going Beyond the Minima

All the chapters in this volume go beyond the minima to more intensive levels of data gathering. These levels of intensity of data collection are hierarchically nested in each other, permitting relational approaches to the database and letting each author use his or her best judgment on the most fundamental data to collect for each data set.

Wilken notes that greater precision in the assessment of climate can be obtained from having data on insolation differences across the year, which permit a better assessment of evaporation rates and seasonal drought stress or wilting. Most of the additional data Wilken recommends are actually consistent with that suggested by Netting et al. and Nicholaides and Moran: socioeconomic and ethnoecological figures about management strategies of farmers to deal with existing local climatic constraints.

Soils data beyond the minima could focus on changes in pH, macronutrients, cation exchange capacity (CEC), and organic matter under different management regimes and crops. Of particular interest today is how populations manage organic residues to achieve sustainable yields. Attention and observation of these folk approaches to mulching and recycling will become increasingly important and ensure that one's work will be used rather than ignored. Beyond the minima, crop varieties and their characteristics can be discussed in terms of how well they resist drought, pests, and other problems and what their yields seem to be. Is yield important to the population? Is plant protection and reduction of risk important to them? Why?

Going beyond the ethnoecology of production and labor organization, Netting et al. suggest a gradual intensification beginning with household surveys to examine intrahousehold labor dynamics and gather detailed data on demography, health, exchange, and nutrition—thereby fulfilling many objectives simultaneously and efficiently. Demographically, at this higher level of intensity the focus ought to be on maternal and child health, especially mortality and fertility rates. Beyond the economic data in household surveys, a third level of intensity would have us explore the dynamics of marketplaces, which play such an important role in either encouraging or dampening producers' incentive, and use twenty-four-hour-recall surveys and diaries of food consumed to quantitatively establish dietary intake. Less intensive may be the anthropometric measurement of children, with special attention to age, sex, height, and weight. These can be used to establish their growth and development rates compared to "standard" populations. Such comparisons help determine whether the population experiences chronic or acute malnutrition, whether children of different ages are at different degrees of risk, and whether they catch up by the time they become adolescents and enter the reproducing population.

Conclusion

In this brief introduction I have not done justice to the complex and detailed chapters that follow. I have tried to tantalize the reader to go to the particular chapters and to engage each author in a dialogue on method. As

Kuper has reminded us, "advances in anthropology actually occur through the development of new observational techniques, the refinement of models, the definition of new foci and above all by the continual interplay of new studies and old studies; that is, by comparison" (1983:204). There is plenty of room in these tasks for creativity and imagination—without the need to revert to fiction. If our colleagues are provoked to question their ethnographic writing and data collection and are moved to come up with better (and still broadly applicable) standards, our task will have been successful. Each author has found this exercise difficult as well as thought provoking. Not one of them has felt that his or her ethnographic practice has lived up to the standards proposed herein. This is as it should be. If we are to strive in earnest for greater reliability, our studies will need to have more comparable data, and we will have to encourage, rather than discourage, restudies of previously researched communities. Our goal in this volume has been to start the process of discussion on standards for data collection and reporting so that data sharing and comparison may become more possible in the future than it is now.

Notes

The author thanks Robert Netting, Robert Hunt, and Sutti Ortiz for constructive suggestions on this discussion.

1. Pelto and Pelto (1978) remind us that researchers need to develop methods to protect themselves from their own biases and value judgments: "[T]raining in anthropology does not rid the investigator of conscious and unconscious biases" (p. 36). They cite several examples from the ethnographic literature.

2. Cf., for example, Royal Anthropological Institute 1874, Radin 1933, Epstein 1967, and Ellen 1984 in England; Griaule 1957, Cresswell and Godelier 1976 in France; Jongmans and Gutkind 1967 in Holland; and Murdock et al. 1971, Williams 1967, Pelto and Pelto 1970, and Bernard 1988 in the United States.

3. In the words of the volume, "to be a handy *aide-memoire* to the trained anthropologist doing field work and also to stimulate accurate observation and the recording of information thus obtained" (RAI 1951:27). It is still widely used in countries whose anthropological research communities are in early stages of development and is appreciated there because it takes little for granted—always good advice in training novices into the practice of a discipline.

4. Described by Ellen (1984:3) as "naive guidance for amateurs."

5. The sixth edition was delayed because of World War II. The committee formed in 1936 had to be reconstituted in 1947 and was able to produce the edition only in 1951. The committee that prepared it was an impressive one, including H. J. Fleure, Le Gros Clark, Evans-Pritchard, C. D. Forde, J. H. Hutton, Radcliffe-Brown, R. Firth, M. Fortes, and F. Myers. They were assisted by, among others, E. R. Leach, S. F. Nadel, F. B. Steiner, and I. Schapera. The volume was divided into two parts—physical anthropology and social anthropology—with the bulk of the 369 pages of text devoted to social anthropology.

6. The first edition of the *Outline* (1945) was a revision of a draft prepared

in 1937 and circulated to approximately "100 specialists in various fields of knowledge" (p. v).

7. This is not surprising, given that a discussion of method inevitably means exposure of the self, "from which many anthropologists have shrunk. . . . Nevertheless, the attempt has to be made if anthropologists are to retain credibility in the face of charges that their work is primarily a series of aesthetic constructs, a set of ego-trips into the exotic" (Ellen 1984:vii).

8. This myopia is not a purely anthropological failing. Ecologists have faulted some of their colleagues in a similar fashion for making the particular the basis for theory rather than seeing it as one case among many, requiring systematic testing and comparison to be validated to the status of theory (Franklin, Bledsoe and Callahan 1990).

9. The development of a postmodern anthropology has exacerbated whatever lack of standards of ethnographic reporting may have existed. Postmoderns revel in the uniqueness and individuality of ethnographic writing (some even making their ethnographic writing into explicit ethnographic novels and other forms of fiction). Insofar as such writing is judged to be great literature, it may be read beyond the current generation of postmoderns. In far too many cases, the ethnographies give too little information about the people, their ecological and economic context, their health, their growth and decline in numbers, or even their forms of religiosity. The aggressiveness of postmodernists has intimidated far too many colleagues into practicing social science outside the academy or into not teaching firmly grounded social science standards to a new generation.

10. Note how many of the sources cited in note two came out in the late 1960s and early 1970s.

11. And at other times critical of our data as well. But that is how sciences advance—by making improvements in the precision with which we can describe and explain phenomena in terms of reproducible data.

12. Thus, the topic most important to the core of anthropology, social organization, may very well be one of the shortest chapters in this volume, because most practitioners have considerable expertise in this area and may only require a brief discussion of minima to collect and report on this data. By contrast, health, nutrition, and demography are less often adequately covered in training; thus, the chapters on these subjects are longer, showing both the relevance of such data and how to collect it and report it.

13. The meaningful period of record is a function of the purpose of the study. Twenty years is generally acceptable for most purposes but not for all. The amplitude of events increases with time. It is probable that during a twenty-year period, higher and lower temperature and rainfall will occur than, say, in a ten-year period. However, twenty years may not be sufficient if the study is focused on erosion or on infrequent natural hazards such as earthquakes, which require a longer time-series for confidence.

14. I want to thank Jeanette Rawlings, who came up with this fascinating and complex system of weights and measures while pursuing her doctoral studies in the Sucre market region. This brief explication is but a summary of her rich material.

15. Again, in *Notes and Queries* anthropologists were advised in considerable detail on this type of data, but with a greater emphasis on kinship and politics (RAI 1951:63–171).

16. Consumption and distribution, by contrast, were given short treatment in *Notes and Queries* (1951:171–173).

17. *Notes and Queries* included demography among its basic data but warned against the use of data gathered by others (1951:59). It advised, instead, that the favored procedure was to personally carry out a village census. For populations too large to census completely, they gave advice on sampling and estimating population trends that is still useful.

18. The standard intervals are 0–4, 5–9, 10–14, 15–19, 20–24, 25–29, 30–34, 35–39, 40–44, 45–49, 50–54, 55–59, 60–64, 65–69, and 70+ for each sex and commonly laid out in a pyramid for effectiveness of presentation. The construction of innovative intervals may be useful for some questions, but it should not replace reporting standard intervals if data sharing and comparison are to be possible. Nor is it useful to aggregate intervals—say, by using a 50+ interval if the number of people over 50 is small—as this leads to data loss and reduces the potential for comparison.

19. *Notes and Queries* suggested enumerating name, origin, area, sex, age, names of parents with ages if living or with ages at time of death, kin or status group, association membership, material condition, and children with their ages (RAI 1951:61.

References

Baker, P., ed., 1978. *The Biology of High Altitude Populations.* Cambridge: Cambridge University Press.

Baker, P., and M. Little, eds., 1976. *Man in the Andes.* US/IBP Synthesis Series, Volume 1. Stroudsburg, PA: Dowden, Hutchinson and Ross.

Bernard, H. R., 1988. *Research Methods in Cultural Anthropology.* Newbury Park: Sage Publ.

Cernea, Michael, 1988. *Putting People First.* New York: Oxford University Press.

Cresswell, Robert, and Maurice Godelier, eds., 1976. *Outils d'enquete et d'analyse anthropologiques.* Paris: François Maspero.

Edgerton, Robert, 1970. *The Individual in Cultural Adaptation.* Berkeley: University of California Press.

Ellen, Roy, ed., 1984. *Ethnographic Research: A Guide to General Conduct.* London: Academic Press.

Epstein, A. L., ed, 1967. *The Craft of Social Anthropology.* London: Tavistock.

Epstein, T. S., 1988. *A Manual for Culturally-adapted Market Research in the Development Process.* East Sussex: RWAL Publications.

Franklin, Jerry, Caroline Bledsoe, and James Callahan, 1990. Contributions of the long-term ecological research program. *BioScience* 40(7):509–523.

Frisancho, R. 1990. *Growth and Nutrition Standards.* Ann Arbor, MI: University of Michigan Press.

Griaule, Marcel, 1957. *Methode de L'Ethnographie.* Paris: Presses Universitaires de France.

Hildebrand, Peter, 1981. Combining disciplines in rapid appraisal: The Sondeo Approach. *Agricultural Administration* 8:423–432.

Jamison, P., S. Zegura, and F. Milan, eds., 1978. *The Eskimo of Northwest Alaska: A Biological Perspective.* US/IBP Synthesis Series Vol. 8. Stroudsburg, PA: Dowden, Hutchinson and Ross.

Jongmans, D. G., and P.C.W. Gutkind, eds., 1967. *Anthropologists in the Field.* Assen: Van Gorcuma and Comp.

Kuper, Adam, 1983. *Anthropology and Anthropologists: The Modern British School,* second edition. London: Routledge.

Lagace, R. O., 1974. *Nature and Use of the HRAF Files: A Research and Teaching Guide.* New Haven, CT: Human Relations Area Files.

McCracken, J., J. Petty, and G. Conway, 1988. *An Introduction to Rapid Rural Appraisal for Agricultural Development.* London: International Institute for Environment and Development.

Merton, Robert, 1989. *Focused Interview.* New York: Macmillan.

Mintz, Sidney, 1985. *Sweetness and Power.* New York: Penguin Books.

Murdock, G. P. et al., 1971. *Outline of Cultural Materials,* fourth revised edition, fifteenth printing with modifications. New Haven, CT: Human Relations Area Files.

Narroll, R. G., and F. Narroll, 1976. *Worldwide Theory Testing.* New Haven, CT: Human Relations Area Files.

Pelto, P. J., and G. Pelto, 1970. *Anthropological Research: The Structure of Inquiry.* New York: Harper and Row. Second edition published by Cambridge University Press, 1978.

Radin, Paul, 1933. *Method and Theory of Ethnology.* New York: McGraw-Hill.

Rhoades, Robert, 1985. Informal survey methods for farming systems research. *Human Organization* 44(3):215–218.

Royal Anthropological Institute (RAI) of Great Britain and Ireland, 1951. *Notes and Queries on Anthropology,* sixth edition, revised and rewritten. London: Routledge and Kegan Paul Ltd. Earlier editions published in 1929, 1912, 1899, 1892, and 1874.

Royce, Anya P., 1977. *The Anthropology of Dance.* Bloomington, IN: Indiana University Press.

Smith, Carol, 1984. Local history in global context: social and economic transitions in western Guatemala. *Comparative Studies in Society and History* 26(2):193–228.

van Willigen, J., and T. Finan, eds., 1991. Soundings: Rapid and reliable research methods for practicing anthropologists. *NAPA Bulletin* No. 10. Washington, D.C.: American Anthropological Association.

Weiner, J. S., and J. A. Lourie, eds., 1969. *Human Biology: A Guide to Field Methods.* Oxford: Blackwell. IBP Handbook No. 9.

Williams, T. R., 1967. *Field Methods in the Study of Culture.* New York: Holt, Rinehart and Winston.

Wolf, Eric, 1982. *Europe and the People Without History.* Berkeley: University of California Press.

Worthington, E., 1975. *The Evolution of the IBP.* Cambridge, UK: Cambridge University Press.

2

Minimum Climate Data for Comparative Analysis in Agriculture

GENE C. WILKEN

Agrarian systems are largely responses to climate. In fact, the crops and management practices by which farming systems are commonly distinguished represent adjustments to opportunities and constraints offered by the environment. The primary element of environment is climate, followed by soils and vegetation, which themselves reflect the climate regimes under which they develop.

Although climate sets limits to plant and animal growth, agrarian systems operate in an environment not of absolutes but of climatic probabilities in which success is likely but not certain. The odds are improved by managerial strategies that include selection of climate-tolerant crops and varieties, scheduling of field operations, and climate-modifying practices. As Porter (1965) succinctly put it: "[R]isk is not given in nature, it is a settlement negotiated between an environment and a technology." There are also social strategies for identifying and coping with general climate conditions and extreme events. Thus, the relationship of an agrarian system to its climate is interactive and has three aspects: the climate itself, managerial responses, and socially and economically conditioned perceptions, evaluations, and strategies. Comparative analyses should include data on all three aspects.

Climate Data

Weather consists of atmospheric elements (such as temperature, precipitation, wind) and events (storms, droughts) that occur at a particular time.

Climate is the statistical expression of weather elements over a period of sufficient length to reveal averages, normal variations, and frequency of extraordinary or extreme events. Twenty years is usually considered the minimum period necessary for calculating reliable means and probabilities. Because of the decadal time requirements involved, field studies of agrarian systems must depend on existing weather records and can generate new data only on unusually long-term projects or for specific short-term, small-scale situations such as deviations of microclimates from known local or regional conditions.

For farmers, average conditions are less important than the range of normal variations. Management decisions usually reflect expectations of deviations from the mean. *Normal variations* here mean simply those that occur often enough to enter into year-to-year planning, as opposed to less common, more extreme events, or *hazards*. If records are long enough, hazard probabilities can be calculated after thresholds of intensity or duration are established. Some hazards occur so infrequently (50- or 100-year droughts, floods) or so randomly (hail, tornadoes) that probabilities are difficult to calculate, and even prudent farmers ignore them in routine year-to-year planning. However, rare or long-past events may linger in farmers' memories and influence their decisions (Wilken 1982:33–34). Extreme events also trigger latent social responses, such as local sharing systems and migration, and should be included in minimum data sets no matter how scarce or scattered their occurrence.

Climate also varies with scale depending upon the values used to define different climate types. A climate identified by broad seasonal temperature and precipitation ranges might cover substantial portions of a continent. Within that region a number of more narrowly defined meso scale and local climates could be identified, each occupying a much smaller area, and within these could be found many microclimates with characteristics significantly different from those of the larger divisions. Table 2.1 suggests representative spatial limits. Although such divisions are arbitrary, they are useful for comparing climates.

Table 2.1 Climate Scales

Scale	Horizontal Extent	Descriptive
Macro scale	10^5 to 10^8 m	Region
Meso scale	10^4 to 2×10^5 m	District
Local scale	10^2 to 5×10^4 m	Village
Micro scale	10^{-2} to 10^3 m	Farm/Plot

Source: After Oke (1978:3).

Macro-scale climates are the smallest units customarily represented in global classification systems. Meso-scale climates appear in regional analyses and are often expressed as variations or subtypes of macro-scale categories. Local-scale climates are especially important in broken terrain or mountainous regions, where topography exerts strong influence over radiation and winds. Micro-scale climates are found at the level of individual fields and furrows. Local- and micro-scale climates are seldom identified with major classification systems but instead are associated with the dominant surface controls, such as hillside aspect (sun-facing, leeside) or surface or plant cover (bare soil, forest, crop), from which they draw their distinctive features (Geiger 1966).

Data sources and availability also vary with scale. Macro-and meso-scale data are produced by networks of weather stations that offer the most abundant and available data. If data for local-scale areas are available at all, they are often derived from one or very few stations. Data on microclimates are even less abundant. Thus, diminishing scale also means diminishing data but not diminishing importance. Local climates are farmers' working environments, in which distinctive agrarian systems have evolved, and microclimates are critical to individual farmer decisionmaking. The disparity between significance and availability of data is not easily resolved. In other scientific fields, efforts are underway to collect environmental and management data from meso-scale and even local areas (for example, Nair 1987). But costs for local and microclimate data inventories are substantial, and until their value is recognized it seems unlikely that major efforts will be undertaken (Omar 1980).

Like climates, agrarian systems are found along a continuum of size, also depending in part on definition. Thus, a broadly defined system, such as flooded rice, might extend over thousands of square kilometers, whereas a more narrowly defined system based on flooded rice but including specific water management practices and secondary crops might be limited to a single small valley. Unless scales are congruent, climate data will not accurately reflect conditions throughout an agrarian system. Mapping, now commonly done with geographic information systems (GIS) technology, facilitates spatial correlations of climate distributions and farming systems.

If two or more areas are nearly identical with respect to physical characteristics, environmental variables can be ignored and attention focused instead on managerial and socioeconomic aspects. Although the techniques of analogue area analysis or agroclimatic analogues are not new (Nuttonson 1947), there is no agreement on what constitutes "nearly identical" environments (Chang 1968:1).

Data reliability is often a problem, especially in countries that have neglected or only recently have begun gathering climate data. Among the

factors that adversely affect data quality are instrument location and relocation, discontinuous observations, incorrect or inconsistent procedures, and
nonstandard or faulty equipment (WMO 1971, 1981). Station records should
be carefully checked to determine reliability and note changes in sites or
procedures that might require adjustments to data.

Weather data lend themselves to almost unlimited statistical examination of central tendencies, probabilities, time series, and spatial distributions. For example, from temperature and precipitation, the most commonly measured climate elements, can be derived means, probabilities, and
derivatives such as degree days (heat units) and length of the temperature-
or moisture-limited growing season. Potential evapotranspiration (PET) and
soil moisture can be estimated, especially if soil depths and characteristics
are known. Major stations measure other elements, such as short-wave
radiation, rainfall intensity, wind speed and direction, and wet- and dry-
bulb temperatures. But there are relatively few such stations, and comparative analyses should be based primarily on commonly measured
elements.

Climate Management Data

Average climate conditions, normal variations, and extreme events or hazards make up the working environment of farmers. Climate management is
the technical response of agrarian systems to these norms and vagaries.
Strategies for managing the climate resource include crop selection, scheduling, field practices, and climate melioration.

Selection of crops suitable to a particular climate is a universal
adjustment. Temperature and moisture requirements have been determined
for most major crops. But crops are also genetically malleable, and modern
research, including tissue culture, aims to develop environmentally tolerant
crops. Traditional farmers accomplished the same thing by selecting for
specific characteristics, and over generations they developed many envi-
ronment-adapted varieties, or *land races* (Wilken 1985). Emergency crops
with extreme tolerance or short growth periods offer additional security in
times of stress. Although general crop patterns are usually known from
published sources, information on local and special crops may require field
surveys.

Scheduling field activities is another coping strategy (see Netting et
al., Chapter 4). Plowing, planting, and harvesting are closely attuned to the
progression of seasons. In some cases schedules are published in crop calendars and farmers' almanacs (for example, FAO 1978), although these may
not be reliable, especially if the information comes from distant places.

Most farmers follow *local* schedules, which are best revealed by field inquiries.

Many societies have achieved at least partial control over local climate. In modern societies efforts have focused on cloud seeding to induce additional precipitation. Climate modification at the local or micro level uses much older and more widespread techniques. Irrigation compensates for inadequate or unreliable rainfall; greenhouses and orchard heating are feasible with high-value crops. Other traditional practices are effective, though less recognized. Deforestation increases insolation on field surfaces, whereas shade trees lower radiation loads on young or delicate plants; windbreaks reduce wind damage and evaporation; and surface mulches modify fluxes of heat and moisture between atmosphere and soil. Although climate-modifying practices are common in traditional systems, data are almost nonexistent (Stigter 1987; Wilken 1972, 1987).

Plants are so closely attuned to climate that they frequently are used as climate indicators and as the basis for climate classifications. Similar crops and agricultural systems are often found in similar environments (for example, the corn belt and the wheat belt) even though cultural differences are great. For example, large-scale grain systems are found in similar climates in the United States, Ukraine, and People's Republic of China. Distinctive Mediterranean agriculture is closely associated with summer-dry conditions in such widely scattered locations as California, Chile, and South Africa.

Emergency and medicinal crops (including weeds) could also serve as climate indicators, although supporting data are scarce (Duke 1976; Duke, Hurst, and Kluve 1977). Special crops, seemingly out of place in a general climate region, may represent distinctive natural environments, managed microclimates, or climate-tolerant varieties. The evidence must be verified, as socioeconomic aspects complicate these relationships. Favorable or managed climates often are devoted to high-value crops that justify greater risk. But risk tolerance is also a social factor. For example, affluent commercial farmers might be willing to incur the risk of early or late frosts for potential gains from high-profit market crops, whereas subsistence farmers would find the same climate probabilities unacceptable. Thus, economic and social conditions limit the reliability of crops alone as indicators of climate.

Socioeconomic Data

The term *agrarian societies* implies close links between economic activity and social organization. But identifying the separate set of agricultural factors and subset of climate within agrarian societies would exceed the scope of this chapter. Instead, only a few social responses that pertain to production decisions will be considered here. These include perception and definitions of climatic events, risk perception and avoidance, ceremony, insurance, and prediction.

Farmers' perceptions of and responses to climate are conditioned by cultural factors. They do not consider all possible crops or feasible strategies, only those familiar to their particular system. Overall evaluation of the climate is also filtered through local experience, as when recent migrants misinterpret the constraints of a new environment (Wilken 1991).

Climatic elements and events are usually expressed in terms of supply—so many degrees of temperature or millimeters of precipitation. But it is equally valid to view the elements in terms of demand. Crop requirements determine the need and thus the definition of shortages or surpluses. Farmers evaluate weather events by crop responses, especially stress or loss of value, regardless of absolute levels (Gibbs 1975:11); in assessing the severity of drought, for example, crop loss is a more significant measure than precipitation shortfall.

Risk perception and avoidance also vary between systems. Farmers must weigh not only the hazards of the physical environment but also the rewards, penalties, and relief measures of the social environment. These factors and the thresholds, or decision points, derived from them offer another basis of comparison between systems.

Given the uncertainties, it is not surprising that there is considerable ceremony associated with weather. Whether they take the form of colored streamers in an African field or special prayers at a church in Kansas, appeals to higher powers for relief from devastating events are widespread. But information on ceremony and its impact on farmers' decisions is mostly anecdotal. Information on ritual is noted in Table 2.3 as being desirable but not essential. The data need rigorous analysis to clarify the role of ritual and ceremony in on-farm decisionmaking (cf. Rappaport 1967).

Similarly, although crop insurance mitigates the effects of designated climate hazards, the effect on farmer decisionmaking is uncertain (see, for example, Dandekar 1977). Furthermore, the concept tends to be narrowly defined to include only the formal premium-and-policy approach of modern societies and ignores other relief measures, such as the food exchanges found in traditional societies, that could rightly be classed as insurance. The data could be significant for comparative analysis but must be considered optional until the subject is better understood.

Predicting weather conditions and events is one of man's earliest and most consistent efforts to link effects with causes or, at least, with correlatives or indicators. A fundamental dilemma of agriculture underlies this effort: Planning is based on climate (statistical averages and probabilities), whereas outcomes are largely determined by weather (what actually happens). Having selected particular crops or strategies, farmers are committed to the months- or years-long growth and maturation cycles, which are much longer than the days or weeks that weather endures. They have few opportunities to make short-term responses and a great need for long-term forecasting.

Most farmers have access to two forecasting systems: formal predictions issued by official agencies based on meteorological patterns, and traditional or informal predictions based on farmers' experience. Unfortunately, neither method is reliable for more than a few days, which is too short for anything but emergency measures. Consequently, the effect of forecasts on agrarian systems may be negligible (NRC 1980). Nevertheless, formal and informal weather information and forecasts provide one more set of data for comparative analysis and are included in Table 2.2.

Minimum Data for Comparative Analysis

The foregoing introduction suggests major categories of data for comparing weather and climate in agrarian systems. Table 2.2 is a guide to that data and to suggested sources and uses. Table 2.3 deals with climate management related to agriculture. Both tables have one section for macro- and meso-scale climates and one for local- and micro-scale climates to reflect differences in data sources and characteristics. These divisions correspond roughly to large regions and districts, on the one hand, and large farms or villages and small farms or fields, on the other. But, as noted earlier, the divisions are arbitrary, and scales appropriate to the agrarian systems should be used.

Table 2.2 also indicates which data are essential for comparative analysis. Minimum data were determined on two criteria: utility and availability. *Daily maximum and minimum temperatures and precipitation amounts are two of the most important variables* (radiation is the third) and are among the most universally available data. Although these measurements leave much of the agroclimatic spectrum uncovered, they, and the characteristics derived from them, can reveal a great deal about basic crop and farming environments and provide the basis for reasonably valid comparisons. Where sources are generous, other data suggested in Table 2.2 can be collected.

Table 2.2 Minimum Climate Data and Useful Derivations* Thereof

Macro/Regional Climates*

Minimum Data	Source	Calculated/Derived	Comments
Latitude	Maps	Day Length	
Altitude	Maps		Reflected in temperatures
Daily maximum/ minimum temperatures	Weather records	Average* monthly temperature Average monthly maximum temperature Average monthly minimum temperature	Average conditions based on latest twenty years of record.
		Average first/last frost Probabilities of other critical temperatures	Average for period of record*
		Occurrence of other extreme temperature events (hazards)*	Longest possible record (may not be able to compute probabilities).
		Degree days* (heat units)	Average for period; special seasonal values
Daily precipitation amounts	Weather records	Average monthly precipitation Average seasonal precipitation Normal ranges	Average conditions based on latest twenty years of record.
		Probabilities* of extreme events (hazards)*	Longest possible record (may not be able to compute probabilities)
		Agroclimatic analogues*	Compare temperature/ precipitation amounts and regimes with other stations at similar latitudes and altitudes.
Hail	Weather records	Summarize for regional patterns	Data unreliable due to point occurrence
Other hazards and special conditions	Weather records	Summarize for frequency and regional patterns	e.g., periodic flooding, typhoons; longest possible record (may not be able to compute probabilities)
Native vegetation	Field inquiry	Plant-climate relationships	Correlate with numerical data

Other Useful Data

Daily radiation; sunshine duration	Weather records	Average monthly and normal ranges	Average conditions for record period (often not available)
Wind speeds; direction	Weather records	General wind conditions/ patterns	
Weather information	Field inquiry	Crop-climate relationships; forecasts	Check availability, coverage, accuracy, receipt, use

continues

Table 2.2 continued

Local/Microclimates

Minimum Data	Source	Calculated/Derived	Comments
Altitude	Maps		
Daily maximum/ minimum temperatures	Weather records; extrapolate; measure	Monthly average maximum and minimum temperatures Average first/last frost	Average for period of record; special local/seasonal values
		Probabilities of other critical temperatures	Identify special micro-environmental situations
		Occurrence of other extreme temperature events (hazards) Degree days (heat units)	Longest possible record (may not be able to compute probabilities) Local/seasonal values
Farmer perception	Field inquiry	Average conditions, variations, hazards Frost	Correlate with numerical data Identify local definitions/indicators; correlate with agroclimatic frost
Daily precipitation amounts	Weather records; measure	Average monthly/seasonal precipitation; normal ranges	Average for period of record; special local/seasonal values
		Probabilities of extreme events (hazards)	Identify special micro-environmental situations
Farmer perception of hazards	Field inquiry	Normal moisture conditions/ranges; drought	Correlate with numerical data; occurrence of extreme events Identify local definitions/indicators; correlate with agroclimatic drought data and indicators
Agroclimatic analogues	Weather records	Agroclimatic analogues	Compare temperature/ precipitation amounts and regimes with other nearby and distant places at similar latitudes and altitudes
Farmer perception	Field inquiry	Agroclimatic analogues	Farmer identification of environmentally similar nearby areas
Hail	Weather records	Summarize for local patterns	
Farmer perception	Field inquiry	Identify local patterns and characteristics	Correlate with recorded data
Other hazards and special conditions	Field inquiry	Summarize for frequency and regional patterns	Correlate with recorded data; how differ from macro/mesoclimates?

continues

Table 2.2 continued

Other Useful Data

Daily evaporation	Records; compute	Average weekly/ monthly evapotranspiration*	Compare with/ precipitation Calculate from temperature/ precipitation data
Soil moisture*	Records; compute; measure	Weekly/seasonal soil moisture* storage/depletion	Compare with crop needs Compute from temperature/ precipitation data
Native vegetation	Field inquiry	Plant-climate relationships	Correlate with numerical data (reinforcing)
Wet/dry bulb temperatures*	Weather records	Vapor pressure; humidity	
Dew/fog	Weather records	Frequency; seasonal patterns	Possible sources of moisture
Wind speed; direction	Weather records	Intensity; seasonal patterns	
Weather information (formal)	Field inquiry	Crop-climate information; forecasts	Availability; media coverage, accuracy, receipt and use
Weather information (informal)	Field inquiry	Local crop-climate information Prediction of future conditions; events	Correlate with broadcast information/forecasts. Local indicators: plant, animal, biological, behavioral
		Farmer evaluation of macro/meso weather information	

*Refer to Appendix 2.A for suggestions on deriving data and definitions of terms with asterisks.

Table 2.3 Climate Management

Macro-/Regional-scale Climate Management

Data	Comments
Common crops; crop combinations; sequences/rotations	Correlate* with general environmental conditions; normal variations; identify marginal crops, unfilled crop niches (re: analogues)
Land races	Crops specially selected for tolerance to climate events (e.g., frost, drought)
Emergency crops	Identify with specific conditions (could include gathered foods)
Field schedules	
Clearing	Associate with general climate conditions;
Plowing	seasons; specific dates/conditions
Planting	
Cultivation	Use of climatic indicators: atmospheric
Harvesting	conditions, plants (phenology), animals
Storage	(biology, behavior) Use of calendars (native or foreign?)

continues

Table 2.3 continued

Macro-/Regional-scale Climate Management

Data	Comments
Extreme measures	Crop abandonment; herd destruction; migration
Climate modification	E.g., irrigation, frost defenses
Emergency/contingency	National/regional/local relief; reallocation;
plans and procedures	food reserves; relocation (migration)
	Crop insurance
	Ritual

Micro-scale Climate Management

Data	Comments
Local crops, crop	Correlate with general environmental conditions; reinforce field
combinations	measurements; reveal unfilled crop niches (re: analogues)
Special crops;	Identify distinctive microenvironments; effects
land races	of climate management practices; tolerance
Emergency crops	Identify with local emergency conditions
Land tenure	Dispersed fields in different ecozones to reduce risk
Field schedules	
Clearing	Associate with local climate conditions; seasons;
Plowing	specific dates
Planting	
Cultivation	Use of climatic indicators: atmospheric
Harvesting	conditions, plants (phenology), animals
Storage	(biology, behavior)
	Use local calendars?
Temperature	Heat soil/air (e.g., heaters; modify surface)
Evapotranspiration*	Reduce evapotranspiration (e.g., retard moisture transfers;
	reduce wind speeds)
Soil moisture*	Augment infiltration; reduce evaporation
	(e.g., modify surface/substrate)
Fog/dew	Induce deposition (e.g., fog screens, dew ponds)
Short-wave radiation	Augment/reduce short-wave radiation (e.g., reflectors,
	shading structures, trees)
Long-wave radiation	Augment long-wave radiation; conserve heat (e.g.,
	structures, surface modifications)
Wind	Reduce speed, reduce evapotranspiration, preserve microclimates
	(e.g., windbreaks)
Hail	Reduce hail damage (e.g., protective shelters)
Prediction	Less important in managed microenvironments
Field schedules	Special situations/control over environmental
	variables may allow market-driven rather than
	climate-driven schedules (e.g., greenhouses)
Emergency measures	Need possibly reduced by control over environmental variables
Emergency/contingency	Local relief/reallocation;
plans and procedures	food storage; food sharing
	Ritual

Appendix 2.A
Some Terms and Procedures for
Calculating/Deriving Values in Tables 2.2 and 2.3

Analogues

> *Comments:* Allow comparison of agricultural and other cultural and managerial practices in places with similar physical environments.
> *Methods:* Use climate classification maps to establish gross similarities, check individual station data to identify local areas with near-identical temperature and precipitation regimes.

Average (also *arithmetic mean;* erroneously *normal*)

> *Comments:* One of the most useful and familiar measures of central tendency of data.
> *Methods:* Sum all values of a variable; divide by number of observations.

Climate

> *Comments:* Statistical expression of weather elements at a place over a long period of time.
> *Methods:* Calculate averages, normal ranges and variations, and probabilities of extreme events. Twenty years of continuous record is usually the minimum for calculating reliable means. Probabilities of extreme events may require longer periods.

Day length

> *Comments:* Varies with latitude and time of year. Middle latitude crops that need long periods of summer daylight to mature do poorly in the tropics, where day length varies little throughout the year.
> *Methods:* Take values from tables constructed for each latitude.

Degree days/heat units

> *Comments:* For each species of plant there is a minimum temperature (MinT) below which growth does not take place and a maximum temperature (MaxT) where growth ceases. Active growth occurs between these two points. For example, MinT for peas has been established at 40°F (4.4°C) and for sweet corn (maize) at 50°F (10°C). MaxT is less important and seldom given. Although still useful, the technique has been criticized (for example, see Wang 1960).
> *Methods:* Consult agronomy manual for degree days (heat units) needed by specific crops. To calculate:

$$\frac{(\text{Daily max. temp.} + \text{daily min. temp.})}{2} - \text{MinT} = \text{degree days}$$

The number of degree hours is obtained by multiplying degree days by 24. Thus:

Daily max. temp.	= 80°F
+ Daily min. temp.	= 50
	130 ÷ 2 = 65 (daily mean)
	− 40° (MinT peas)
	25 degree days
	x 24
	600 degree hours

In degrees celsius, the example is:

Daily max. temp.	= 26.7°C
+ Daily min. temp.	= 10.0
	36.7°C ÷ 2 = 18.4°C = daily mean
	− 4.4 (MinT peas)
	14.0 degree days
	x 24
	336 degree hours

Use caution when converting from °C to °F. For example, 36.7°C does *not* equal 130°F.

Evapotranspiration (ET); Potential Evapotranspiration (PET)

Comments: Combined term (evaporation + transpiration). Amount of water evaporated and transpired from water, soil, and plants in a given area. PET is the water loss that would occur if there were no deficiency of water so that evaporation could reach the full potential determined by available energy.

Methods: Difficult to measure directly, although sometimes evaporation losses from an open pan are used. Calculations range from simple relationships with one or more weather variables to equations based on physics of the evaporation process. For example, in the Blaney-Criddle method the only measured value is mean daily air temperature:

$$PET = \frac{[0.0173 \text{ (TA)} - 0.314] \text{ (KC) (TA)}}{(DL/4465.6)}$$

Where TA = mean daily air temperature
KC = a growth stage factor for alfalfa (from tables)
DL = day length in hours (from tables)
4465.6 = constant to convert day length to a fraction of total day-time hours of the year

More complicated procedures can be simplified. For example, Frére and Popov (1979) use Penman's PET formula, which combines energy balance and aerodynamic equations. But by means of work sheets and tables the procedure is made suitable for field use.

Expediency

> *Comments:* Field studies do not always have access to the best instruments and records. The first step is to decide whether available data are reliable enough for intended purposes. The data suggested here are among the most commonly collected.
>
> *Methods:* Despite the growing popularity of powerful microcomputers, it seemed advisable to match minimum data with minimum technology. The calculations suggested here require nothing more than a handheld calculator. Gommes (1983) derives probabilities, periodicities, solar radiation, PET according to Penman, and mean daytime/nighttime temperatures from daily maximum/minimum temperatures using only a programmable pocket calculator.

Hazards

> *Comments:* Sporadic events such as hurricanes or tornados or extreme variations such as droughts or floods that exceed normal variations of dry seasons or stream flows. Although infrequent, the sheer magnitude of hazardous events may have major impacts on landscapes and climate means.
>
> *Methods:* Calculate probabilities from long-term weather records.

Interpolation/correlation

> *Comments:* If data are unavailable for a particular site, it is tempting to interpolate with average data or correlate with data from other years or nearby stations.
>
> *Methods:* The procedures must be used with caution. The one characteristic that all climate data share is variability over time and space. Particular care is required in hilly or mountainous regions, where temperature and precipitation gradients are not uniform and data even from nearby stations may need substantial adjustments for differences in altitude, aspect, and so forth.

Microclimate:

> *Comments:* Climate of a small area that may differ markedly from the general climate. Slow heat and moisture transfers can create extreme gradients over short vertical and horizontal distances.
>
> *Methods:* Measure weather elements in zones defined by activity being studied (for examples, plant zone; interior of houses).

Missing Data

> *Comments:* Missing data is a frequently encountered problem that complicates calculations of means and probabilities.
>
> *Methods:* 1) Ignore periods with missing data and adjust value of *n;*

2) interpolate from average sequences or comparable previous years; 3) correlate with nearby stations; or 4) use various combinations of these. For example, in the United States degree days are adjusted when there are fewer than ten days of missing data but are left blank when there are ten or more missing days (Haggard 1965). Clearly there is less risk in estimating continuous data, such as temperature, than sporadic data, such as precipitation.

Period of record

Comments: Period of time in which reasonably valid calculations can be made of means and normal variations. Twenty years is generally accepted for most but not all climate data. Calculating probabilities of infrequent events (such as droughts and hurricanes) requires longer periods.

Methods: Field studies are usually too short to generate original records of adequate length. Thus, data availability is determined for most places; if it doesn't already exist, it can't be created during the few months or years of a project. Instead, field studies must rely on existing records or collect short-term local data and attempt correlations with nearby stations that have longer records.

Probability

Comments: Frequency with which an event is expected to occur. Probabilities are usually calculated from minimum data in one of two forms: probability of certain values for a season or year (e.g., above average temperature; adequate moisture), or probability that an event will occur by a particular date (e.g., date of last/first frost; beginning/end of rainy season). Of the two, the latter is the more useful.

Methods: Consult standard statistical texts for procedures and probability tables.

Soil moisture

Comments: Because plants take their water from the soil, precipitation measurements provide only a rough index of water available in the root zone.

Methods: Measure soil moisture directly or calculate using one of several procedures (e.g., Baier, et al. 1972; Frére and Popov 1979).

Weather

Comments: State of the atmosphere at a particular time, including radiation, pressure, temperature, precipitation, wind speed and direction, humidity, and clouds.

Methods: Measured with radiometers, barometers, wet- and dry-bulb thermometers, rain and snow gauges, and anemometers.

References

Baier, W., D. Z. Chaput, D. A. Russello, and W. R. Sharp, 1972. *Soil Moisture Estimator Program System.* Ottawa: Agrometeorology Section, Canada Department of Agriculture, Technical Bulletin 78.

Chang, J., 1968. *Climate and Agriculture: An Ecological Survey.* Chicago: Aldine Publishing Co.

Dandekar, V. M., 1977. *Crop Insurance for Developing Countries.* Washington, D.C.: Agricultural Development Council, Teaching and Research Forum No. 10.

Duke, J. A., 1976. Perennial weeds as indicators of annual climatic parameters. *Agricultural Meteorology* 16:291–294.

Duke, J. A., S. J. Hurst, and J. L. Kluve, 1977. Botanicals as environmental indicators. *Herbarist* (Supplement 1977):1–12.

Food and Agriculture Organization (FAO), 1978. *Crop Calendars.* Rome: Food and Agriculture Organization of the United Nations, FAO Plant Production and Protection Paper 12.

Frére, M., and G. F. Popov, 1979. *Agrometeorological Crop Monitoring and Forecasting.* Rome: Food and Agriculture Organization of the United Nations, FAO Plant Production and Protection Paper 17.

Geiger, R., 1966. *The Climate Near the Ground,* translated from fourth German edition. Cambridge: Harvard University Press.

Gibbs, W. J., 1975. Drought—its definition, delineation, and effects. In *Drought: Lectures Presented at the Twenty-Sixth Session of the WMO Executive Committee,* pp. 1–39. Geneva: World Meteorological Organization, Special Environmental Report No. 5, WMO No. 403.

Gommes, R. A., 1983. *Pocket Computers in Agrometeorology.* Rome: Food and Agriculture Organization of the United Nations, FAO Plant Production and Protection paper 45.

Haggard, W., 1965. Configuraciones sinoptico-climatológicas asociadas con ciclogenesis tropical Noratlantica. *Geofísica Internacional* (Mexico City) 5(3):97–113.

Nair, P.K.R., 1987. *Agroforestry Systems in Major Ecological Zones of the Tropics and Subtropics.* Nairobi: International Council for Research in Agroforestry (ICRAF), Working Paper No. 47.

National Research Council (NRC), Committee on Weather-Information Systems, Board on Agriculture & Renewable Resources, 1980. *Weather Information Systems for On-farm Decision Making.* Washington, D.C.: National Research Council/National Academy of Sciences.

Nuttonson, M. Y., 1947. *Ecological Crop Geography.* Washington, D. C.: American Institute of Crop Ecology.

Oke, T. R. 1978. *Boundary Layer Climates.* London: Methuen & Co., Ltd.

Omar, M. H. 1980. *The Economic Value of Agrometeorological Information and Advice.* Geneva: World Meteorological Organization, Technical Note 164.

Porter, P. W., 1965. Environmental potentials and economic opportunities—a background for cultural adaptation. *American Anthropologist* 67:409–420.

Rappaport, Roy, 1967. *Pigs for the Ancestors: Ritual in the Ecology of a New Guinea People.* New Haven: Yale University Press.

Ray, P. K., 1974. *A Manual on Crop Insurance for Developing Countries.* Rome: Food and Agriculture Organization of the United Nations.

Stigter, K., 1987. Tapping into traditional knowledge. *Ceres* (FAO Review) 20(3):29–32.

Wang, J. Y., 1960. A critique of the heat unit approach to plant response studies. *Ecology* 41:785–790.

Wilken, G. C., 1972. Modification of microclimates by traditional farmers. *Geographical Review* 62:544-560.

————, 1982. *Agroclimatic Hazard Perception, Prediction, and Risk-avoidance Strategies in Lesotho.* Boulder: University of Colorado, Natural Hazard Research Working Paper #44.

————, 1985. Role of traditional agriculture in preserving biological diversity. In *Technologies to Maintain Biological Diversity,* Vol. II, Part D. Washington, D. C.: Congress of the United States, Office of Technology Assessment (U.S. Department of Commerce, National Technical Information Service).

————, 1987. *Good Farmers: Traditional Resource Management in Mexico and Central America.* Berkeley: University of California Press.

————, 1991. *Sustainable Agriculture is the Solution, but What's the Problem?* Washington, D.C.: USAID, Board for International Food and Agricultural Development and Economic Cooperation (BIFADEC), Occasional Paper No. 14.

World Meteorological Organization, 1971. *Guide to Meteorological Instrument and Observing Practices,* fourth edition. Geneva: WMO Scientific and Technical Publication No. 8.

————, 1981. *Guide to Agricultural Meteorological Practices,* second edition. Geneva: World Meteorological Organization (WMO No. 134).

General References

Agricultural Compendium 1989 (third revised edition). Amsterdam: Elsevier Science Publishers, B.V.

Bishnoi, O. P., 1989. *Agroclimatic Zoning.* Geneva: World Meteorological Organization, Agricultural Meteorology, Center for Agricultural Meteorology Report No. 30 (WMO/TD No. 238).

Biswas, A. K., 1980. Crop climate models: A review of the state of the art. In Ausubel, J., and A. K. Biswas, eds., *Climatic Constraints and Human Activities.* New York: Pergamon Press.

Brooks, C.E.P., and N. Carruthers, 1978 [1953]. *Handbook of Statistical Methods in Meteorology.* New York: AMS Press [London: HMSO].

Griffith, D. A., and C. G. Amrhein, 1991. *Statistical Analysis for Geographers.* Englewood Cliffs: Prentice Hall.

Griffiths, J. F., ed., 1972. *World Survey of Climatology.* Amsterdam: Elsevier Publishing Co.

Oliver, J. E., ed., 1987. *Encyclopedia of Climatology.* New York: Van Nostrand Reinhold Co.

World Meteorological Organization, 1987. *Glossary of Terms Used in Agrometeorology.* Geneva: CAgM Report No. 20.

3

Soil Indices for Comparative Analysis of Agrarian Systems

JOHN J. NICHOLAIDES III AND EMILIO F. MORAN

One of the most fundamental processes in nature is the conversion of solar energy into plant biomass, or tissue. It is from this conversion that all biological processes are possible and that animals such as ourselves can exist. Plant growth and production are dependent on a number of factors, among them temperature, rainfall, soil nutrients, and soil texture. Human use of plants depends upon the plants' ability to produce a net yield that can be harvested. Because energy transfers are inherently inefficient, plants must absorb and convert far more energy than they can yield. A major portion of this energy goes into keeping the plant alive; the rest goes into energy to ensure its reproduction. This portion may be available to consumers. A great deal of attention has been spent in human history trying to understand how we came to domesticate plants and animals—and how in so doing we made many plants and animals dependent on our care for their very survival (Cohen 1977). Yet we depend to this day on a very small number of domesticated plants, leaving much of the biotic richness of the earth still unmanaged (National Academy of Science 1978).

The study of plants is intimately tied to the soils upon which they grow. Although temperature, rainfall, and other climatic factors are as important as soil, there is very little humans can do to manage or control these forces of nature (but see Wilken, Chapter 2, for the efforts to try to alter the odds; cf. Wilken 1987). By contrast, soils can be and often are managed by human groups. Most populations, particularly those dependent upon farming, possess ethnoecological expertise about soils and their characteristics. This is important information that may in many cases be superior in its richness of detail to that available from agricultural ministries and research stations (Conklin 1957; Carter 1969; Moran 1981, 1993; Posey and Balée, 1989).

The soil is not an undifferentiated medium but is rather a dynamic one that is constantly in formation and undergoing transformation. Soils are distinguishable from bedrock and unconsolidated debris by their relatively high content of organic matter, an abundance of roots and soil organisms, and the presence of clearly distinguishable layers, or horizons (Brady 1984:9–10). Soils may vary even within short distances of each other. These differences may be the result of variations in surface, slope, weathering conditions, and plant activity. For example, soils originating from chemically basic (or alkaline) parent material (bedrock) will have a pH close to neutral (7.0), whereas those originating from acid rocks will tend to be acid (4.0–5.0). Soils on steep slopes will be shallower than those on gentler slopes if the steep slopes are not covered in vegetation capable of breaking the eroding impact of water and light.

Color is one of the most obvious things to notice about soils. It is an important indicator of various characteristics but not a foolproof determinant of soil type. When weathered, a red shale or sandstone may yield a red-colored soil, although the oxidation of iron is not the major process responsible for redness. In interpreting the nature of the soil, color must be used in conjunction with broader knowledge of the weathering factors in a given climatic zone. But color is always important data to report. In temperate regions dark-colored soils are usually high in organic matter. In the tropics, however, some dark clays may be poor in organic matter, whereas others may very well be rich organic soils. Bright red and yellow soils in the tropics may suggest high levels of iron oxides, but they also indicate good drainage and aeration (as compared with grayish mottling, which suggests poor drainage). This observation can be very important in evaluating plant performance and in planning management approaches to a given area. In poorly drained areas where oxygen is deficient, reduced iron yields bluish-gray soils, whereas sites of good drainage lead to oxidation of iron, producing red colors. Soil color data is commonly reported using the Munsell color charts.

Because chemical weathering, slope, and other influences vary at different depths, distinctive layers, or horizons, develop in most soils. These horizons, when taken as a group, form what is known as a soil profile, which expresses the types of processes experienced by the soil in the past and the factors important to the use of that soil in the future. Profiles are two-dimensional slices through a soil. Soils, in general, are said to have four major horizons: an organic horizon (O) and three mineral horizons (A, B, and C).

Of all the horizons, the organic layer is the most critical for plant growth (see Figure 3.1). This layer usually contains a disproportionately

Figure 3.1 Soil Profiles

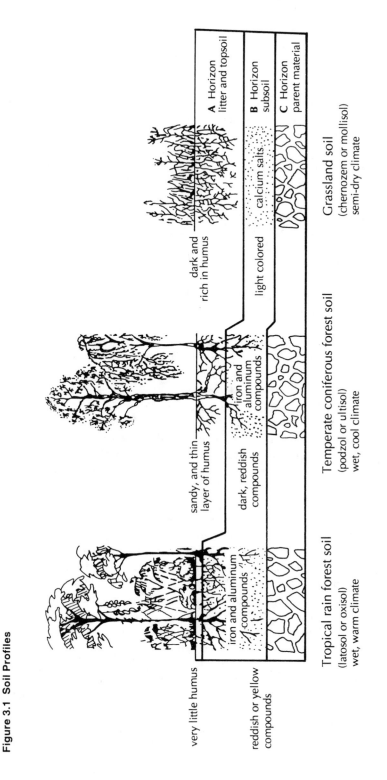

A Horizon
litter and topsoil

B Horizon
subsoil

C Horizon
parent material

dark and
rich in humus

calcium salts

light colored

Grassland soil
(chernozem or mollisol)
semi-dry climate

sandy, and thin
layer of humus

iron and
aluminum
compounds

dark, reddish
compounds

Temperate coniferous forest soil
(podzol or ultisol)
wet, cool climate

very little humus

iron and aluminum
compounds

reddish or yellow
compounds

Tropical rain forest soil
(latosol or oxisol)
wet, warm climate

Source: Moran 1979: 76-77.

large portion of the total humus in a soil. Humus is important because it is capable of retaining water and nutrients and thus facilitates exchange of these elements (Brady 1984:266). Organic matter is also responsible for the loose, friable condition of productive soils. It is the source of phosphorus, sulfur, and nitrogen inputs, providing most of the sustenance for soil microorganisms. The majority of the domesticated plants utilized by the human population rely primarily on this humic layer for their nutrition (Brady 1984:14–16). That is why most soil sampling for estimating soil fertility and fertilizer needs takes place in the top few inches of soil ("the plow layer," or 0–20 cm). Sampling of the entire soil profile usually aims at soil classification rather than at practical assessments of fertility. Most ethnoecological systems give priority to the plow layer in making classificatory choices, although Western soil classification tends to give priority to subsoil characteristics. This difference reflects a greater interest in soil genesis in Western classifications than in the more pragmatic folk classifications, which correctly focus on the environment for the plants of local interest.

The mineral horizons are characterized by lesser concentrations of organic matter and varied particulate structure. The A-horizon is richer in organic matter than B or C and characterized by the presence of granular, platy, or crumb structures. The B-horizon is marked by alluvial concentrations of silicates, clay, iron, and aluminum and by the development of blocky, prismatic, or columnar structures. The C-horizon lies above the consolidated bedrock and has even larger particulate matter. It is the zone of transition between the B-horizon and the bedrock proper.

Knowledge of soil properties is useful when an investigation includes a focus on human management of land resources. Soil phenomena are of such complexity that a system of classification can be helpful in grouping soils that share natural properties. Native systems of classifying soils exist in most farming populations. Over four thousand years ago, the Chinese developed one based on color and structural characteristics (Steila 1976:64). The Hanunóo of the Philippines based theirs on vegetative cover (Conklin 1957:39), which is perhaps the most widely used criteria worldwide. The Kekchi of Guatemala used color, texture, drainage, root content, and vegetation cover (Carter 1969:21).

The distribution of major soil orders affects what forms of agriculture are possible and what levels of productivity can be achieved. Because soils are the product of the weathering of rock materials, the prevalent climatic conditions play a crucial role in the formation of soils and help determine their characteristics. Thus, oxisols are dominant in wet, humid areas, whereas mollisols are characteristic of temperate grasslands.

Map 3.1 illustrates the distribution of soils on a worldwide scale. The association is not perfect, as pockets of unexpected soil types may be found

Map 3.1 Soils of the World

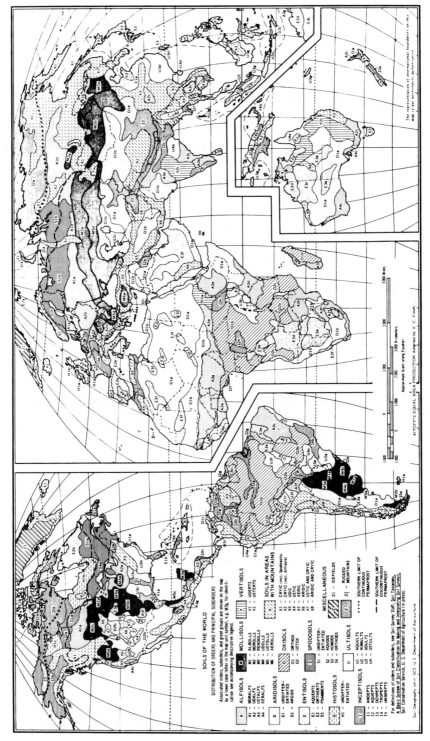

SOILS OF THE WORLD

DISTRIBUTION OF ORDERS AND PRINCIPAL SUBORDERS

Associated orders, suborders, and great groups are shown on the map by a lower case letter in the map unit symbol, e.g. M2a, for identification. See accompanying descriptive legend.

ALFISOLS	VERTISOLS
A	V
A1 BORALFS	V1 UDERTS
A2 UDALFS	V2 USTERTS
A3 USTALFS	
A4 XERALFS	SOILS IN AREAS WITH MOUNTAINS

ARIDISOLS	X
D	X1 CRYIC (incl. Spodosols)
D1 UNDIFFERENTIATED	X2 CRYIC (incl. Alfisols)
D2 ARGIDS	X3 UDIC
	X4 USTIC
	X5 XERIC
ENTISOLS	X6 ARIDIC
E	X7 ARIDIC AND CRYIC
E1 AQUENTS	X8 ARIDIC AND CRYIC
E2 ORTHENTS	
E3 PSAMMENTS	MISCELLANEOUS
	Z
HISTOSOLS	Z1 - ICEFIELDS
H	Z2 - RUGGED MOUNTAINS
H1 UNDIFFERENTIATED	

INCEPTISOLS	ULTISOLS
I	U
I1 ANDEPTS	U1 AQUULTS
I2 AQUEPTS	U2 HUMULTS
I3 OCHREPTS	U3 UDULTS
I4 TROPEPTS	U4 USTULTS
I5 UMBREPTS	

MOLLISOLS	
M1 ALBOLLS	
M2 BOROLLS	
M3 RENDOLLS	
M4 UDOLLS	
M5 USTOLLS	
M6 XEROLLS	

OXISOLS	
O1 ORTHOX	
O2 USTOX	

SPODOSOLS	
S1 UNDIFFERENTIATED	
S2 AQUODS	
S3 HUMODS	
S4 ORTHODS	

···· SOUTHERN LIMIT OF CONTINUOUS PERMAFROST

—·—· SOUTHERN LIMIT OF DISCONTINUOUS PERMAFROST

For definitions of orders and suborders, see *Soil Survey Staff, Soil Taxonomy: A Basic System of Soil Classification for Making and Interpreting Soil Surveys.* Soil Conservation Service, U. S. Department of Agriculture (in press).

Soil Geography Unit, SCS, U.S. Department of Agriculture

ATOFF'S EQUAL AREA PROJECTION Adapted by V. C. Finch

The representation of international boundaries on this map is not necessarily authoritative.

Approximate Scale along Equator

0   1000   2000   3000 Miles

1000   2000   3000 Kilometers

anywhere and can be very important in terms of local agrarian potential. Still, the association of soil orders with ecosystem types is remarkable. Tundra regions are dominated by inceptisols (young soils), deserts by aridisols (rocky, gravelly soils), temperate grasslands by mollisols, tropical savannas by ultisols, and tropical moist forests by oxisols. The areal significance of these major soil orders is variable. Aridisols, which present problems of high salt levels and high concentrations of other minerals, are the most extensive (19.2 percent of the total) and occur in regions with very low rainfall. The second most extensive soils (15.8 percent) are the inceptisols, which also can be problematic for farming because they are rocky or gravelly and still in the process of development. It is only with the third most extensive soil type, the alfisols (14.7 percent), that we get to a relatively fertile soil in regions with adequate rainfall and temperature for plant growth. Even these can present problems, as they do in West Africa. Thus, a crucial problem of farming populations is to locate areas of land with the best possible soils, given their scarcity. Location of such land requires knowledge of soil characteristics and their effective management.

The Minimum Data

Investigators should collect and report as minima the proportions of the major soil types and/or orders in the area of interest, their texture, color, pH, and the vegetation that grows on them. Crop productivity on the various soils can also be useful to colleagues in comparisons (see Hunt, Chapter 9). In most cases, these should be available from local agricultural research stations and will not require direct field collection.

Ten major soil orders are recognized at present: entisols (soils with little if any profile development); inceptisols (slightly more profile development than entisols, but less than other orders); mollisols (dark soils of temperate grasslands); alfisols (moist soils of medium to high fertility, often under forest); ultisols (moist soils found in the tropics, with percentage of clay increasing with depth); oxisols (most highly weathered soils, often found in the tropics); vertisols (dark swelling clays); aridisols (soils of dry areas); spodosols (soils with a subsurface horizon with organic matter accumulation, low in nutrients and often acid); and histosols (peat or bog soils, developing in water-saturated environments) (Brady 1984:436–453).

Texture is determined by the relative proportions of particles of various sizes in the soil. It is not subject to rapid change: A sandy soil tends to remain sandy, and a clayish soil remains dominated by the clay fraction. Soil analyses can include textural analysis, which provides the percentage of particle sizes for each category. Silt, clay, sand, and gravel (or coarse particles) are often used as categories in making textural discriminations (Brady 1984:36–37). The size of particles is important because it influences the adsorption of water, nutrients, and the tilth of a soil. Clay tends to hold water better than sand or silt. A textural class known as loam is hard to explain because it is a mixture of sand, silt, and clay particles "that exhibit light and heavy properties in about equal proportions" (Brady 1984:42).

Color is determined in the field with the use of the Munsell color charts. It is important to note if the soil is dry or wet. Color can be misleading in some cases, but it is relatively important in soil descriptions and thus facilitates comparison. The acidity or alkalinity of a soil is expressed by pH, which tends to fall on most mineral soils between 3 (acid) and 10 (alkaline). The range for productive cultivated soils is narrower, generally between 5 and 7 in humid regions and 7 and 9 in temperate regions. Soil nutrient availability tends to increase significantly if a soil's pH is raised from 5 to 6 or 7. At pHs below 5, aluminum, iron, and manganese are soluble enough to become toxic to many plants. At very high pH values, bicarbonates can have similar effects on plants. Some plants are more able to remain productive at the extremes of the pH gradient than others, and this knowledge constitutes an important component of how people manage soil-plant relationships (Jeffrey 1987).

In the process of conducting field study, effort should be spent on getting the local names for the soils and the population's assessment of each one, particularly as to what crops do better on which named soils and what specifically named soils present outstanding properties or are unacceptably infertile (Moran 1987; Behrens 1989; Johnson 1974; Conklin 1957). This effort can go hand in hand with the minima collected in connection with the ethnoecology of farming and the listing of locally cultivated crops (see Netting et al., Chapter 4).

Second-Level Intensity of Data Collection

Students of agrarian systems and ecology may very well want to go beyond the above minima, particularly by paying attention to soil sampling or making greater use of available local data. Soil sampling may take either of two forms, each of which reflects different research objectives. These forms are known as core sampling and profile sampling. In core (or surface) sampling, a soil sample is taken to a depth of between 10 and 20 centimeters (more commonly the latter). As this is the zone from which most domesticated plants obtain their nutrients, core sampling is the method commonly used to assess the soil nutrients available. The sample is taken with a core sampler. A single soil sample consists of fifteen to twenty "cores" collected in a random manner from a homogeneous soil surface area. A zigzag pattern is usually used. The cores that make up a single sample are deposited in a bag and thoroughly mixed before being sent to the laboratory for analysis. Each sample should be numbered and described in terms of where the sample was taken; what vegetation was in the area; what texture the soil had; what color it was (using standardized color charts, such as Munsell); and what the past use of the soil was (if known). Any other remarkable features (for example, drainage problems and slope) should also be noted.

Profile sampling goes to greater depth in the soil. A depth of 1 to 3 meters provides a fairly comprehensive cross-section of soil horizons applicable to the study of land uses such as tree farming or cultivation of special plants with deep tap roots. In profile sampling, a soil auger is used unless a pit is dug (which is far more time consuming). The aim of this type of sampling is to establish the various horizons and their characteristics. As the auger is turned, each layer is laid out on a sheet of plastic or other material in the order in which it was extracted. Each horizon is then described in terms of the same information noted in core sampling. Such descriptions help reveal the alternatives open to cultivators and can serve to test the accuracy of the population's ethnoecological knowledge. At this level it is desirable to construct more fully the local population's taxonomic knowledge of soils, noting which plants are indicative of which soils and the distinctive criteria for identifying them.

Third-Level Intensity of Data Collection

At this level, it becomes more appropriate to engage in assessment of soil fertility. It is important to note that soil fertility is a term with numerous connotations. A "fertile" soil may be one that needs no fertilizer additions, but the term is somewhat vague until some clear level of expected production is defined. Soil that has sufficient fertility to produce maize yields of 1 ton per hectare can be judged infertile when yields of 9 tons per hectare are anticipated. Infertility can also relate to soil water conditions, toxic salt concentration, a root-restricting hardpan, nematodes, or low soil temperatures.

Soil fertility, broadly conceived, connotes the ability of soil to grow plants. It does not connote, in itself, what is right or wrong with the many factors that influence plant growth. Crop yields are a function of at least four major factors—crop, soil, climate, management—and each one has various aspects that must be considered (Fitts 1959).

Evaluation of soil fertility should address not only what limits plant growth but also what steps may be taken to overcome those limitations, including a reassessment of what is planted on such soils. Soil fertility evaluation and extrapolation can be viewed as major tools in the comparative analysis of agrarian systems. Various groups make use of these tools, including researchers (both agronomic and anthropologic), extensionists, land-use policy planners, and farmers themselves. The primary constraint to soil fertility evaluation and extrapolation—and, as a consequence, to comparative analysis of agrarian systems—is the lack of a systematic technical grouping of surface soil properties by which research workers can define the limits of the uncontrolled variables within which field fertility research can be extrapolated (Buol and Nicholaides 1980). The alleviation of this constraint would be useful.

One of the most important things to note in this regard is that, for all practical purposes, soil classification and soil fertility management are usually at cross-purposes (Buol and Nicholaides 1980). Because the basic goal of soil classification is to record features that are at least quasi-permanent and not subject to management alteration, soil properties in the surface horizons are usually considered only at the lowest categories of most soil classification systems. Surface soil chemistry of the type directly related to fertilizer manipulation is usually not included in soil classification criteria to avoid the confusion that may result from the transient nature of the values encountered when soils are subjected to management. Thus, soil properties considered for taxonomic purposes (Dudal 1980) are not necessarily relevant for soil fertility management—nor should they necessarily be (Buol and Nicholaides 1980).

Conversely, soil fertility evaluation and improvement approaches (Cate and Nelson 1971; Waugh et al. 1975; Fitts 1974), though valuable, have not always related the numerous analytical data to kinds of soils via any classification system. Several such approaches have implied wide applicability over many soils, although the soil classification information usually is not given (Cate and Nelson 1971).

Most management practices for cultivated crops occur in the upper 20 centimeters of soil, and the effects of these management practices are reflected in this layer. Thus, soil taxonomic systems often do not use surface soil criteria. Likewise, soil fertility evaluations do not utilize the classification systems because the latter do not reflect soil management practices. Neither group, therefore, provides a strong basis for consequent extrapolation of soil fertility evaluation and improvement (Buol and Nicholaides 1980) or for comparative analysis of agrarian systems.

It should be reemphasized that subsoil properties do not have as great an effect on crop yields as do surface properties. For example, a survey of 441 field trials in North Carolina found that properties of topsoils, individually and collectively, better explained crop yield variability than did the corresponding subsoil properties (Sopher and McCracken 1973).

Nearly forty years ago, it was written that some problems related to soil fertility evaluation and extrapolation could be overcome by technical classifications for specific, applied, practical purposes (Cline 1949). One such technical classification is the Fertility Capability Classification system, or FCC (Buol et al. 1975). Technical classification systems do not replace soil taxonomic information and soil surveys but rather build on them to become useful in practical agricultural development initiatives (Johnson 1980).

The FCC was developed (Buol et al. 1975) to group soils with similar limitations of fertility management (Buol 1972) and thereby provide a guide for extrapolating fertilizer response experiences (Buol and Couto 1981). It centers on surface soil properties most directly related to field crop management, and it can be related to a more inclusive natural soil classification system (Buol and Nicholaides 1980).

The proposed system consists of the following three labels:

1. Soil type—texture of surface soil (0–20 centimeters).
2. Substrata type—texture of subsoil if within 50 centimeters of surface.
3. Condition modifiers—specific properties noted if a specific range of conditions is encountered.

Thus every soil is named at the highest category by the surface texture present, and further properties are noted as needed in a systematic fashion. The description of type, subtype, and condition modifiers (Buol et al. 1975) follows:

Soil Type. Definition: Texture of plow layer or surface 10 centimeters, whichever is shallower.

1. S = sandy topsoils: loamy sands and sands. High rate of infiltration, low water-holding capacity.
2. L = loamy topsoils: <35 percent clay but not loamy sand or sand. Good water-holding capacity, medium infiltration capacity.
3. C = clayey topsoils: >35 percent clay. Low infiltration rates, potential high runoff if sloping, difficult to till except when *i* modifier is present (see below).
4. O = organic soils: >30 percent O.M. to a depth ≥50 cm or more. Artificial drainage is needed, and subsidence will take place. Possible micronutrient deficiency, high herbicide rates usually required.

Texture of subsoil. Used only if there is textural change from the surface or if a hard root restricting layer is encountered within 50 centimeters.

S = sandy subsoil
L = loamy subsoil
C = clayey subsoil
R = rock or other hard restricting layer.

Condition modifiers. Where more than one criterion is listed for each modifier, only one needs to be met. The criterion given is preferred, but additional criteria are selected to facilitate semiquantitative use in the absence of desired data.

1. g = (gley): Soil or mottles ≤2 chroma within 60 centimeters of surface and below all A horizons or saturated with water for >60 days in most years. Limitations: Denitrification frequently occurs in anaerobic subsoil and tillage operations, and certain crops may be adversely affected by excess rain unless drainage is improved by tiles or other drainage procedures.

2. d = (dry): Ustic, aridic, or xeric soil moisture regimes (subsoil dry >90 cumulative days per year within 20–60 centimeter depth). Limitations: Soil moisture is limited during the growing season unless irrigated. Planting date should take into account the flush of N at onset of rain.

3. e = (low cation exchange capacity or CEC): <4 meq/100 g soil by bases + KCl extractable Al, or >7 meq/100 g soil by cations at pH 7, or <10 meq/100 g soil by cations + Al + H at pH 8.2. (Applies only to plow layer or surface 20 centimeters, whichever is shallower.) Limitations: Low ability to retain nutrients, mainly Ca, K, Mg, for plants. Heavy applications of these nutrients should be split. Potential danger of overliming.

4. a = (aluminum toxic): >60 percent Al saturation of CEC by bases +KCl extractable Al within 50 centimeters, or >67 percent exchangeable acidity (EA) saturation of CEC by cations at pH 7 within 50 centimeters, or >86 percent EA saturation of CEC by cations at pH 8.2 within 50 centimeters, or pH <5.0 in 1:1 H_2O except in organic soils. Limitations: Plants sensitive to aluminum toxicity will be affected unless the lime is deeply incorporated. Extract of soil water below depth of lime incorporation will be restricted. Lime requirements are high unless an e modifier is also indicated. Aluminum tolerant varieties should be considered in these soils.

5. h = (acid): 10–60 percent Al saturation of CEC by bases + KCl extractable Al within 50 centimeters, or pH in 1:1 water between 5.0 and 6.0. Limitations: Strong to medium soil acidity. Requires liming for most crops. Aluminum-tolerant varieties should be considered in these soils.

6. i = (high phosphorus fixation by iron): percent free Fe_2O_3 divided by percent clay >0.15 and >35 percent clay, or hues of 7.5 YR or redder and granular structure. Limitations: High P fixation capacity. Requires high levels of P fertilizer. Sources and method of P fertilizer application should be considered carefully. (Used only in clay (C) types.)

7. x = (X-ray amorphous): pH >10 in 1N NaF, or positive to field NaF test, or other indirect evidence of allophane dominance in clay fraction. Limitations: High P fixation capacity. Amount and most convenient source of P to be determined. (Applies only to plow layer or surface 10 centimeters, whichever is shallower.)

8. v = (Vertisols, very sticky plastic clay): >35 percent clay and >50 percent of 2:1 expanding clays; COLE >0.09. Severe topsoil shrinking and swelling. Limitations: Clayey textured topsoil. Tillage is difficult when too dry or too moist, but soils can be highly productive.

9. k = (potassium deficient): <10 percent weatherable minerals in silt and sand fraction within 10 centimeters of soil surface, or exchangeable K <0.20 meg/100g, or K <2 percent of bases, if bases <10 meg/100 g. Limitations: Low ability to supply K. Availability of K should be monitored and K fertilizers may be required frequently for plants requiring high levels of K.

10. b = (basic reaction): Free $CaCO_3$ within 10 centimeters of soil surface (effervescence with HCl), or pH >7.3. Limitations: Basic reaction. Rock phosphate and other water insoluble phosphates should be avoided. Potential deficiency of certain micronutrients, principally iron and zinc.

11. s = (salinity): >4 mmho/centimeters of saturated extract at 25 C within 1 meter depth. Limitations: Presence of soluble salts. Requires special soil management practices for alkaline soils.

12. n = (natric): >15% Na saturation of CEC within 50 centimeters of soil surface.

13. c = (cat clay): pH in 1:1 H_2O is <3.5 after drying and jarosite mottles, with hues of 2.5 Y or yellower and chromas 6 or more are present within 60 centimeters. Limitations: Potential acid sulfate soil. Drainage is not recommended without special practices. Should be managed with plants tolerant of flood and high water table levels.

Interpretation of FCC condition modifiers. When only one condition modifier is included in the FCC class nomenclature, the above limitations or management requirements apply to the soil. Interpretations may be slightly modified when two or more modifiers are present simultaneously or when textural classes are different.

A worldwide survey of published descriptions and analytical data of 244 soil profiles representing a broad geographical and morphological range grouped the soils into 117 fertility capability classes (Buol et al. 1975). Types L, C, LC, and S represented 92 percent of the total, and 10 condition modifiers accounted for 515 of the population. Five modifiers (v, n, s, x, i) never occurred alone, reflecting the fact that several fertility-related parameters occur together in many soils. Soil profiles of 678 Brazilian soils were grouped into 84 fertility capability classes (Buol et al. 1975).

Soils from 73 potato fertilization trials (McCollum and Valverde 1968) in Peru were grouped into five classes by FCC (Buol et al. 1975). Gross returns to fertilizer applications were higher when recommendations were based on a combination of the FCC and surface soil test results. This strongly emphasizes that there is no substitute for on-site reporting of the soil properties, including both soil characteristics and soil test determinations, to arrive at the most accurate recommendations.

A strong push for more complete soil characterization at experimental sites and more careful on-site soil evaluation in extrapolation work was made in a solid discourse on fertility management interpretations and soil surveys of the tropics (Buol and Couto 1978). Such a combination of the FCC, using data from soil survey reports and standard soil test results following on-site sampling, allowed extrapolation of proper fertilization practices for peanuts and soybeans from a Haplustox with a clayey textured surface soil in Brazil and a Paleudult with a loamy surface soil in Peru to a Paleustult with a loamy textured surface soil in Bolivia (Nicholaides et al. 1978). A slight modification (Pope and Buol 1976) of the FCC was used when the FAO/UNESCO soil map of South America was converted to FCC units (Sanchez et al. 1982).

The FCC, or some modification thereof, can serve as the basis on which to group soils for specific soil management evaluations and land-use planning. An example is CIAT's computerized tropical America land-resource study, which also uses climatic data and satellite and side-looking radar imagery (Cochrane et al. 1979). Recent work (Sanchez and Benites 1987) has shown that the FCC could be useful in identifying soil constraints that could affect low-input cropping systems' performance in other soils.

However, as one views the possibilities with FCC, it is important to note that one can transfer the results of research and experience on named kinds of soil between countries and continents in order to estimate potential for use. But farming systems are developed and used by people, and what they can and should do also depends on their social habits and goals (Kellogg, personal communication 1975).

Only one example (Moran 1987) was found in the anthropological literature where the FCC was used in an attempt to explain why some immigrants in colonization schemes have succeeded while others have not. In that study, just as important as (and perhaps more important than) the soil fertility levels of the various farmers was their farm management experience. Those with more farming and management experience did better than those with less.

Conclusions

The need to regard soils as a fundamental element to be assessed in the study of agrarian systems can hardly be doubted. No less important is to understand how people modify the soil environment within which plants grow in order to achieve their goals. Thus, reports should begin by indicating people's understanding of their soils (their ethnopedology, if you will). This can be supplemented with basic information such as color, texture, pH, and vegetation associated with particular soils. Major soil constraints can be reported, although it can be just as useful to note what soils are good for what crops according to the local classification. Additional data based upon core sampling and soil profile samples can also be given should greater detail be appropriate. The need for a quantitative grouping of surface-soil properties that define the boundary conditions of the uncontrolled variables within which field research is conducted is the most critical constraint to soil fertility evaluation and extrapolation of research results— and, as a consequence, a constraint to comparative analysis of agrarian systems. All user groups of soil fertility evaluation, anthropologists, land-use planners, extension workers, and both small and large farmers rely on information developed first by soil researchers. Soil researchers should, in turn, rely more on available anthropological data to ascertain the applicability of their extrapolations in diverse sociological settings.

A technical classification system such as the FCC, built upon quantitative natural soil classification systems, is suggested as the most immediate, obtainable tool in the extrapolation of soil-related research results. Each technical classification system has to be organized using quantitative criteria of practical significance to the applied technology. However, no single technical classification will equally serve all purposes.

When properly used (by building on soil taxonomic information) and combined with soil testing, the FCC could enable soil researchers to help farmers—no matter how small or remotely located—reduce risks and increase their chances of producing economical crop yields. The FCC can provide an initial basis for comparing agrarian systems' soil capabilities.

However, systems of interpretation must provide flexibility to adapt to local conditions and to specific uses and users of the land. In judging the reliability of the FCC, we must consider the fact that agricultural productivity of agrarian systems depends as much on the differing social habits and goals of people as it does on any soil index. This fact should not deter one from trying to characterize this important information on the physical conditions for plant growth. In so doing anthropologists, geographers, and agronomists have much to learn from each other.

References

Behrens, C., 1989. The scientific basis for Shipibo soil classification and land use. *American Anthropologist* 91:83–100.

Brady, N., 1984. *The Nature and Properties of Soils,* ninth edition. New York: Macmillan.

Buol, S. W., 1972. General soil conditions in tropical Central and South America. *Agronomic-Economic Research on Tropical Soils 1971–1972 Annual Report,* pp. 6–9. Raleigh: North Carolina State University.

Buol, S. W., and W. Couto, 1978. Fertility management interpretation and soil surveys of the tropics. In M. Drosdoff, R. B. Daniels, and J. J. Nicholaides, III, eds., *Diversity of Soils in the Tropics,* pp. 65–75. American Society of Agronomy Special Publication No. 34. Madison, Wisconsin.

Buol, S. W., and W. Couto, 1981. Soil fertility-capability assessment for use in the humid tropics. In D. J. Greenland, ed., *Characterization of Soils,* pp. 254–261. London: Wiley.

Buol, S. W., and J. J. Nicholaides III, 1980. Constraints to soil fertility evaluation of extrapolation of research results. In *Soil-Related Constraints to Food Production in the Tropics,* pp. 425–438. Los Baños, Phillipines: IRRI.

Buol, S. W., P. A. Sanchez, R. B. Cate, Jr., and M. A. Granger, 1975. Soil fertility capability classification. In E. Bornemisza and A. Alvarado, eds., *Soil Management in Tropical America,* pp. 126–141. Raleigh: North Carolina State University.

Carter, W., 1969. *New Lands and Old Traditions.* Gainesville: University of Florida, Latin American Studies Monograph Series.

Cate, R. B., and L. A. Nelson, 1971. A simple statistical procedure for portioning soil test correlation data into two classes. *Soil Science Society of America Proceedings* 35:658–659.

Cline, M. G., 1949. Basic principles of soil classification. *Soil Science* 67:81–91.

Cochrane, T. T. , J. A. Porras, L. G. de Azevedo, P. G. Jones, and L. F. Sanchez, 1979. *An Explanatory Manual for CIAT's Computerized Land Resource Study of Tropical America.* Cali, Colombia: CIAT.

Cohen, M., 1977. *The Food Crisis in Prehistory.* New Haven, CT: Yale University Press.

Conklin, H. C., 1957. *Hanunóo Agriculture.* Rome: Food and Agriculture Organization.

Dudal, R., 1980. *Soil Map of the World and Legend.* Rome: FAO/UNESCO.

Fitts, J. W., 1959. Research plus extension equals bigger farming profits. *Plant Food Review* 5:10–12.

Fitts, J. W., 1974. Proper soil fertility evaluation as an important key to increased crop yields. In H. Hernando, ed., *Fertilizers, Crop Quality and Economy,* pp. 5–30. New York: Elsevier Scientific Publishing Co.

Jeffrey, D. W., 1987. *Soil-Plant Relationships: An Ecological Approach.* Portland, OR: Timber Press.

Johnson, A., 1974. Ethnoecology and planting practices in a Swidden agricultural system. *American Ethnologist* 1:87–101.

Johnson, W. M., 1980. Soil-related constraints, soil properties and soil taxonomy. In IRRI, *Soil-Related Constraints to Food Production in the Tropics,* pp. 41–54. Los Baños, Phillipines: IRRI.

McCollum, R. E., and C. Valverde, 1968. The fertilization of potatoes in Peru. *North Carolina Agricultural Experimental Station Technical Bulletin* 185.

McCracken, R. J., 1987. Soils, soil scientists and civilization. *Soil Science Society of America Journal* 51(6):1395–1400.

Moran, E. F., 1979. *Human Adaptability: An Introduction to Ecological Anthropology.* North Scituate, MA: Duxbury Press.

———, 1981. *Developing the Amazon.* Bloomington: Indiana University Press.

———, 1987. Monitoring fertility degradation of agricultural lands in the lowland tropics. In P. D. Little, M. M. Horowitz, with A. E. Nyerges, eds., *Lands at Risk in the Third World: Local Level Perspectives,* pp. 69–91. Boulder: Westview Press.

———, 1993. *Through Amazonian Eyes: The Human Ecology of Amazonian Populations.* Iowa City: University of Iowa Press.

National Academy of Science, 1978. *Conservation of Germplasm Resources.* Washington, D.C.: NAS Press.

Nicholaides III, J. J., F. R. Cox, G. S. Miner, W. Couto, R. E. McCollum, S. W. Buol, and E. Hinojosa, 1978. Extrapolation fertilizer trials in Bolivia. *Agronomical Abstracts* 36:43.

Pope, R. A., and S. W. Buol, 1976. Improving the "i" modifier. In *Agronomic-Economic Research on Soils of the Tropics,* 1975 North Carolina State University Tropical Soils Program Annual Report, pp. 245–250.

Posey, D., and W. Balée, eds., 1989. *Resource Management in Amazonia.* Advances in Economic Botany No. 7. New York: New York Botanical Garden.

Reynolds, W. U., and G. W. Petersen eds., 1987. *Soil Survey Techniques.* Madison, WI: Soil Science Society of America, Special Publication No. 20.

Sanchez, P. A., W. Couto, and S. W. Buol, 1982. The fertility capability soil classification system: Interpretation, capability and modification. In *Geoderma* 27:283–309.

Sanchez, P. A., and J. R. Benites, 1987. Low-input cropping for acid soils of the humid tropics. In *Science* 238:1521–1527.

Sopher, C. D., and R. J. McCracken, 1973. Relationships between soil properties, management practices and corn yields in N. Atlantic coastal plain soils. *Agronomic Journal* 65:595–600.

Steila, D., 1976. *The Geography of Soils.* Englewood Cliffs, NJ: Prentice-Hall.

Waugh, D. L., R. B. Cate, Jr., L. A. Nelson, and A. Manzano, 1975. New concepts in biological and economical interpretation of fertilizer response. In E. Bornemisza and A. Alvarado, eds., *Soil Management in Tropical America,* pp. 484–501. Cali, Colombia: CIAT.

Wilken, G. C., 1987. *Good Farmers: Traditional Agricultural Resource Management in Mexico and Central America.* Berkeley: University of California Press.

4

The Social Organization
of Agrarian Labor

ROBERT McC. NETTING, GLENN D. STONE,
AND M. PRISCILLA STONE

> It must . . . be stressed that it is the social organization of labor, and not
> the tools and resources themselves, that are the proper subjects of our
> study [of cultural ecology], for it is only through the process of labor that
> nature and technique play their parts in molding society (Murphy
> 1970:157).

It is curious to observe that fieldwork for cultural anthropologists, even for
those who study farmers, has seldom dwelt on their subjects' work in the
fields. As a well-known Africanist observed to me once, "You can't very
well follow people around with a stopwatch, now, can you?" Agrarian
labor is so omnipresent, so diverse, and so mundane as to be uninteresting,
and when it does become complex, hierarchical, and industrial, then the
time/motion people from sociology and business management can take
over with their vaguely threatening flow charts and tables of time allocation. But if Murphy was right and the empirical, quantitative and qualitative, *scientific* study of labor is both necessary and possible, we must
devise the methods to collect standardized minimum data sets that permit
comparisons of agricultural task performance, both within societies over
time and cross-culturally (Epstein 1979).

Though the structure and function of human groups has always been
a prime object of anthropological study, and although the social relations of
production are basic for many more than merely Marxists, adequate studies
of nonmechanized agriculture are usually seen as requiring too much time

and effort, as being labor intensive for the investigator. But we can learn a lot about labor by fitting the scale of inquiry to the available research time and the questions at issue, building cumulatively from a basic descriptive profile to successively more precise and comprehensive characterizations of the system of farm work. The graded levels of investigation are: 1) descriptive, ethnoecological interviews with key farmer informants on the farming system, the agricultural labor task calendar, and the local types of work-group organization; 2) household surveys of membership, production, occupations, income, wealth, land tenure, and extrahousehold exchange and hired labor; and 3) labor time allocation, derived from observation, randomly sampled time frames, or daily records kept throughout the agricultural year.

An Ethnoecology of the Farming System

Until we know the names of things and the place of activities in space and time, we cannot ask meaningful questions or design useful research. If anthropologists have any slight advantage over agronomists and economists, it is the priority we give to learning the native model, assuming the existence of an ethnoecology of work and a system of cognitive categories reflecting a shared folk culture of utilitarian agrarian behavior (Hunn 1982). Knowledgeable local farmers or key informants (Connell and Lipton 1977:90) can teach us the agricultural vocabulary and provide the broad general outline of successive activities. Just such a summary (though perhaps in less emic terms) was collected by a farming system rapid reconnaissance team on the *Sondeo*[1] that includes a description of the cropping or farming system, a characterization of the farmers' socioeconomic situation, and a report on the availability of labor and its periodic scarcity (Hildebrand 1981; Collinson 1981).

Informal, open-ended questions can elicit material on the following matters with a minimal lexicon of terms in the local language.

1. *What* is produced?—major crops, domestic animals, gathered products, fish, and game.
2. *When* do major activities take place according to the seasonal schedule or calendrical designations marked by climatic features? Learning the yearly cycle of agriculture through such a conducted "grand tour of time" (Werner and Schoepfle 1987:329) is not threatening to the local consultant, nor need it be as detailed as a cognitive ethnoscience ethnography would require.
3. *For what purpose* are agricultural products produced?—subsistence, exchange, sale for cash (including estimated proportions for various purposes).

4. *How* are agricultural tasks done?—major tasks with distinctive names that reflect typological differences (for example, the variety of terms for hoe cultivation/ridging/mounding in a West African society); tools and equipment used.

5. *Who* works?—division of labor by gender, age, status; social units of production at the level of individual, family segment (married couple, co-wives, teenaged girls, etc.), household, suprahousehold local group (descent group, neighborhood, village, age set), ad hoc work group (exchange or reciprocal labor, friends, emergency aid, festive labor), or patron-client network; corvée, or tribute labor; and wage work (in kind, shares, piece work, permanent employment).

6. *Constraints*—folk explanations of limiting factors such as shortages of labor, seasonal bottlenecks (Collinson 1981:445), cash for wage labor, preferences for types of labor organization (for example, beer party work over paid contract labor).[2]

7. *System* operations—a synthetic outline (by the investigator as checked with local consultants) of crop, season, task and tool, agency or labor group. May form contrasting specializations (dairy, wine, small grains) or levels of operation (cottager, smallholder peasant, traditional estate, agribusiness). Simplified models of the farming cycle can be represented by tables (Figure 4.1) showing months, crops, and operations (Netting 1968:66) or by circular graphs (Figure 4.2) of the annual round (Schultz 1976: 140).

The timing of labor—in addition to its relative amount, its quality, and the special skills and knowledge it requires—becomes more important as the agricultural system becomes more intensive (Boserup 1965; Turner and Brush 1987). The management of labor, especially within the corporate household, becomes a critical element when the smallholder must face conditions of heavy local population density and the demand for both subsistence and cash production (Netting 1993). In conceptualizing the complexity of such ecosystems, it can be useful to graphically model the link between significant environmental variables (topography, soils, water) and land use for crops and livestock (Figure 4.3). Such an approach has been used in agricultural development to specify problems and opportunities for beneficial change (McCracken et al. 1988). Farmers themselves can draw pictures (Figure 4.4) of integrated systems of cultivation and aquaculture, as in this Vietnamese system comprising irrigated rice; mulched, dike-grown onions, peanuts, and cassava; tree crops of mango, coconut, and eucalyptus; cattle and poultry; and shrimp for market (Lightfoot and Tuan 1990). The diversity and scheduling of farm labor can only be adequately comprehended in the context of a distinctive and highly differentiated agrarian ecology.

Figure 4.1 Kofyar Farming Calendar

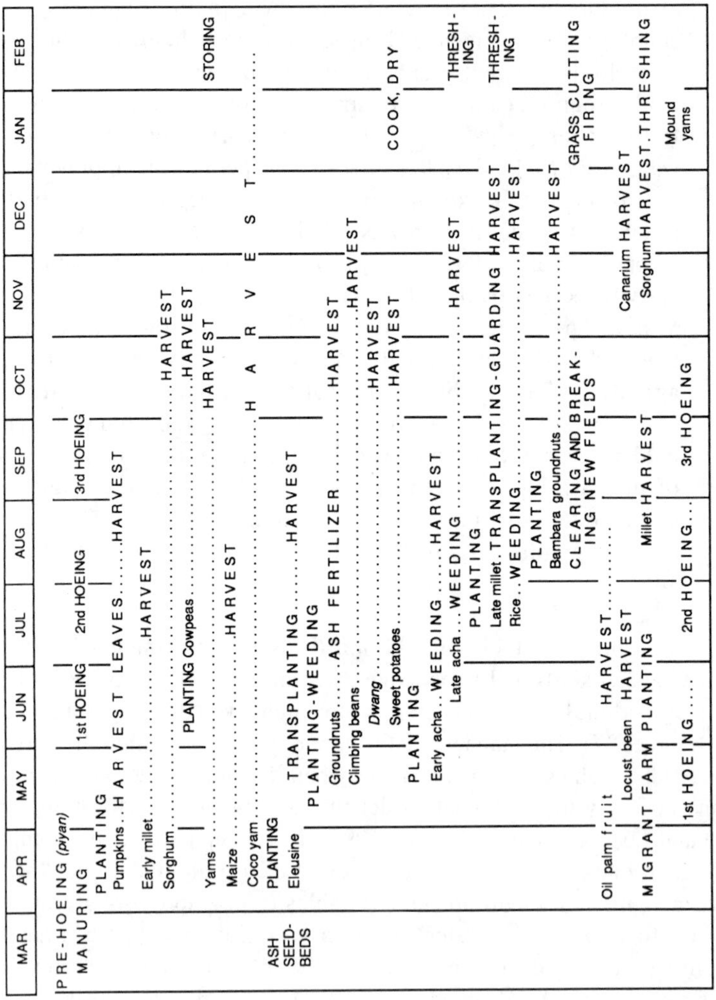

Source: Netting 1968:66. Reprinted with permission.

Figure 4.2 Hausa Farming Calendar, Soba District, Nigeria

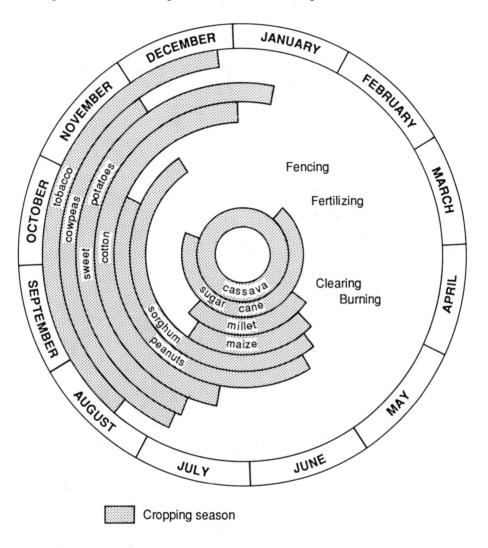

Cropping season

Source: Schultz 1976: 140.

Figure 4.3 Transect of Village in North Pakistan

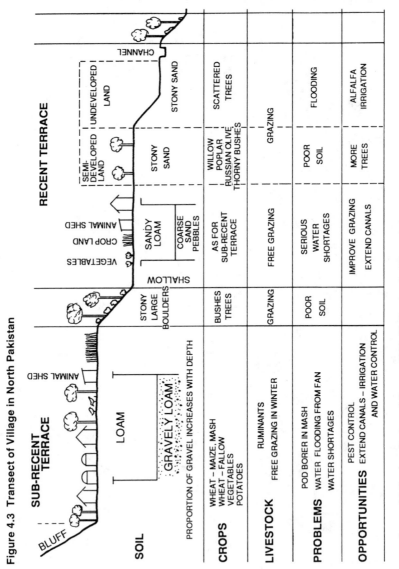

Source: McCracken, Pretty, and Conway 1988: 36. Reprinted with permission.

**Figure 4.4 Material Flows in a Vietnamese Integrated Farming System, Based
on Local Farmers' Drawings**

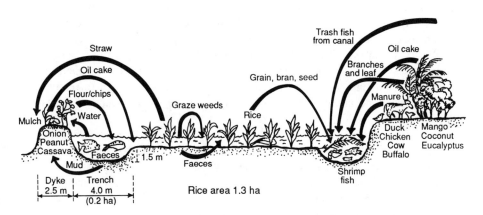

Source: Lightfoot and Tuan 1990. Reprinted with permission.

Household Survey

A fundamental instrument for the collection of data on farming in
most rural communities is the household survey, an interview schedule
encompassing the membership, composition, and economic activities of
coresidential social units of production and consumption (Netting, Wilk,
and Arnould 1984). Covering whole communities, random samples, or
stratified samples from a number of communities, the household survey can
reflect significant differences in labor supply and productiveness between
various farming systems, stages of the household developmental cycle, or
physical environments as well as between contrasting ethnic, religious,
occupational, property holding, or class groupings. A well-formulated census of a representative sample structures data collection for maximum
information and greatest comparability (Colson 1954) and allows efficient
coding and computer analysis. Carefully trained and supervised local enumerators can conduct quite extensive interviews using their own linguistic
skills, rapport, and fund of cultural knowledge, thereby reaching a broader
cross-section of the population than the investigator could and relieving the
primary researcher of a routine task. Constructing and testing a survey is an
ideal way to develop familiarity with the population and create a staff of
assistants early in field research (Pelto and Pelto 1978:193).

Though it is relatively quick, cheap, and simple and provides the "statistic documentation" advanced by Malinowski and practiced by his students (Bennett and Thaiss 1970), the household survey is a methodology taken for granted and scarcely mentioned in fieldwork manuals. Taking a census is a prosaic, residual job, good for doing, as Sol Tax once said, when you can't think of anything else to do. But a proper set of household protocols can check and document an investigator's impressions, open up unsuspected lines of inquiry, and provide tabulations crucial to testing hypotheses and analyses developed long after the field research is complete.

The household—as opposed to the individual (cf. Bernard 1988:47), the mother-child dyad, the lineage, the business firm, or the manor—was selected as the unit of survey because of the banal observation that among farmers the family household is a significant unit of production and consumption, often, though not invariably, distinguishable by common residence, reproduction and socialization, and intergenerational transmission of rights to the means of production (Wilk and Netting 1984; Netting 1993). Furthermore, even if cooking, agricultural work, and landholding do not take place exactly in the same unit (Leach 1967), and even if the household is not an autonomous unit of production and consumption with a single male head (Sanjek 1982; Woodford-Berger 1981; Guyer 1981; McMillan 1986), households continue to mobilize a great deal of agricultural labor, and they provide the most functional, easily recognizable, and frequently surveyed socioeconomic unit cross-culturally.

Household surveys have infinite variations but the theme is common. At the minimum, a census should determine sex, age, and place of residence for each member of a community (Johnson 1978:84). These questions are conveniently asked in the household context, where the other important demographic and social characteristics of kinship or other relations to the household head, marital status and history, parents (of adults), place of origin, and migration history are also easily determined. Members' education, religion, and occupation can also be specified. The elementary facts of household size and composition or type (Netting 1965, 1979; Hammel and Laslett 1974) open the way to consideration of labor organization and economic adaptation as being contingent on stage in the developmental cycle of the household (Goody 1958), dependency ratio (Chayanov 1966), the contribution of nonagricultural labor (Levine 1977), or the influence of cash cropping. If restudies or historical records show a change in household form through time (Figure 4.5), the role of the household in accommodating to changing labor needs and economic constraints may be a primary explanatory variable (Netting 1979). Repeated censuses of the same population (Scudder and Colson 1978) allow the construction of household histories (Carter 1984) that relate labor mobilization to the developmental cycle and the domestic group.

Figure 4.5 Kofyar Household Size and Composition, by Years Spent in Cash Cropping

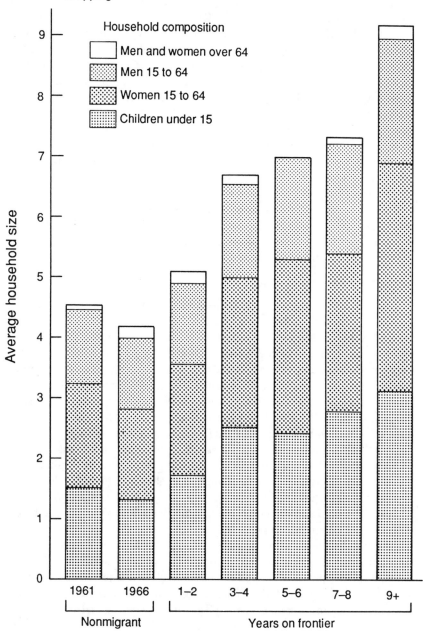

Source: Netting 1993:90. Reprinted with permission.

The household survey should include information on production of all major crops, amounts sold, and prices, preferably for the last two harvests. Individual members may, like Kofyar married women (Stone 1988), also have individual production and income, and where there are nonagricultural employment opportunities it may be useful to have estimates of the proportion of time (weekends only, school vacations, evenings, etc.) spent in farming. Livestock should also be counted, and appropriate measures of land owned or used, its location, type of tenure, and how and when acquired[3] are desirable. Indices of household wealth may also include vehicles, dwellings, purchased materials, and amenities such as iron beds, radios, and lamps. The definition of socioeconomic strata provides perhaps the most powerful discrimination of major differences in agricultural choices of farming system, types of labor, and relative returns to labor (Bartlett 1982; Hart 1986). The interview schedule can also include summary information on nonhousehold labor by sources utilized in the last year (such as exchange, festive, communal corvée, wage), agricultural task, days or hours in each task, number of workers, origin of workers (neighborhood, village, district, migrant), and cost in cash or kind.

Labor Time Allocation

The household survey gives only the rough outlines of labor resources, available land, and some indication of capital along with estimates of total farm production and returns. A more refined description and economic analysis of labor requires some study of actual labor time allocation. Though societies may be differentially involved in the market and have varying monetary standards for the measurement of economic activities, time is a common resource of all groups, always in some sense scarce, subject to choices about alternative uses and to quantitative assessment (Epstein 1967:156; Carlstein 1982). Because farm labor is applied to a wide variety of tasks over an entire agricultural year by individuals of different ages and sexes and by variously constituted groups, collection of scientifically valid data is likely to require sustained field observations, carefully controlled record keeping, and considerable research expense. Direct observation by the investigator of who does what for how long sets limits on the number of people potentially observed, the representativeness of the sample, the period covered, and the possible "Hawthorne effect" (wherein the observer's presence leads to changed behavior). It is arduous, often boring, and costly in time and money (Gross 1984; Grossman 1984a), and it may be carried on with stopwatch precision (McSweeny and Freedman 1980) that is probably unnecessary.

More efficient is the use of randomly sampled time frames (Johnson 1975) where a group of households are visited for a brief period on randomly selected days and hours. The observer notes what each individual in the group is doing and gathers information on the activities of absent individuals.[4] Dividing the number of observations of a particular activity by the total number of observations for the entire period (usually close to a year) gives the percentage of time and therefore the average number of hours per day devoted to that activity. Such random spot checks have the virtue of low time requirements (often no more than several hours a week), unbiased coverage of all types of work (including nonfarm activities) by *all* household members, and the creation of a large corpus of observations. Johnson (1975) made 3,495 observations on 134 days over a 10-month period, whereas Grossman (1984a) had 3,262 observations of 13 households on 69 days. Though coded categories may contain a great deal of information— for example, female head preparing food, straining manioc beer (Johnson 1978:89)—time-use categories are often stated in terms of gross contrasts, such as agriculture/hunting/tool-making/leisure or compound/bush/minor crop farming (Tripp 1982). The growing complexity and rapid seasonal change in the mix of activities that characterizes agricultural intensification by smallholders may create important daily and weekly differences in labor allocation that slip through the mesh of this sampling method (Netting 1993:102–122).

Agricultural economists concerned with greater detail and larger samples favor the systematic gathering of individual labor data via repetitive interviews every three or four days, relying on the short-term recall of individuals (Saunders 1979). For an entire farming season this may require expensive, full-time, well-trained local interviewers supervised by a research staff. Norman (1969) used this method for forty-five randomly selected farm families in each of three villages. This approach provides a more extensive set of observations than the unaided single researcher can collect (White 1976), and it has a much higher validity than the one-time questionnaire study, which asks farmers to estimate time in major tasks for the entire year (Saunders 1979).[5]

A middle-range alternative to the organization and payment of a cadre of employed interviewers is the enlistment of literate farmers to maintain labor diaries on the members of their own and perhaps one or two neighboring households. Hildebrand (1981) used such farmer *registros* (Whyte and Boynton 1983), as did Swift (1981) with Sahelian pastoralists. In our own study, (Stone et al. 1990) seven young Kofyar resident enumerators kept daily track of fifteen sample households (including their own) with twenty-six males and thirty-six females over the age of 15 for a total of fifty weeks in 1984 and 1985.[6] For each household, a weekly form was filled out listing each adult, each day, and all tasks by type and duration (if they were 45 minutes or more) rounded to the nearest hour.[7] These returns were checked weekly or biweekly by one of the investigators. Tasks were designated by crop and operation (for example, mounding yams, brewing millet beer, harvesting sorghum) using Kofyar words, and a total of 247 different activities (using 121 tasks and 53 crops or other subjects) were eventually coded for tabulation. The enumerators also indicated whether the task was performed on an individual plot, the homestead farm of the resident household, or someone else's field. For all labor groups of three people or more, we recorded the type (exchange, festive, wage) and the number of participants. Certain categories of workers (such as children) were omitted, leisure time was not specified, and domestic chores were partially neglected,[8] but our approximately 50,000 observations still gave a finely grained depiction of the seasonal sequence and timing of adult agricultural tasks (van de Waal 1975); the division of labor by gender; the means of mobilizing labor by household, exchange, and beer party groups; and the allocation of scarce labor to competing tasks (Figures 4.6, 4.7).

Compiling labor allocation data is itself labor intensive, requiring collection over long periods, sustained supervision of the process, and coding, programming, and computer analysis. If agricultural labor turned out to be as routine, homogeneous, and cross-culturally similar as was once thought, time allocation data would not be worth the effort. But we now know that there is a great deal of theoretical significance riding on the regular differences that the numbers show. If, as Boserup (1965) claims, population density and agricultural intensity are correlated, and if the cost of intensification is often higher labor input per unit produced, then intensive cultivators should be working more and longer hours. Comparative studies (Cleave 1974; Ruthenberg 1971; Norman 1972; Minge-Klevana 1980; Lagemann 1977) show that this is indeed the case. The Kofyar spend approximately 1,600 hours of labor in cultivation a year, double that of their neighbors, the Hausa (Stone et al. 1990). The major contribution of child labor to the household (Nag, White, and Peet 1978; Cain 1980) gives a clear economic rationale for high fertility, and the loss of children to schooling and delayed entry into the farm labor force has a definable cost (Minge-Klevana 1980). Female labor in direct production and domestic work can now be measured and more accurately valued and its often lower marginal returns in the market place ascertained (Hart 1986). Time allocation studies may be particularly important in evaluating the "hidden" work of women in both production and reproduction of the household; it may also help remove biases against unpaid domestic activities (Gross 1984:533; Roberts et al. 1982).

Does cash cropping subtract necessary labor from subsistence production or raise total work inputs? Economic developers should heed the changing labor profiles of New Guinea coffee growers and cattle raisers (Grossman 1984b:210–219). As peasant farmers increasingly pursue seasonal labor migration or take up part-time cottage industrial crafts or trade, labor time may increase, periods of unemployment may menace the landless, and seasonal bottlenecks may worsen in agriculture. We cannot

Figure 4.6 Weekly Agricultural Labor Inputs

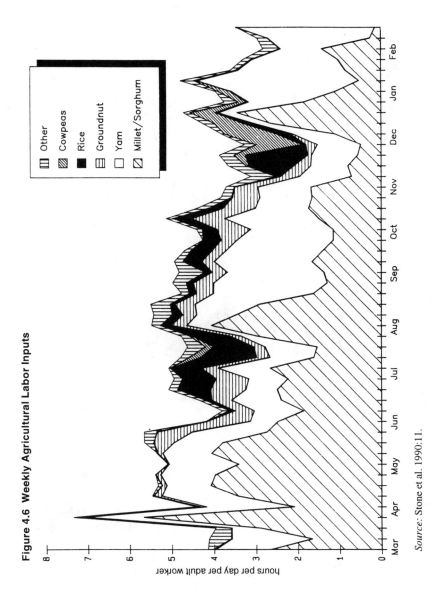

Source: Stone et al. 1990:11.

Figure 4.7 Kofyar Labor Inputs and Work Groups

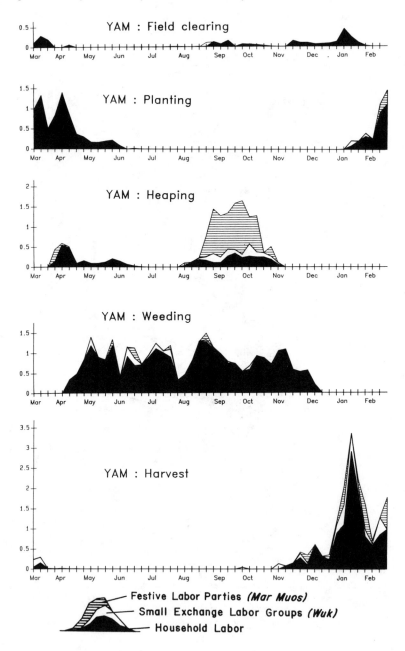

Source: Stone et al. 1990:18.

evaluate the utility of economic choices made in the course of rapid development unless we can estimate returns per hour in a range of available occupations (Barlett 1980).

Times change and with them time allocation, and even our present rudimentary methods can harness time's winged chariot to the cultivation of new knowledge of agrarian systems. But regardless of whether or not we can expend the effort to collect this data, we must begin our investigations of labor with an ethnoecology of farming system crops, calendar, and tasks, followed by a household survey of work and production.

Notes

We are grateful for the research assistance, references, and editorial suggestions provided by Ms. Andrea Smith. Professor Sutti Ortiz and other members of the symposium also commented on the original draft of this paper. The organization of data collection on Kofyar labor allocation was conducted in the field by M. Priscilla Stone, and analysis was done by Glenn D. Stone. Support for this project came from the National Science Foundation (BNS-8318569), the Wenner-Gren Foundation for Anthropological Research, and a University of Arizona Social and Behavioral Sciences Summer Grant. John Hollingsworth redrafted several of the figures.

1. The Sondeo is "a 7-day exercise consisting of: 1) identifying an homogeneous cropping system among farmers in an area; 2) employing a team of five agricultural scientists and five social scientists who work in bidisciplinary pairs to investigate the local conditions with farmer interviews: the pairs change after each of the four days of the field study and daily post-survey team discussions take place; 3) the preparation of a report over the weekend, by amalgamating the reports of each individual team member" (McCracken et al. 1988:52–53).

2. The International Potato Center's Informal Agricultural Survey (Rhoades 1979) asks farmers to rank their production problems in order of importance.

3. Agricultural economists (Norman 1972; Lagemann 1977) often collect their labor data on the basis of particular fields or plots, for which other inputs (such as fertilizer or use of draft animals) are also recorded and from which the outputs of crops are tabulated. Where land is the scarce factor of production and productivity calculations are sought, this procedure may be reasonable, but anthropologists will probably continue to focus on the multifunctional household enterprise as a necessary first step in analyzing farm labor in Third World contexts.

4. For a discussion of other "spot sampling" studies and their limitations, see Bernard 1988:280–289.

5. Landlords or large-farm managers using purchased inputs such as wage labor, draft animals or rented machinery, seeds, fertilizer, and irrigation water may have a fairly accurate perception of annual labor time required for separate operations on specific crops in fields of known sizes, as is the case in India (Epstein 1967).

6. Wagenbuur (1973) used five middle school leavers to collect daily time budgets from five households of Ghanaian lime farmers. The observers actually accompanied the farmers and their wives for four days a week during the first month. For the remaining eleven months of the study, direct observations were con-

fined to one day a week, and a daily interview of about fifteen minutes was conducted each night (Wagenbuur 1973:147).

    7. It can be argued that instead of measuring labor in hours, half-days are a
more useful unit because people tend to do agricultural tasks in half-day chunks
(Levi and Havinden 1982:58). Hours may also be a misleading measurement
because "an hour's work can be carried out more or less energetically," and it is difficult to factor in the health and experience of the worker, the degree of motivation,
and the urgency of the particular task (Levi and Havinden 1982:58–59). Short-term,
repetitive jobs (for example, farm chores such as feeding chickens, milking a cow,
spreading beans to dry in the courtyard, or cleaning out a stall) may also be underrepresented by hour-long time slices. The proliferation of minor husbandry and pro-
cessing tasks may well be characteristic of more intensive agricultural systems.

    8. Levi and Havinden (1982:56) suggest the useful distinction between *req-
uisite* and *productive* labor. Requisite labor is that needed to obtain the final product
but the amount of which may bear no relation to output. An example would be the
time spent walking to and from fields or preparing meals. It may be necessary to
classify leisure activity, such as resting in the course of work or relaxing at the beer
party after a bout of exchange labor, as requisite to production.

References

Barlett, Peggy F., 1980. Adaptive strategies in peasant agricultural production.
    Annual Review of Anthropology 9:545–573.

———, 1982. *Agricultural Choice and Change: Economic Decisions and
    Agricultural Evolution in a Costa Rican Community.* New Brunswick: Rutgers
    University Press.

Bennett, J. W., and G. Thaiss, 1970. Survey research in anthropological fieldwork.
    In R. Naroll and R. Cohen, eds., *A Handbook of Method in Cultural
    Anthropology,* pp. 316-377. Garden City, NY: Natural History Press.

Bernard, H. Russell, 1988. *Research Methods in Cultural Anthropology.* Newbury
    Park, CA: Sage.

Boserup, Ester, 1965. *The Conditions of Agricultural Growth.* Chicago: Aldine.

Cain, Mead T., 1980. The economic activities of children in a village in
    Bangladesh. In H. P. Binswanger, R. E. Evenson, C. A. Florencia, B.N.F.
    White, eds., *Rural Household Studies in Asia,* pp. 218–247. Singapore:
    Singapore University Press.

Carlstein, Tommy, 1982. *Time Resources, Society and Ecology.* London: Allen and
    Unwin.

Carter, Anthony T., 1984. Household histories. In R. McC. Netting, R. R. Wilk, and
    E. J. Arnould, eds., *Households: Comparative and Historical Studies of the
    Domestic Group,* pp. 44–83. Berkeley: University of California Press.

Chayanov, A. V., ed., 1966. *The Theory of Peasant Economy.* Homewood, IL:
    Richard D. Irwin.

Clark, B. A., 1975. The work done by rural women in Malawi. *East Africa Journal
    of Rural Development* 8:80–91.

Cleave, John H., 1974. *African Farmers: Labor Use in the Development of
    Smallholder Agriculture.* New York: Praeger.

Collinson, Michael, 1981. A low cost approach to understanding small farmers.
    Agricultural Administration 8:433–450.

Colson, Elizabeth, 1954. The intensive study of small sample communities. In Robert F. Spencer, ed., *Method and Perspective in Anthropology,* pp.43–59. Minneapolis: University of Minnesota Press.

Connell, John, and Michael Lipton, 1977. *Assessing Village Labour Situations in Developing Countries.* Delhi: Oxford University Press.

De Schlippe, Pierre, 1956. *Shifting Cultivation in Africa: The Zande System of Agriculture.* London: Routledge and Kegan Paul.

Epstein, T. S., 1967. The data of economics in anthropological analysis. In A. L. Epstein, ed., *The Craft of Social Anthropology,* pp. 153–180. London: Tavistock.

———, 1979. Mysore villages revisited. In G. M. Foster, T. Scudder, E. Colson, R. V. Kemper, eds., *Long Term Field Research in Social Anthropology,* pp. 209–226. New York: Academic.

Goody, Jack, ed., 1958. *The Developmental Cycle in Domestic Groups.* Cambridge: Cambridge University Press.

Gross, Daniel R., 1984. Time allocation: A tool for the study of cultural behavior. *Annual Review of Anthropology* 13:519–558.

Grossman, L. S., 1984a. Collecting time-use data in Third World rural communities. *Professional Geographer* 36:444–454.

———, 1984b. *Peasants, Subsistence Ecology, and Development in the Highlands of Papua New Guinea.* Princeton: Princeton University Press.

Guyer, Jane I., 1981. Household and community in African studies. *African Studies Review* 24:87–137.

Hammel, E. A., and Peter Laslett, 1974. Comparing household structure over time and between cultures. *Comparative Studies in Society and History* 16:73–109.

Hart, Gillian, 1986. *Power, Labor, and Livelihood: Processes of Change in Rural Java.* Berkeley: University of California Press.

Hildebrand, P. E., 1981. Combining disciplines in rapid appraisal: The Sondeo approach. *Agricultural Administration* 8:423–432.

Hunn, E., 1982. The utilitarian factor of folk biological classification. *American Anthropologist* 84:830–847.

Johnson, Allen W., 1975. Time allocation in a Machiguenga community. *Ethnology* 14:310–321.

———, 1978. *Quantification in Cultural Anthropology: An Introduction to Research Design.* Stanford: Stanford University Press.

Lagemann, Johannes, 1977. *Traditional African Farming Systems in Eastern Nigeria: An Analysis of Reaction to Increasing Population Pressure.* Munich: Weltforum Verlag.

Leach, E., 1967. An anthropologist's reflections on a social survey. In D. G. Jongmans and P. Gutkind, eds., *Anthropologists in the Field,* pp. 75–88. New York: Humanities.

Levi, John, and Michael Havinden, 1982. *Economics of African Agriculture.* Essex: Longman.

Levine, David, 1977. *Family Formation in an Age of Nascent Capitalism.* New York: Academic.

Lightfoot, Clive, and Nguyen Ahn Tuan, 1990. Drawing pictures of farms helps everyone. *ILEIA Newsletter* 6(3):18–19.

McCracken, Jennifer A., Jules N. Pretty, and Gordon R. Conway, 1988. *Introduction to Rapid Rural Appraisal.* London: International Institute for Environment and Development.

McMillan, Della E., 1986. Distribution of resources and products in Mossi households. In A. Hansen and D. E. McMillan, eds., *Food in Sub-Saharan Africa,* pp. 260–273. Boulder: Lynne Rienner Publishers.

McSweeney, B. G., and M. Freedman, 1980. Lack of time as an obstacle to women's education: The case of Upper Volta. *Comparative Education Review* 24:124-139.

Minge-Klevana, Wanda, 1980. Does labor time decrease with industrialization? A survey of time-allocation studies. *Current Anthropology* 21:279–298.

Murphy, Robert F., 1970. Basic ethnography and ecological theory. In Earl H. Swanson, Jr., ed., *Languages and Cultures of Western North America,* pp. 152–171. Pocatello: Idaho State University Press.

Nag, M., B.N.F. White, and R. C. Peet, 1978. An anthropological approach to the study of the economic value of children in Java and Nepal. *Current Anthropology* 19:293–306.

Netting, Robert McC., 1965. Household organization and intensive agriculture: The Kofyar case. *Africa* 35:422–429.

———, 1968. *Hill Farmers of Nigeria: Cultural Ecology of the Kofyar of the Jos Plateau.* Seattle: University of Washington Press.

———, 1979. Household dynamics in a nineteenth-century Swiss village. *Journal of Family History* 4:39–58.

———, 1993. *Smallholders, Householders: Farm Families and the Ecology of Intensive, Sustainable Agriculture.* Stanford: Stanford University Press.

Netting, R. McC., R. R. Wilk, and E. J. Arnould, eds., 1984. *Households: Comparative and Historical Studies of the Domestic Group.* Berkeley: University of California Press.

Norman, David W., 1969. Labour inputs of farmers: A case study of the Zaria Province of the North-Central State of Nigeria. *Nigerian Journal of Economic and Social Studies* 11:3–14.

———, 1972. *An Economic Survey of Three Villages in Zaria Province.* Samaru Miscellaneous Paper Nos. 37, 38. Zaria: Institute for Agricultural Research, Ahmadu Bello University.

Pelto, P. J., and G. H. Pelto, 1978. *Anthropological Research: The Structure of Inquiry.* Second edition. Cambridge: Cambridge University Press.

Rhoades, R. E., 1979. *The Art of the Informal Agricultural Survey.* Social Science Department Training Document 1979–1981. Lima, Peru: International Potato Center.

Roberts, S. B., A. A. Paul, T. J. Cole, and R. G. Whitehead, 1982. Seasonal changes in activity, birth weight and lactational performance in rural Gambian women. *Transactions of the Royal Society of Tropical Medicine and Hygiene* 76:668–678.

Ruthenberg, Hans, 1971. *Farming Systems in the Tropics.* Oxford: Clarendon.

Sanjek, Roger, 1982. The organization of households in Adabraka: Toward a wider comparative perspective. *Comparative Studies in Society and History* 24:57–103.

Saunders, Margaret O., 1979. Data acquisition. *Workshop on Sahelian Agriculture,* Department of Agricultural Economics, Purdue University, III-A, pp. 1–15.

Schultz, J. F., 1976. *Population and Agricultural Change in Nigerian Hausaland.* Ph.D. dissertation, Columbia University.

Scudder, Thayer, and Elizabeth Colson, 1978. Long-term field research in Gwembe Valley, Zambia. In G. M. Foster, T. Scudder, E. Colson, and R. V. Kemper, eds., *Long-term Field Research in Social Anthropology,* pp. 227–254. New York: Academic Press.

Stone, Glenn D., Robert McC. Netting, and M. Priscilla Stone, 1990. Seasonality, labor scheduling, and agricultural intensification in the Nigerian savanna. *American Anthropologist* 92:7–23.

Stone, M. Priscilla, 1988. Women doing well: A restudy of the Nigerian Kofyar. *Research in Economic Anthropology* 10:287–306.

Swift, J., 1981. Rapid appraisal and cost-effective participatory research in dry pastoral areas of West Africa. *Agricultural Administration* 8:485–492.

Tripp, Robert B., 1982. Time allocation in northern Ghana: An example of the random visit method. *Journal of Developing Areas* 16:391–400.

Turner, B. L., and S. Brush, eds., 1987. *Comparative Farming Systems.* New York: Guilford Press.

van de Waal, Etienne, 1975. Population and development. In J. C. Caldwell, ed. *Population Growth and Socioeconomic Change in West Africa,* pp. 136–153. New York: Columbia University Press.

Wagenbuur, H.T.M., 1973. Labour and development. An analysis of the time budget of lime farmers in Southern Ghana. In I. M. Ofari, ed., *Factors of Economic Growth in West Africa,* pp. 145–157. Legon: University of Ghana.

Werner, Oswald, and G. Mark Schoepfle, 1987. *Systematic Fieldwork. Vol. 1: Foundations of Ethnography and Interviewing.* Newbury Park: Sage.

White, Benjamin, 1976. Population, involution, and employment in rural Java. *Development and Change* 7:267–290.

Whyte, W. F., and D. Boynton, eds., 1983. *Higher Yielding Human Systems for Agriculture.* Ithaca: Cornell University Press.

Wilk, Richard R., and Robert McC. Netting, 1984. Households: changing forms and functions. In R. McC. Netting, R. R. Wilk, and E. J. Arnould, eds., *Households: Comparative and Historical Studies of the Domestic Group,* pp. 1–28. Berkeley: University of California Press.

Woodford-Berger, Prudence, 1981. Women in houses: The organization of residence and work in rural Ghana. *Antropologiska Studier* 30–31:3–35.

5

Minimum Data Sets in the Study of Exchange and Distribution

LILLIAN TRAGER

Exchange and distribution are fundamental to the organization of all societies. As the anthropological literature on a wide range of human societies demonstrates, exchange and distribution are institutionalized in a variety of specific ways. Belshaw pointed out some thirty years ago that

> exchange penetrates through the social fabric and may be thought of as a network holding society together. This applies whether we think of an isolated family group, the members of which give each other support and the benefit of differentiated services; or of a Oceanic culture in which reciprocal service and obligations link together in reflection of social structure and values; or of modern capitalism or communism in which exchange is rationalized by reference to a price system (1965:6).

The anthropological literature includes many important studies of exchange and distribution in specific societies or regions. Malinowski's classic study of the kula system in the Trobriands (1932) has become *the* case used to exemplify reciprocal exchange institutions and is probably referred to in nearly every introductory textbook. Likewise, Bohannon and Dalton's compilation of research on markets in Africa (1962) was for a long time the major reference point for the understanding of market exchange in that region, and Skinner's studies of Chinese markets (1964, 1965) set forth crucial perspectives on understanding marketplaces as systems within which exchange occurs.

Other fields of study have also contributed to the anthropological discourse on exchange and distribution. Geography, in particular, has provided widely used analytical methods such as central-place theory. But most

75

geographical research focuses on markets and retail distribution in First World industrial economies, such as that of the United States, and only touches tangentially on some of the most crucial questions in anthropological studies. For anthropologists, these questions include not simply the economic organization of exchange and distribution but also the social organization of these activities and the ways in which these institutions are connected to other societal institutions and processes (see Netting et al., Chapter 4, for discussion of production).

A major attempt to examine these issues and generalize about them from the data available was Belshaw's 1965 book, *Traditional Exchange and Modern Markets.* This study not only examined the organization of exchange in various types of economic systems but also sought to consider the dynamics of change in those economies as they were affected by worldwide economic developments in the contemporary period. Since the publication of that book, there have been many additional studies of exchange and distribution in societies around the world, and new theoretical perspectives on economic change, such as world systems theory and dependency theory, have emerged. Yet attempts at generalization about these key institutions have been limited; comparative analysis has not kept up with the richness of detailed ethnographic research.

A basic problem with attempts at comparison and generalization is the disparate nature of the data presented. To give a rather simple example: Several years ago, as part of a review of the literature on African rural markets, I sought to determine the extent to which women play key roles as traders in the market systems of Africa (Trager and Spring 1988). I knew they were central in the society I had studied (the Yoruba) and in some other West African societies (for example, the Ashanti). But when I looked for specific information on this question in the extensive literature on African markets, it was simply not there; many studies, addressing a variety of issues, did not provide basic demographic data on who the traders were in the markets under study.

Furthermore, despite the obvious importance of exchange and distribution systems in the study of agrarian economies, there has been relatively little discussion of methodologies for studying these systems. Whereas study of agrarian production systems can focus largely on household and community levels of social organization (see Netting et al., Chapter 4), the study of exchange systems inevitably takes one outside the household and often outside the local community as well. Data collection methods must therefore include ways to consider the linkages to regional, national, and even international economic systems yet remain within the reach of an anthropologist in the field. The basic (i.e., minimum) questions to be considered in studying exchange and distribution systems include the following:

1. What is being exchanged or distributed?
2. Who is involved in these exchanges?
3. How are exchanges organized?
4. When does exchange and distribution take place?
5. Where does exchange and distribution take place?

Some of the institutions that are central to exchange and distribution are highly visible; others are not. For example, markets and marketplaces are usually obvious loci on the landscape and are likely to draw the attention of even the most casual observer. At the same time, however, markets are complex and confusing, with large numbers of people milling about, bargaining over prices, buying and selling goods. Even though the activity is obvious, it is not self-evident how best to go about studying it. Conversely, exchange between households may be very difficult to observe and may therefore be totally overlooked; but such exchanges—for example, the remittances sent by urban migrants to family in rural areas—may be very important aspects of local economic systems.[1] In discussing minimum data sets in the study of exchange and distribution, we need to consider data on both the visible and the less visible institutions.

My goal in this chapter is to set out some of the ways to obtain data in the consideration of fundamental questions in the study of exchange and distribution and to suggest the types of minimum data sets that can be utilized as a basis for comparative analysis. I also indicates type of data that go beyond minimum data sets and that can be used for more in-depth study. I consider four levels of data that can be used for comparative analysis, beginning with the data that is most accessible and leading to that which involves more work on the part of the investigator. The utilization of available data, including locally published and government records, is considered first. Second, key informant interviews, particularly of specialists involved in distribution and trade, are discussed. Third, the value of survey data is examined; surveys at the household level and beyond are suggested. Finally, data from observations and more detailed interviewing are considered. The chapter is organized around these four types of data, and I point out how each can provide the information needed to engage in comparative discussion of the basic questions listed above.

I suggest that these sources of data can provide minimum data sets and serve as the basis for moving to more detailed analysis. Existing published data can yield information on some questions, whereas key informants can be utilized to obtain other minimum data. Survey data and participant observation can also assist in answering some basic questions and, if desired, can be the basis for more extensive study of exchange and distribution. At the end of the chapter, these different types of data are divided into four levels, from the minimum to the most comprehensive (see Table 5.1).

Throughout the discussion, I emphasize the necessity to move beyond the household level to consider distribution and exchange networks both within and beyond local communities. In a sense, then, the chapter begins where Netting et al. left off in Chapter 4. Minimum data sets in the study of exchange and distribution provide information not only on household involvement in exchange but also on issues such as flows of goods, setting of prices, and organization of markets. These are crucial questions, especially as anthropologists study changing economies and societies. A central concern in recent anthropological work has been to move beyond the description and analysis of exchange institutions in isolation ("the Yoruba marketplace") to the study of these institutions in the context of wider systems of socioeconomic change. In recent years, some anthropologists interested in these issues have adopted perspectives from the study of political economy (e.g., C. Smith 1975, 1978; Babb 1989), whereas others have examined the relationship of exchange systems to economic development (e.g., Dannhaeuser 1985). Underlying these analyses, however, is the anthropological study of the social and economic organization of specific exchange institutions in specific social and cultural contexts. As anthropology seeks to understand the local in its national and global context—the interaction between local institutions, people, and processes at wider levels of social organization—the analysis of exchange institutions will continue to be central.

Utilization of Available Data

At a minimum, anthropologists doing research in many regions of the world today can draw on existing data for basic information about some aspects of exchange and distribution. Though there is considerable skepticism about the validity and accuracy of such data, some data may be of greater value than is generally thought. Two types of data are considered here—price and other market information collected by the government, and locally published data on markets and trade.

Many governments today collect some type of information about goods that are bought and sold, typically with an emphasis on prices. For example, in the Philippines in 1979 I obtained from the Bureau of Agricultural Economics a typed listing of all goods sold in the marketplace in the city where I was doing research, with monthly average wholesale and retail prices for all of 1978. At a minimum, such a list indicates what agricultural commodities are available for sale in the market. In addition, it is possible to compare average prices over time to note seasonal changes; if similar lists for earlier years are obtained, one could also investigate changes in prices from year to year.[2]

Problems certainly arise when relying on such data, as Jones pointed out in discussing the utilization of government price data in Nigeria:

> It was generally believed that the price quotations were based on erratic and casual observation; it was obvious from the statistics themselves that some were faked; and the reports contained no information about the quality of the product priced, the date within a month when the price prevailed, the unit of sale to which the price referred, or how customary units and volumes of sale were converted into weights for which the prices were reported (1972:121–122).

However, he found the data of better quality than expected, as "preliminary investigation of seasonal price movements indicated that those for some commodities and some markets displayed regularities consistent with time of harvest and relative storability" (Jones 1972:122). Therefore, he used these data as the basis for a major study of staple food marketing in Nigeria.

I am suggesting that such data be used mainly as a preliminary guide to products being exchanged. If, however, one wants to examine price variation on a seasonal or longer-term basis, it is best to look for consistency (or inconsistency) in the data. There is no single method used by economists to test the reliability of price data; hence, local knowledge of how the data were collected and examination for consistency are the most useful guidelines to apply in deciding whether published price data can be used in a specific context.

Locally published information may also provide a useful initial guide. In Nigeria, for example, market calendars are available for sale and provide information on the meeting dates for periodic marketplaces in a specified region. Data in such calendars can be verified and supplemented in interviews with key informants; in some communities in Nigeria there are individuals who specialize in keeping records and calendars of market days.

Key Informant Interviews

Published and government data, though useful, are limited in many ways and should be verified by other types of data. They cannot provide the information needed to answer all of the basic questions outlined initially. For this, one must turn to other types of data, especially key informant interviews and surveys.

Interviews with key informants can provide valuable data on a number of important topics. Key informants are "people who are particularly knowledgeable and articulate" (Patton 1990:263) about the topics being studied. An important first step, then, is the selection of appropriate key informants, people with the requisite knowledge of exchange and distribution. In many societies, there are specialists who engage in these activities. In societies where most exchange takes place in marketplaces, market traders are clearly the logical specialists to serve as key informants. Even traders themselves may, have limited knowledge, however; they may know mainly about one commodity or one set of marketplaces. In societies without marketplace specialists there may be "big men" or others who engage in trade and redistributive activities. Whatever type of specialist is interviewed, it is important for the researcher to attempt to evaluate the extent of the source's knowledge; some will have a better grasp of the overall system than others. It may also be useful to train key informants so that they understand the objectives of the researcher and have a sense of the context into which the information they provide is being placed (Pelto 1970:95–98).

Key informants can provide valuable information on several of the questions outlined above. First, they can assist the researcher in learning about *who* is involved in exchange activities. Are there people who specialize in these activities? If so, are distinctions made among them? For example, among the Hausa, there are several named categories of traders active in the marketplace (Scott 1981:27–28). By contrast, in Sierra Leone, where historically trade took place without marketplaces, distinctions could be made between "big men," who operated households as trading firms, and caravan leaders who acted as wholesalers (Howard 1981:6–8).

Second, key informant interviews can be used to address the question of *what* is being exchanged. What types of goods are bought and sold? What things are exchanged in other ways? Where there are marketplaces, simple observation and counting (discussed in the section on surveys below) may be most useful. But it is easy to miss some items, especially as there is likely to be seasonal variation. Furthermore, not all goods are bought and sold in marketplaces; there may be significant exchanges that do not enter the marketplace at all. Hence, interviews with specialists can provide basic information on the types of goods bought and sold in markets as well as on exchanges that take place in other contexts.

Third, key informants can provide basic information on *where* and *when* exchanges take place. In most peasant societies, a large portion of exchange takes place through trade in periodic marketplaces. Such marketplaces are located in both space and time on the landscape. Crucial factors in understanding distribution through such markets include where they are located, when they meet, how they are related to one another, and how buyers and sellers operate in them.[3]

Using a combination of published market calendars and key informant interviews, it is possible to map the location and periodicity of marketplaces in a region; geographer R.H.T. Smith has done this for most of Africa. Such data are needed for making intra- and interregional comparisons of the periodicity of marketplaces. Distinctions among types of marketplaces can also be discovered. In some regions there are both daily and periodic markets. In other areas, there may be specialized wholesale markets or retail markets. Distinctions may also be made between local markets, those that serve local populations, and regional markets that serve those engaged in long-distance trade. Again, much of this information can be mapped.

Maps showing the location and timing of marketplaces can be constructed initially from published market calendars (if available) and checked with informants. Although this information can be supplemented with survey data, as discussed below, mapping alone is valuable in several respects. The location and timing of markets provide information on their accessibility within a region; if, for example, they are evenly distributed across the landscape and meet at regular intervals, then it is likely that producers in the region have good access to market outlets and that consumers can be easily supplied. These factors relate directly to political economic issues of access to and control over distribution within a region. Where markets have been established primarily for the purpose of export trade, for example, they tend to have locational patterns suitable for the collection of goods for resale elsewhere rather than for the effective distribution of goods within the region (cf. Johnson 1970).

Mapping of the location and timing of markets is essential for comparative study. A number of models have been proposed in the literature, and it is possible to compare local and regional maps against those models. For example, in his study of spatial organization in developing countries, Johnson called attention to "dendritic" market systems, organized and controlled largely to export goods from rural areas to dominant cities. Although additional information on the local political economy would be necessary to fully analyze whether a particular system is a dendritic one, minimum data on the timing and location of markets provides a crucial basis for comparing specific systems with the model and, over the long term, in building new models based on comparative study from a number of systems.

Key informants are even more important in answering "where" and "when" questions in situations where there are no marketplaces. Here trade specialists can describe their movements and timing of exchanges, whether these take place through individual exchange networks, households, or in some other type of institution (such as seasonal fairs). It is almost inevitable that exchange and distribution involve movement, typically of both goods and people. In using key informants for information on where and when exchange takes place, then, we are essentially trying to get a basic understanding of those movements. More detail on such movements can be obtained from surveys, as described below.

Another set of questions involves *how* goods are exchanged and distributed. Here, too, key informants can provide essential information. If trade involves movement, then how are goods moved? What system of transport is used, and who is involved in it? Are there specialists who act as transporters? Historically in southern Nigeria, as elsewhere in Africa, goods were transported by headloading (carrying containers on one's head), and there were people who did this on a regular basis; for example, there are elderly women who can recall headloading agricultural produce from the interior to the coast in the first part of the twentieth century and returning with imported cloth. Today, long-distance trade in that region involves transport mainly by truck, and the transporters are integral to the established exchange and distribution networks. Knowledge about transport provides basic information about how goods are moved and who is involved. Access to transport facilities, either by producers themselves or by distributors, is vital for effective distribution. Even if there are markets or other distribution outlets, they are useless if there is no way to move goods to them. The importance of transportation becomes apparent when the system breaks down, as it did in the 1980s in Ghana. In such a situation, distribution depends largely on those who still have access to and control over whatever transport remains available. Later, when transport became available once again and road conditions improved,

> [f]aster trips and more frequent and reliable schedules reduced the amount of capital and labor tied up in slow trips, long waits and searches for truckers, risk reserves for truck breakdowns, and fatigue-related illness. . . . Specialist traders based in urban areas found their familiarity with transport facilities and operators brought less competitive advantage now over traders from district towns and villages (Clark and Manuh 1991:229).

Minimum data on the structure of transport are valuable for comparative analysis as well, especially in seeking to examine issues such as the comparative structure of market systems and questions of control over and access to exchange and distribution institutions in the context of wider political economic change.

Another important aspect of how exchange and distribution are carried out is the question of what types of measures and standards of value are used in the distribution process. Here again, key informant interviews with specialists can be particularly useful. For example, Mintz has described the various units of measure employed in a Haitian marketing system, including two types of liquid measures and a system of measures for solids that is fairly well standardized. The measures for both liquids and solids are based on standard-size bottles, tin cans, and other such containers (Mintz 1961a). Similarly, in Nigeria certain types of bottles and cans are widely used as measures for produce in marketplaces. Disputes and bargaining can occur over how full the container is, but the use of a particular container is not in question. Other products, such as yams, onions, and tomatoes, are sold by the quantity in a pile. Negotiation and bargaining focus mainly on the quality of the goods and the possibility of adding additional items to the pile; after the sale, a "dash," or small gift, may be given in the form of one or two additional items. Knowledge of such units of measure is necessary to understand how prices are determined. For those commodities measured in containers, it is possible and necessary to convert the container size to metric measures. Where goods are sold by piles, one can inquire whether there are specific numbers in the piles—for example, are yams usually sold by threes or fives? are oranges sold by ten? is quantity in the pile variable? Finally, the researcher needs to note whether a dash is usually given and if so in what form; although the dash probably cannot be incorporated into the measures, the existence of this form of exchange is important to note, especially as it usually has implications for the social organization of exchange (indicating, for example, the existence of a special relationship).

Standards of value are typically based on national currencies. However, earlier systems of currency denominations may be in use, as well as modifications of contemporary denominations. For example, market traders in southern Nigeria frequently use pounds and shillings and sometimes even cowries and readily convert from those to the current Naira and kobo denominations. They have also developed some terminology of their own; "muri" indicates twenty Naira bills, based on the fact that the picture of former Nigerian head of state Muritala Muhammed appears on the note. Thus, even when national currencies are in use, it is helpful to have a key informant describe the terminology used by specialists.

Price setting may well involve negotiation and bargaining. Knowledge of the system of currency and of the units of measure is needed to understand these negotiations. Though key informants can describe the bargaining methods in general, more detailed understanding of how prices are negotiated requires firsthand observation as well.

Finally, key informant interviewing can provide basic information on aspects of the social organization of exchange. In many societies with marketing systems, regular named relationships exist between buyers and sellers—*onibara* among the Yoruba (Trager 1981a), *suki* in the Philippines (Davis 1973), *pratik* in Haiti (Mintz 1961b). In other societies, there may be regular exchange relationships—for example, between "big men" and others—based on prestige. From interviews, one can learn of the existence of such relationships and whether there are specialized terms for them, as well as something of the content of the relationships. Similarly, one can learn about other social relationships that may be involved in exchange, such as the granting of credit. However, detailed understanding of the specific content of these relationships and of variations in them require survey and observational data, as considered below.

Survey Data

Key informant interviews can be used to gain a basic outline of the system of exchange and distribution and provide data needed for certain types of comparative analyses. Survey data can be used to fill in this outline. Three types of survey data are discussed here—household surveys; surveys of traders and other specialists; and, for those situations where most exchange takes place in marketplaces, market surveys.

Household Surveys

Questions about exchange can be added to the basic questions asked by Netting et al. on production (Chapter 4). Questions can be asked about what is sold to or otherwise exchanged with people outside the household, to whom it is sold, and where. Likewise, information about what is bought or otherwise received by the household and from whom should be sought. It is important to ask not only about the items bought and sold but also about reciprocal exchanges in which household members may be involved. For example, research on urban migration has shown the significant role of remittances from urban migrants to people remaining in rural areas (see, for example, Trager 1984, 1988), and research on low-income urban residents shows that there are numerous reciprocal exchanges of goods and money between households (Stack 1974; Lomnitz 1977).

Trader Surveys

Where there are traders or others who specialize in exchange and distribution, a sample survey is useful to provide additional information on a number of questions. First, such a survey helps define who the traders are by asking for basic socioeconomic information, including age, sex, educational background, other work experience, and so forth. Basic demographic data of this sort are often unavailable. Second, traders can provide information on what they sell and where—whether in marketplaces or elsewhere. Details on the trading process can also be obtained. For example, do traders travel to markets in other communities to buy or sell goods? What mechanisms do they use in their trade activities—is there bargaining? do they have regular customers and/or suppliers? do they grant or receive credit?

Appendix 5.A provides an example of an interview schedule for traders. Such data can be especially helpful in contributing to a comparative analysis of the movements of people, of goods involved in transactions, and of the networks and linkages that facilitate exchange.

Market Surveys

In most agrarian societies, most exchanges occur in marketplaces. Hence, great attention must be paid to data on the system of markets in the region being studied. Three types of market survey data, each of increasing degree of complexity and difficulty to collect, are discussed here. At the simplest level, market surveys involve the counting of vendors and/or commodities in marketplaces. The next level of complexity involves surveys of the flows of people and/or goods into marketplaces. Third, the counting of people and goods can allow for analysis of the organization of marketplaces in a central-place system. All three approaches have value for the comparative study of exchange.

The first step is counting; as C. Smith has pointed out, the basic procedure in studying markets is "counting onions and other commodities" (1985:52). However, counting is not as simple as it sounds, especially in confusing and busy marketplaces. The two basic things one wants to count are vendors and commodities (or commodity groups), leading to compilation of information about the number of different commodities and the number of sellers of each for every marketplace under consideration.[4] For example, in a comparison of two market systems in the Gambia River Basin, Appleby used vendor counts as the basis of his analysis. He grouped vendors into five functional categories based on type of commodities—foodstuffs, manufactured goods, service, wholesaling, and animals—and showed that whereas in one of the systems half of all vendors sold merchandise, in the other system foodstuffs predominated, with two-thirds of all vendors selling local produce (1985:91–92).

Appleby used vendor counts as the basis for comparison within a region, but the approach has wider applicability, especially in its grouping of vendors into several broad functional categories. Basic categories that could be used for comparative purposes are locally produced food, manufactured goods, and services. It may also be useful to include imported foodstuffs and imported merchandise as separate categories. Appleby found it useful to distinguish wholesalers from retailers, but it is not always possible or useful to do so. Likewise, others have suggested a sharp distinction between urban and rural markets (and between urban and rural vendors), but such a distinction is not necessarily found in all market systems. Counting vendors in the different categories within a market system provides a minimum basis for comparison, showing, for example, the extent to which locally produced foodstuffs dominate in different systems.

Beyond counting vendors and commodities, it can also be useful to examine flows, or what Bromley terms "market movement censuses" (1985). Bromley's censuses in Ecuador "measured the flow of people, vehicles, and livestock into each center during the build-up period of market activity" (1985:330). Such a survey focuses on the people entering the markets, including information on place of origin, how they traveled to the market, and whether they are selling goods, as well as basic socioeconomic data. Surveys of this sort require considerably more resources than does the counting of vendors in the marketplace. Bromley describes how the movements of pedestrians, livestock, vehicles, and bicycles into market centers were recorded; as many pedestrians as possible were questioned, and vehicles were stopped with the assistance of police to determine the place of origin (1985:330–332). As a result, Bromley was able to map the flows of people (including consumers) and goods to specified markets.

Maps of this sort can be valuable for the study of specific market systems at specific points in time to show, for example, the distances traveled and the numbers of people who travel those distances. If used in specific systems at different points in time, they may show the increasing importance of vehicular travel. This approach has potential as well for the comparative study of market systems in analyzing the geographic reach of marketplaces on different landscapes and in varying socioeconomic systems. For example, it has been suggested that in some contexts cultural rather than geographic barriers may determine the specific markets people buy and sell at; maps showing people's movements could aid in providing evidence for this contention. Likewise, socioeconomic constraints may affect movements—lack of transport or lack of money to pay transport costs may affect the extent to which pedestrian or vehicular transport predominates in given systems and hence the extent to which people tend to buy and sell primarily in local markets or in larger markets at greater distances.

However, neither counting of vendors and commodities nor tracking of flows of people and goods provides a comprehensive picture of marketplaces as organized into an interconnected economic system. For this, additional data are needed, along with mapping and analysis utilizing methods developed in the study of central-place systems. As C. Smith has argued, central-place measurement procedures

> can help one find the patterns and functions of regional marketing systems in a systematic way, whether that system is rural or urban, permanent or periodic. What they help one see is the hierarchical organization of market trade, a pattern of organization that varies in accordance with the complexity of a particular commodity economy, but a pattern of organization that is basic to all commodity-based economies (1985:50).[5]

The basic method for studying markets within a central-place system begins with counting commodities—or groupings of commodities—and vendors in the markets under study. These counts form the basis of a centrality index that makes it possible to measure a marketplace both by its size (number of vendors) and by the variety of commodities for sale there. All markets in the system can then be compared in terms of a single measure. In using this approach in research on Yoruba markets, I followed the method of calculating a centrality index proposed by Marshall:

> For each function [commodity] the amount of centrality contributed to a place is taken to be proportional to the number of establishments of that function present in the place, with the total number of establishments of that function in the entire system having a combined centrality value of 100. . . . The centrality value of a single establishment of any function [is termed] the *location coefficient* of that function and [is defined] as follows: C=100.t/T where: C is the location coefficient of the function t; t is unity, representing one establishment of function t; and T is the total number of establishments of function t in the system.
>
> Once the location coefficient of every function has been calculated in this way, the number of establishments of each function in each place are multiplied by the appropriate location coefficients to obtain the amounts of centrality conferred on each place by each function. Addition of these amounts then gives the final index of centrality for each center (Marshall 1969:85–86).

Using this method, I was able to determine a spatially arranged hierarchy of Yoruba marketplaces (Trager 1976, 1981b). However, C. Smith has argued that the method may need modification. In her study of western Guatemala, she found it necessary to distinguish types of sellers, such as long-distance traders, producer-sellers, and middlemen. She then grouped marketplaces in terms of the proportion of each type. What is particularly at issue here is the separation of retail and wholesale functions, which tend to take place in the same marketplaces and yet which have different functions in the system. She states:

> Centrality indices based on the variety and quantity of goods found in agrarian marketplaces, therefore do not measure the reach of those centers to consumers alone, they measure the importance of those centers to traders as well as to consumers. And if locally produced goods are sold in local market places . . . rather than sold through distinct market channels, one needs to discriminate between the retail goods and the wholesale goods supplied in each market place. Otherwise, one risks lumping into a single type centers with high retail functions but no wholesale functions and centers with low retail functions but high wholesale functions. And there is reason to believe that these two types of market center, which may appear equivalent through measures of goods but which are not equivalent because they perform different functions in the marketing system, may have a special locational relationship in an agrarian economy (Smith 1985:55).

Determining the hierarchical organization of marketplaces within a central-place system by using central-place methods and modifications appropriate in studying agrarian economies can provide the basis for examination of a range of questions about regional economies and their organization. Smith has probably taken this approach further than anyone else, basing her extensive analysis of the political economy of western Guatemala on her study of the market system. Among the issues she raises are the differing roles in the economy of the region's two main ethnic groups and the differing functions of rural and urban markets in meeting the needs of producers, traders, and consumers.

From a comparative perspective, questions may be raised about these issues, as well as others. For example, how are market systems integrated in regions where traders, producers, and consumers are of the same ethnic group and where sharp distinctions are not found between rural and urban populations, as is the case in much of Africa? Comparative analysis of central-place hierarchies can assist in addressing such questions by allowing results from specific systems to be compared with the available central-place models and with specific actual systems—such as those of western Guatemala, China, and other areas—where this type of analysis has been carried out.

In sum, surveys of marketplaces can begin with the counting of goods and vendors. From there one can do a census of the movements of people and goods in order to examine the linkages and movements between places. Finally, methods for determining the size and function of marketplaces within a system can form the basis for analysis of the ways in which sets of marketplaces are interrelated within a hierarchical system. This analysis, in turn, can provide the basis for examination of a range of comparative questions about regional economies and their organization. However, extensive surveys of market flows and central-place systems are likely to go beyond the requirements and resources of most researchers interested in minimum data sets.

Observations and In-Depth Interviews

Although surveys can provide a great deal of information on the movements of people and goods involved in networks of distribution and exchange, they yield limited insights into the social organization of exchange relationships. Similarly, key informant interviews can be valuable in outlining the basic characteristics of types of traders and their relationships, but they are not as useful in providing detail on the content of those relationships. For detailed understanding of the social organization of exchange, data obtained through observation and in-depth interviewing are especially valuable.

Two brief examples may serve to demonstrate this point. Among the Yoruba of Nigeria, as in most peasant marketing systems, bargaining is basic to price negotiation in marketplace transactions. Trade specialists can provide a description of the basic method of bargaining, which happens to be quite different from that used elsewhere in Nigeria or, for that matter, in many other areas of the world. That is, bargaining among the Yoruba involves gradual price reduction: The seller quotes a price, the buyer proposes a slightly lower price. If the seller agrees to that, the buyer then suggests a still lower price, and so on, until the seller refuses to go any lower, thereby letting the buyer know that the last-agreed price is the "final price." Usually the total reduction is very small; in fact, it is possible to circumvent the negotiation by simply asking for the seller's final price. A description by a specialist, however, is likely to leave out a number of important aspects to these bargaining methods. For example, there is extensive bargaining on some commodities and little or no bargaining on others. For some goods, such as those that are sold in piles (tomatoes, yams, etc.), negotiation focuses on improving the quality of a particular pile and on getting a dash of additional tomatoes. Furthermore, if the buyer is a regular customer, there may be little bargaining, although a dash may be expected to signify the continuing social relationship. Only observation and in-depth interviews based on such observation are likely to enable an investigator to describe such bargaining relationships in any detail. (See Alexander 1987 for an extended description of bargaining in a Javanese market.)

A second and related example involves the existence of named exchange relationships. As pointed out earlier, among the Yoruba there are people termed *onibara;* the relationship between them is also called onibara. Although this term is usually translated as "customer relationship," it in fact refers to a reciprocal relationship involving both a buyer and a seller who regularly trade with one another. Both people involved call each other their onibara. It is relatively easy to learn of such relationships through interviews with key informants. But the content of the relationship is not uniform throughout the exchange system; it may or may not involve granting of credit, giving of gifts, and other multiplex ties. Variations result from differences in the commodity traded, the distance over which the transaction takes place, and other variables affecting the extent of risk (Trager 1981a). Data obtained through observation and in-depth interviewing are again important for this type of more detailed analysis.

Such examples can be easily multiplied. Recent studies of markets by Alexander (1987) and Babb (1989), for instance, emphasize that their data collection depended largely on observation and interviewing. Clark's study of social relationships among traders in Kumasi, Ghana, during a period of economic instability likewise depended heavily on participant observation and interviews (1991). Such studies, of course, go far beyond minimum data sets to include detailed description and analysis of the markets, those who trade in them, and their role in the local and regional economy. Especially as anthropologists move beyond description and analysis of exchange at local levels and consider how exchange is articulated with the wider economy, a wide range of data is required. Though published data, survey data of various types, and key informant interviewing can all be very valuable, observation and in-depth interviews remain extremely important methods of data collection.

Conclusion

It is perhaps worthwhile to emphasize some of the difficulties involved in collecting data for the study of exchange and distribution. By its very nature, exchange and distribution involve movement, always of goods and often of people. When it takes place in highly visible marketplaces, the activity is obvious but also confusing. There are many people, they move around, the same people may engage in both buying and selling, and so forth. In situations where exchange takes place not in marketplaces but in other arenas, it may be difficult even to pinpoint what is being exchanged, who is involved, and where exchanges take place. Furthermore, the networks and linkages that are created through exchange and distribution and that facilitate continued exchange are crucial. Whether a situation involves interhousehold exchange within an urban area or long-distance trade in a regional marketing system, it is important that data be obtained on the nature of those networks and linkages.

Table 5.1 summarizes the types of data discussed in this chapter, indicating the kind of information it is possible to obtain as well as some of the problems associated with each method. It suggests that the data sets may be divided into four levels, from those that provide basic, minimum data to those that provide increasingly comprehensive data about exchange and distribution. The first level includes government records and published information (where available) and key informant interviews. The second level includes some of the survey data discussed, including household survey data and trader surveys; these can provide basic demographic profiles as well as an outline of what is being exchanged and how exchanges are carried out. This level also includes one type of market survey, the counting of vendors and commodities. The third level, applicable where marketplaces are important loci of exchange, includes the other market surveys—market movement censuses and the data collection necessary for

Table 5.1 Summary of Data Sets in the Study of Exchange and Distribution

Level	Type of Data	Information Obtained	Problems
Minimum	Government records and published information	Government price records and other market information; market calendars	Reliability
	Key informant interviews	Trader types; commodity types; overview of organization of exchange—who, where, when, what, how; transportation information; units of measures and standard of value; bargaining methods	Reliability and knowledge of key informant(s)
Second	Household surveys	What is bought/sold/ exchanged	Resource limitations in carrying out surveys
	Trader surveys	Demographic information; information on organization of exchange: social relationships, credit, bargaining; movements of traders	Design of appropriate questions
	Market surveys (where marketplaces are main sites for exchange)	Number of vendors and types of vendors; number of commodities and types of commodities; functional groupings	Determination of set of markets to study
Third	Market surveys	Movement of people (vendors, consumers), movement of vehicles and commodities	Resource limitations
		Number of commodities (functions) and vendors as basis for determining central-place hierarchy of market system	Modify central-place methods for specific system, especially separate wholesale and retail functions
Most Comprehensive	Observation and in-depth interviews	Details on social organization of exchange— bargaining, customer relations, social networks, etc.; additional information on basic questions (who, when, what, how)	Time and intensive work by researcher

central-place analysis. Finally, the most comprehensive data set is that which relies on observation and in-depth interviews, which are especially valuable for data on the social organization of exchange. A truly comprehensive study of exchange and distribution would attempt to include all four levels of data.

The first two levels of data collection discussed here provide the minimum necessary data for comparative study of exchange and distribution. Together with the other two levels, the data sets range from the utilization of already collected information to labor-intensive surveys, observation, and in-depth interviews. There are limitations to these data sets; reliance on already collected price data is problematic, and there may be problems with surveys and key informant interviews, including the basic issue of knowing the right questions to ask. However, a focus on the fundamental questions outlined at the start of the chapter—what is exchanged, who is involved, how exchanges are organized, when exchange takes place, and where exchange takes place—and utilization of the data collection approaches recommended here should result in an overview of the system of exchange and distribution, with the possibility for greater depth and detail.

Appendix 5.A
Interview Schedule for Survey of Traders

1. Name of Respondent
2. Location: 1) marketplace (name of market)
   2) street (name)
   3) other (specify)
3. Sex: 1) female   2) male
4. Age
5. What are you selling?
   (List primary item for sale, and then list anything else being sold in the shop).
6. Do you ever sell anything else? What?
7. For how long have you been selling (first item listed)?
8. Did you ever sell anything else before then? If yes,
   8a. What did you sell?
   8b. Why did you decide to stop selling that and to start selling (commodity now trading)?
9. If no to question 8:
   Why did you decide to start trading in (the commodity you are now selling)?
10. Have you ever worked at any other occupation besides trading? If yes,
    10a. What occupation(s)?
    10b. Do you still work at that (those) occupations?
11. What is your wife/husband's occupation? If a trader,
    11a. What does s/he sell?
    11b. Where?
12. Do you have other family members who are traders? If yes,
    12a. What is the relationship?
    12b. What does s/he sell?
13. Where were you born?
14. Where do you live now?
15. Do you sell goods in the town where you live?
16. Where else do you sell goods? (It may be useful to provide a list of other towns and markets and ask if respondent sells at specific locales.)
17. Do you buy goods in the town where you live?
18. Where else do you buy goods?
19. Do you have anyone who helps you with your work? If yes,
    19a. Are they   1) family member?
    2) employee?
    3) apprentice?

20. Are there other traders in the market who regularly buy and sell with you?
    20a. How many?
    20b. Are they related to you?
    20c. What is the relationship?
21. Do you belong to any organizations or associations of traders?
22. Do you make sales on credit?
    1) often   2) sometimes   3) never
23. Do you buy on credit?
    1) often   2) sometimes   3) never
24. Are there people from whom you regularly buy?
25. Are there people to whom you regularly sell?
26. How much schooling have you had?
27. When you began trading, did anyone help you with money to begin? Who? Did you have savings that you used?
28. How much money did you need to begin?
29. What is your approximate income every week?
30. For what kinds of things do you use the money you earn? (E.g., household expenses, reinvest in business, savings; a list may be provided and each item asked about.)
31. What do you estimate your profit to be from your trade in one week?

Notes

1. This chapter is concerned with data to be used in the study of exchange *outside* the household, although intrahousehold exchange has recently been noted as a topic of considerable importance. (See, for example, Netting, Wilk and Arnould 1984.)

2. Price information in such data is, of course, given in local currency. One can compare average prices over time in local currency but must keep in mind any changes that may have occurred in the value of the currency (such as major devaluations or changes to new denominations). To convert such data into dollars, one can use the exchange rate at each point in time; in many cases, the black market exchange rate is more appropriate than the official exchange rate.

3. There is a vast literature on periodic marketplaces. Much of it is based on research done by geographers, but some particularly significant contributions have come from anthropologists who have applied central-place theory to the study of periodic markets. See, for example, R.H.T. Smith (1979, 1980), Brian J. L. Berry and John B. Parr (1988), C. Smith (1976), and G. W. Skinner (1965).

4. As Smith points out, a preliminary step in analyzing a regional system of marketplaces is to determine the boundaries of the region to be considered (1985:50–51).

5. Smith's discussion of methods for central-place analysis of marketing systems is especially valuable for anyone wishing to go beyond minimum data collection and analysis to a more thorough study of market systems. Also useful in this regard are Berry and Parr (1988), Marshall (1969), and C. Smith (1976).

References

Alexander, Jennifer, 1987. *Trade, Traders and Trading in Rural Java.* Singapore: Oxford University Press.

Appleby, Gordon, 1985. Marketplace development in the Gambia River Basin. In Stuart Plattner, ed., *Markets and Marketing,* pp. 79–97. Lanham, MD: University Press of America.

Babb, Florence, 1989. *Between Field and Cooking Pot: The Political Economy of Marketwomen in Peru.* Austin: University of Texas Press.

Belshaw, Cyril S., 1965. *Traditional Exchange and Modern Markets.* Englewood Cliffs, N.J.: Prentice Hall.

Berry, Brian J. L,. and John B. Parr, 1988. *Market Centers and Retail Location: Theory and Applications.* Englewood Cliffs, N.J.: Prentice-Hall.

Bohannan, Paul, and George Dalton, eds., 1962. *Markets in Africa.* Evanston, IL: Northwestern University Press.

Bromley, Ray, 1985. Circulation within systems of periodic and daily markets: The case of central highland Ecuador. In Mansell Prothero and Murray Chapman, eds., *Circulation in Third World Countries,* pp. 325–349. London: Routledge and Kegan Paul.

Clark, Gracia, 1991. Colleague and customers in unstable market conditions: Kumasi, Ghana. *Ethnology* 30(1):31–48.

Clark, Gracia, and Takyiwaa Manuh, 1991. Women traders in Ghana and the structural adjustment program. In Christine H. Gladwin, ed., *Structural Adjustment and African Women Farmers,* pp. 217–236. Gainesville, FL: University of Florida Press.

Dannhaeuser, Norbert, 1985. Urban market channels under conditions of development: The case of India and the Philippines. In Stuart Plattner, ed., *Markets and Marketing,* pp. 179–203. Lanham, MD: University Press of America.

Davis, W. G., 1973. *Social Relations in a Philippine Market: Self-Interest and Subjectivity.* Berkeley, CA: University of California Press.

Howard, Allen M., 1981. Trade without marketplaces: The spatial organization of exchange in northwestern Sierra Leone to 1930. *African Urban Studies* 11:1–22.

Johnson, E.A.J., 1970. *The Organization of Space in Developing Countries.* Cambridge, MA: Harvard University Press.

Jones, William O., 1972. *Marketing Staple Food Crops in Tropical Africa.* Ithaca, NY: Cornell University Press.

Lomnitz, Larissa, 1977. *Networks and Marginality: Life in a Mexican Shantytown.* New York: Academic Press.

Malinowski, Bronislaw, 1932. *Argonauts of the Western Pacific.* London: Routledge and Kegan Paul.

Marshall, John U., 1969. *The Location of Service Towns: An Approach to the Analysis of Central Place Systems.* Toronto: University of Toronto, Department of Geography.

Mintz, Sidney, 1961a. Standards of value and units of measure in the Fond-des-Negres market place, Haiti. *The Journal of the Royal Anthropological Institute* 91(1):23–38.

———, 1961b. Pratik: Haitian personal economic relations. In *Proceedings of the 1961 Annual Spring Meeting of the American Ethnological Society,* pp. 54–63.

Netting, Robert McC., Richard R. Wilk, and Eric J. Arnould, eds., 1984.

Households: Comparative and Historical Studies of the Domestic Group.
Berkeley, CA: University of California Press.

Patton, Michael Quinn, 1990. *Qualitative Evaluation and Research Methods,* second ed. Newbury Park: Sage.

Pelto, Pertti J., 1970. *Anthropological Research: The Structure of Inquiry.* New York: Harper & Row.

Scott, Earl, 1981. Organizational and structural aspects of trade in peripheral regions: The case of Nigeria. *African Urban Studies* 10:21–41.

Skinner, G. W., 1964. Marketing and social structure in rural China, part 1. *Journal of Asian Studies* 24:3–43.

————, 1965. Marketing and social structure in rural China, Part II. *Journal of Asian Studies* 24:195–228.

Smith, Carol A., 1975. Examining stratification systems through peasant marketing arrangements: An application of some models from economic geography. *Man* 10:95–122.

————, ed., 1976. *Regional Analysis,* Vol. I. New York: Academic Press.

————, 1978. Beyond dependency theory: National and regional patterns of underdevelopment in Guatemala. *American Ethnologist* 5:574–617.

————, 1985. How to count onions: Methods for a regional analysis of marketing. In Stuart Plattner, ed., *Markets and Marketing,* pp. 49–77. Lanham, MD: University Press of America.

Smith, Robert H. T., 1979 and 1980. Periodic market places and periodic marketing. *Progress in Human Geography* 3(4):471–505 and 4(1:)1–31.

Stack, Carol, 1974. *All Our Kin: Strategies for Survival in a Black Community.* New York: Harper and Row.

Trager, Lillian, 1976. Yoruba markets and trade: Analysis of spatial structure and social organization in the Ijesaland marketing system. Ph.D. dissertation, University of Washington.

————, 1981a. Customers and creditors: Variations in economic personalism in a Nigerian marketing system. *Ethnology* 20:133–146.

————, 1981b. Yoruba market organization—A regional analysis. *African Urban Studies* 10:43–58.

————, 1984. Migration and remittances: Urban income and rural households in the Philippines. *The Journal of Developing Areas* 18:317–340.

————, 1988. *The City Connection: Migration and Family Interdependence in the Philippines.* Ann Arbor, MI: University of Michigan Press.

Trager, Lillian, and Anita Spring, 1988. Gender issues in rural-urban marketing networks. Paper prepared for USAID/Office of Women in Development, for the Eleventh Conference on Housing and Urban Development in Sub-Saharan Africa. Lilongwe, Malawi.

6

Minimum Data Sets for the Description of Diet and Measurement of Food Intake and Nutritional Status

DARNA L. DUFOUR AND NICOLETTE I. TEUFEL

The description of diet and the measurement of food and nutrient intake can provide valuable insights into a people's relationship with their sociocultural and biological environment. For any human group, the choice of foods is ultimately limited by the physical environment and by access to trade networks. Within these broad constraints, however, both the types of foods included in the diet and the quantities consumed are defined by social, economic, political, and cultural factors. Anthropology has a long tradition of including information on diet in the basic description of human groups. However, the cacophony of ways in which dietary data have been collected and presented has limited their usefulness in making cross-cultural comparisons and in accurately describing the "typical" diet of a group. In this chapter we will suggest techniques for collecting, interpreting, and presenting information on diet and nutritional status within a framework easily understood by other researchers and suitable for cross-cultural comparison. In preparing this chapter, we had in mind the needs of field researchers whose primary interest is not diet or nutritional status but who see these as associated variables for which they want descriptive control.[1]

A description of a people's diet begins with general, ethnographic information on food habits: What foods are eaten? How they are obtained and prepared? What are their social and cultural significance? A comprehensive description of food habits based on observations and informant interviews provides the basic framework upon which more detailed quantitative data collection and analyses can be built. Quantitative information on food consumption can be obtained through 1) food frequencies, 2) food lists, and 3) food records. These three forms of data can be thought of as hierarchical levels of investigation. In progression, each level provides a more detailed and quantitative description of the diet. Each level also requires a greater time commitment from both the researcher(s) and the respondents. The advantages and disadvantages of each are summarized in Table 6.1.

Table 6.1 Methods for Assessing Diet

Method	Advantages	Disadvantages
Food Habits		
Participant observation and interview	Data can be collected in context of ethnographic observations using techniques familiar to anthropologists; respondent burden minimal; does not require respondent literacy	Data may not be representative of all groups or of annual cycle; provides only qualitative data
Nonquantitative food frequencies	Rapid technique to get a description of frequency of use of different foods; low respondent burden	Does not provide quantitative information on intake, cannot be used to generate nutrient intake
Food Intake of Groups		
Food lists	Time efficient, one session (twenty to forty-five minutes); low respondent burden; does not require respondent literacy; most effective with a large sample size and low dietary diversity	Does not measure habitual intake unless collected for three or more days; relies on respondent's memory and ability to estimate food quantities
Food records	Moderate time expense (four-day minimum); data can be used to compute prevalence of households meeting nutritional standards; does not require literacy if record is maintained by an outsider observer	Moderate respondent burden, requires continued cooperation; if respondent-maintained, literacy required; may cause respondent modification of food behaviors

Source: Adapted from Sanjur (1982: 173–175).

Nutritional status is not the same as diet or food intake. Nutritional status refers to the biological state of an organism with regard to the balance between what the diet supplies and what the organism needs (McLaren 1976). Assessments of nutritional status are based on "indicators," sets of variables that provide a measure of this state of balance. The simplest and most widely used indicators of nutritional status are anthropometric measurements of relative body size. For children, these measurements are height-for-age and weight-for-height. For adults they are weight-for-height and body mass index (BMI).

Dietary intake measurements of individuals are sometimes used as indirect indicators of nutritional status. This use of dietary data is based on the assumption that "adequate" intake results in satisfactory nutritional status. However, the data sets needed for an assessment of nutritional adequacy are maximal, not minimal. For the purposes of this chapter, the use of dietary intake data to assess nutritional status will not be discussed further.

Assessing Food Habits

"Food habits" refers to the patterns of food selection and consumption, methods of food preparation, and factors affecting these behaviors (such as seasonality of food availability and socioeconomic status). Good examples of discussions of food habits are presented in Mead (1943), Sanjur (1970), Pagezy (1985), Orlove (1987), Delgado (1991), and Milton (1991).

Observation and open-ended interviews with key informants can provide a great deal of information about food habits. Observations can be used to define the kinds of food grown locally in agricultural fields and kitchen gardens and those sold in markets and by street vendors. Interviews with key informants can be used to obtain the local names of foods; to learn how people talk about foods; to define patterns of food use (what is eaten in a meal, a day, or a season), seasons of availability, and consumption patterns of age-sex groups; and to gather basic information on the economic dimensions of food distribution and exchange (see Trager, Chapter 5). The objectives of the observations and interviews conducted to assess food habits should be to answer the following questions:

1. *What foods are consumed?* Food items should be clearly identified by both the local and scientific name. The part eaten should be specified—for example, leaves of "au" (*Phytolacca rivinoides*). The investigator should be alert to substances not considered "food" by the investigator or respondent, such as clay, laundry starch, or herbal teas consumed for medicinal purposes. Local names for foods can be obtained through interviews. However, local names alone are insufficient for the purposes of comparative analysis. Taxonomic identifications are usually more difficult to obtain but should be pursued. Museum herbariums and biologists familiar with local flora and fauna are often helpful. Plants and animal specimens can also be collected for later identification (Messer and Kuhnlein 1986).

2. *Which foods are dietary staples and which are supplementary foods?* Dietary staples are the most common components of ordinary meals. They provide the bulk of energy and nutrient intake and are typically considered essential to the maintenance of well-being by the local group. They are the most important food emotionally and symbolically (Sanjur 1982:25) as well as nutritionally. Supplementary foods are those consumed less frequently and/or those that make a smaller contribution to the diet. This category includes side dishes, or "relishes," as well as foods that might only be eaten on a weekly basis. Supplementary foods should be distinguished from foods eaten seasonally, occasionally, or under particular circumstances—for example, foods eaten in times of acute food shortages (famine foods) or clay used for medicinal purposes. Compared to simple lists of foods, inventories that make distinctions as to the relative importance of foods provide a clearer picture of the nutritional quality of the diet and the patterns of resource use.

3. *How are foods categorized?* What are the important cultural-linguistic distinctions between "foods" and other categories of edibles (Pelto 1989)? These distinctions are likely to be particularly important with regard to supplementary foods. For example, Fleuret (1979) found that the Shambaa in East Africa did not consider wild greens food per se, even though they were eaten at almost one-third of all meals. Classifications of edibles with regard to social acceptability and prestige value can also affect people's willingness to report their use, and these factors also need to be considered (Pelto 1989).

4. *How are foods processed and/or prepared for consumption?* Methods of food preparation have important implications for nutrient content and bioavailability and for the release of toxins. Is the food eaten whole, husked, or peeled? Is it eaten fresh, fermented, or cooked? If cooked, is it baked unpeeled, boiled in a stew, grilled, or fried? If fried, is fat added to the food during the cooking process? What type of fat is added?

5. *How and when are foods consumed?* Which foods are components of ordinary meals and which are only eaten on festive occasions? When are supplementary foods used? Which foods are consumed as snacks? Are harvested foods eaten during work in agricultural fields? Are some animal parts eaten during or immediately preceding the butchering process?

6. *By whom are these foods consumed?* Are all foods consumed by all age and gender groups in the population? Are some foods consumed only by pregnant women, only by young children, and so forth? Are some foods avoided by certain age-gender groups—pregnant women? men on a hunting trip?

7. *How and when are foods obtained?* How are different foods obtained (agricultural production, gathering, hunting, purchase, trade and/or gift, etc.)? Who obtains them and controls their use? Which foods

are available throughout the year and which only during certain seasons? How frequently and when is marketing done? Are any foods provided through local food supplementation programs or emergency relief programs?

A description of food habits can be presented in prose, with specific foods listed in tables. Prose descriptions should address the questions listed above and should include information on how and when data were collected. A good example can be found in Messer (1977). Tables should include both local and scientific names, and foods should be categorized by relative importance. An example of data presentation is shown in Table 6.2. Typical daily menus can also be reported to provide an indication of the types and diversity of food consumed as "meals" (Table 6.3).

A description of food habits can provide valuable information on food resource use in a particular geographical region and can provide a basis for assessing food use cross-culturally and diachronically. Such a description may also indicate how food is used to mark ethnic boundaries or social standing within a population. A description of food habits does not provide sufficient information to quantify the contribution of particular foods to the diet nor to assess the adequacy of the diet. However, overall patterns of food use may suggest where problems of inadequacy would be most likely. For example, they may suggest seasonal shortages or very restricted diets in particular age-sex groups.

Assessing the Frequency of Food Use

Once basic information about food habits has been collected, more detailed information on patterns of food used can be obtained from a food frequency questionnaire. This tool provides information on how often specific foods are consumed. The standard technique is a semistructured interview, during which a list of common foods (determined from a food habits assessment) is presented and the respondent is asked how often each food is consumed within a given time interval (Sanjur 1982). When the specified interval is greater than a month, the food frequency interview is often used to yield a description of the "typical" pattern of intake (Block et al. 1992; Willett et al. 1987). The time frame specified and the "typicalness" of the diet should be guided by consideration of seasonal variability. If the diet does vary seasonally, food frequency questionnaires should focus on seasonally defined time intervals (postharvest, preharvest, rainy season, dry season, etc.). Some seasons have a disproportionately high number of festive occasions in which special foods are eaten. The prevalence of these occasions should not be over- or underrepresented in the food frequency data.

The food frequency interview requires the respondent to perform a

Table 6.2 Cultivated Vegetable Foods Used by Tatuyo Indians in the Northwest Amazon

Name and Part Eaten	Preparation and Use
Staple	
Cassava, bitter, roots (*Manihot esculenta*)	as bread, coarse flour, in drinks
Common Supplementary Foods	
Bananas and plantains, fruit (*Musa* spp.)	raw as snack, boiled as drink consumed with meals
Cassava, leaves (*Manihot esculenta*)	mixed with fish.
Coca, leaves (*Erythroxylum coca*)	toasted and powdered (used by adult men only)
Naranjilla, fruit (*Solanum*)	raw as snack, cooked in a drink consumed with meals
Papaya, fruit (*Carica papaya*)	raw as snack
Pepper, fruit (*Capsicum* sp.)	boiled in pepper pot,[a] served with meals
Occasionally Used Foods	
Arrowroot, root (*Maranta ruiziana*)	roasted as snack,[b] ingredient in beer[c]
Breadfruit, seeds (*Artocarpus communis*)	boiled as a snack
Cassava, sweet, roots (*Manihot esculenta*)	roasted as a snack,[b] ingredient in beer[c]
Coconut meat (*Cocos nucifera*)	raw as snack
Maize, seed (*Zea mays*)	ingredient in beer[c]
Malanga, stem (*Xanthosoma* sp.)	ingredient in beer[c]
Root (*Heliconia hirisuta*)	ingredient in beer[c]
Sugarcane, juice (*Saccharum officinarum*)	raw as snack, ingredient in beer[c]
Sweet potato, root (*Ipomoea batatas*)	roasted as snack,[b] ingredient in beer[c]
Taro, corn (*Colocasia aff. esculenta*)	ingredient in beer[c]
Seasonally Available Foods	
"Guama" fruit (*Inga* sp.)	raw as snack
Peach palm, fruit (*Bactris gasipaes*)	boiled as snack, ingredient in beer[c]
Pineapple, fruit (*Ananas sativa*)	raw as snack
Uvilla, fruit (*Pourouma cercopiaefolia*)	raw as snack

Source: Data collected during fieldwork in 1976–1978 (Dufour 1983).

Notes: All foods are consumed by all age-sex groups except as noted. "Snacks" are foods eaten between meals.

a. A dip made for cassava bread by boiling thirty or more hot peppers in about 1 liter of salted water. The pepper pot is reheated at each meal and often used to cook small fish.

b. Roasting done in ashes of cooking fire.

c. With the exception of maize, all of these starchy vegetables are peeled and boiled, masticated or mashed, and then added to cassava beer. The basic ingredients in the beer are boiled manioc juice ("manicuera") and a thin cassava bread. Maize is generally ground and cooked as a cake before being masticated. Beer is drunk principally by adults on festive occasions.

fairly complex judgmental task and may not be appropriate for use with nonindustrialized populations in which people are unaccustomed to thinking in terms of numbers or frequencies. It would be especially problematical in groups that have traditional counting systems of "1, 2, 3, many." In groups such as these, a more suitable method would be to simply obtain a

Table 6.3 Sample Diets of "Newyorican" Families of Puerto Rican Ancestry Living in New York City in 1960s

Sample No. 1	Breakfast	Orange juice Unsalted soda crackers Gouda cheese Coffee with milk
	Lunch	*Serenata*[a] *Viandas*[a] Coffee with milk
	Dinner	Rice *Habichuelas*[a] Fried pork chop Canned fruit cocktail Canned peas and carrots Coffee with milk
Sample No. 2	Breakfast	Orange juice Unsalted soda crackers Gouda cheese Coffee with milk
	Lunch	Fried eggs Ripe plantain Canned vegetables and lettuce salad Coffee with milk
	Dinner	Rice *Rosita* (pink) beans Beef stew Lettuce and tomato salad with oil and vinegar Coffee with milk
		Steak with onions Rice with pigeon peas *Tostones*[a] Coffee with milk

Source: Modified from Sanjur (1982).
Note: a. *Serenata* is a mixture of hard-boiled eggs, onions, green pepper, tomatoes, lettuce, oil, vinegar, garlic, and codfish. *Viandas* is the generic name for plantains and starchy foods. *Habichuelas* are dried beans such as kidney beans and pinto beans. *Tostones* are slices of green plantain, fried, flattened, and fried again.

list of the foods eaten the previous day and determine the number of times each was eaten. This process could then be repeated periodically during the time period of interest. An average of five repeats per individual should yield food frequency data comparable to that of the standard method (Hunt et al. 1979).

Using either method, the interviewer works from a list of local foods or categories of foods (wild green leaves, wheat flour breads, sugar sweetened beverages, etc.) developed from the ethnographic information on food habits. Depending on the research objectives, it might be useful to record source and/or acquisition information, such as where or how the food is usually obtained (received as a gift, gathered, produced, etc.). Because the food list can unintentionally limit informant response, it is a good idea to close food frequency interviews with an open-ended question about foods consumed that the respondent did not have the opportunity to report. A sample recording form is shown in Appendix 6.A.

A second type of food frequency questionnaire, referred to as a semi-quantitative questionnaire, includes an estimate of food quantity using general serving-size categories such as "large," "medium," or "small." The use of semiquantitative questionnaires requires additional ethnographic information on population-specific definitions of serving sizes (in both local and metric units) for each food item, and whether or not they vary with age and/or gender. The addition of quantitative information to the food-frequency questionnaire makes tool development a lengthy process, and the resulting data set is more than minimal.

The sample of individuals to be interviewed should be representative of the study population. Because of the level of cooperation needed in collecting this type of data, it is usually not possible to get a truly random sample, and any sampling design should allow for a high rate of refusals. If age, gender, or social rank appear to affect food use, the sample could be stratified relative to these variables. Other sampling considerations are addressed later in the discussion of household sample selection.

Data can be analyzed to show the frequency of individuals or households reporting consumption of each food at least once a day or once a week during a selected time period. For example, Table 6.4 indicates that in a sample of fifty-two households, 98 percent reported consuming corn

Table 6.4 Percent of Households[a] (n = 52) in Nopalcinco, Mexico, Reporting the Consumption of Common Foods During the Previous Week

Food	Percent	Food	Percent
Vegetable foods		*Animal foods*	
Tortillas, corn	98	Beef	60
Bread, wheat	86	Eggs, hen	49
Beans	78	Cheese	20
Fruit	59	Chicken	12
Vegetables	34	Pork	8
		Fish	2

Source: Adapted from DeWalt and Pelto (1977).

Note: a. Data were obtained by asking how many times a week particular foods were consumed.

tortillas the previous week. Table 6.5 shows the frequency of use of a supplementary food: Milk was served as an accompaniment to the staple in 25.3 percent of all Sandawe meals recorded in five households during selected time periods. Food frequency data can be reported in day, week, month, and even year intervals. Shorter time intervals are probably more suitable for non-Western populations experiencing seasonal and/or annual fluctuations in food availability.

Table 6.5 Frequency of Consumption of "Relish" Dishes at *Ugali*-Based Meals Consumed by Sandawe (Central Tanzania)[a]

Source	Percent	Source	Percent
Vegetable		*Animal*	
gathered		*wild*	
Ceratotheca sesamoides, Corchorus		Fish (*Claris mossembicus, Labeo*	
trilocularis, Gynandropsis gynandra		*cylindricus*)	2.4
Sesamum augustifolium	29.3	Dik Dik (*Rynnchotrogus kirkii*)	1.3
Mushrooms (unidentified)	1.7	Gazelle (*Gazella granti* and	
Baobab seeds		G. *thompsonii*)	0.7
(*Adansonia digitata*)	0.3	Impala (*Aepyceros melampus*)	0.7
Unidentified	9.7	Francolin (*Francolinus sephaens,*	
		F. squamatus, F. coqui)	0.5
		Guinea Fowl (*Numida mitrata,*	
		Guttera pucherami)	0.3
		Klipspringer (*Oreotragus oreotragus*)	0.2
		Hare (*Lepus capensis*)	0.2
		Unidentified	3.2
Subtotal	41.0	Subtotal	9.5
Cultivated		*Domestic*	
Groundnuts (*Arachis hypogaea*)	2.9	Cow milk (zebu variety)	25.3
Cassava leaves (*Manihot esculenta*)	2.4	Cow meat	6.7
Haricot beans (*Phaseolus vulgaris*)	1.3	Goat meat	6.4
Cowpea (*Vigna* spp.)	0.7	Chicken meat	4.2
Sweet potato leaves			
(*Ipomoea batatas*)	0.7	Eggs, hen	1.5
Cowpea leaves (*Vigna* spp.)	0.5	Sheep meat	0.8
Cassava (*Manihot esculenta*)	0.2		
Bambara nuts			
(*Voandzeia subterranea*)	0.2		
Subtotal	8.9	Subtotal	44.9
Total	49.9	Total	54.4

Source: Adapted from Newman (1980:29).

Note: a. Relish dishes are those foods served as accompaniments to *ugali,* a stiff porridge usually made of maize, which is the staple food of the Sandawe. Totals in the table exceed 100 percent because more than one relish is served at some meals. Data are based on records of foods eaten by five households for three separate one-month periods. Records were kept by a school-aged child in each household.

Figure 6.1 Percent of Households (n=52) in Nopalcinco, Mexico, Reporting the Consumption of Common Foods During the Previous Week

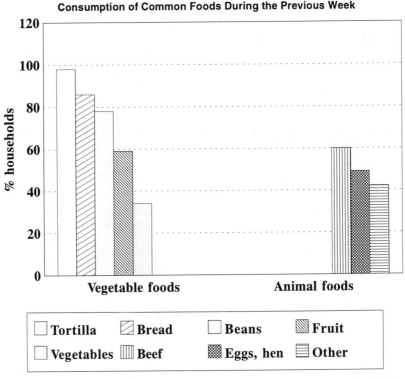

Legend:
☐ Tortilla ▨ Bread ☐ Beans ▨ Fruit
☐ Vegetables ▥ Beef ▦ Eggs, hen ☰ Other

Source: Plotted from data in Table 6.4, which was adapted from DeWalt and Pelto (1977).

Examples of food frequency data presented graphically are shown in Figures 6.1 and 6.2. Any presentation of data, graphic or tabular, should be accompanied by a clear description of how, where, and when (year and time of year) the information was gathered.

Food frequency data provide a more detailed picture of local diets and a better indication of the relative importance of different foods in the diet than does a description of food habits and is often used in addition to the latter. Food frequency data can also provide useful descriptive data on seasonal or socioeconomic differences in food use. For example, Table 6.6 shows that whereas maize is a dietary staple throughout the year, millet and, to a lesser extent, rice are seasonally important. The diet is lowest in diversity in October, suggesting food availability might be a problem during this season. Graphing the data (Figure 6.2) emphasizes the seasonal contrasts.

Figure 6.2 Seasonal Differences in Food Use in a Rural Community

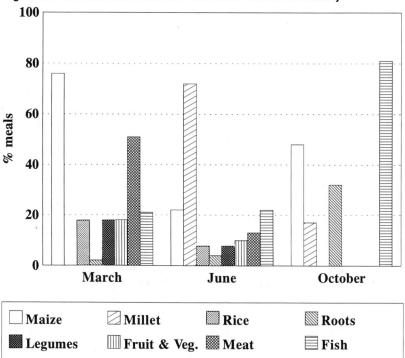

Source: Plotted from data in Table 6.6, which was adapted from den Hartog and van Staveren (1983:91).

Note: Based on interviews with eighty adults repeated in March, June, and October.

Table 6.6 Seasonal Differences in Food Use in a Rural Community

	Meals with Each Food Item, Percent		
Food	March	June	October
Vegetable Foods			
Grains: Maize	76	22	48
Millet	0	72	17
Rice	18	8	0
Roots and tubers	2	4	32
Pulses, groundnuts	18	8	0
Leafy vegetables	16	9	0
Other vegetables and fruits	2	1	0
Animal Foods			
Meat	51	13	0
Fish	21	22	81

Source: Adapted from den Hartog and van Staveren (1983:91).

Note: Based on interviews with eighty adults repeated in March, June, and October.

Food frequency data that do not provide information on the quantity of food consumed cannot be used to evaluate the adequacy of the diet. They can, however, suggest potential nutritional problems in the population or particular subgroups. For example, if the principal source of vitamin A in the diet is green leafy vegetables and these are eaten only during a short harvest period, the vitamin A adequacy of the diet might be questioned.

Food frequency data recalled in an interview is subject to the limitations of all recall data (Bernard et al. 1984). First, respondents' memories are not perfect, and some foods (especially snacks) may be forgotten (Sanjur 1982). Second, because of the emotional and symbolic value of foods, respondents' recall may be modified to an unknown extent by images of what they think they should have or would like to have eaten or what they think *you think* they should have eaten. For example, Tukanoan Indians typically omitted the consumption of wild vegetable foods because these were of low prestige (Dufour, unpublished data).

Assessing the Amount of Food Consumed by Households and Small Social Groups

Information about the type and amount of food consumed by households or small social groups can be used to answer questions such as which types of food and/or which individual foods are consumed in the greatest quantities, how food quantities vary throughout the year, and how the quantities of foods consumed vary between subgroups within the population. Measuring the food consumption of households requires considerable time and cooperation from both investigators and respondents. It yields a maximal rather than a minimal data set and probably should not be attempted without the collaboration of individuals familiar with this type of research. Further, this level of quantification should not be attempted until a detailed ethnographic description of food habits has been completed.

Most of the current research on food consumption in industrialized societies is focused on individuals. However, in nonindustrialized populations the household, the family, or some other social group may be a more appropriate unit of study. In such populations the household is often the primary unit within which economic, social, and cultural resources are organized (Pelto 1989); hence, food production, distribution, and consumption are strongly influenced by household size and composition. Furthermore, when household members eat from common serving dishes (Quandt 1986) or share foods from a household larder, it is often easier to determine the amount of food consumed by a group than by individuals during a meal. In the following discussion, we refer specifically to the assessment of *household* intake, but the same techniques can be used to assess food intake of other small social groups. Similar techniques can also be used to assess the food intake of individuals.

Factors affecting household food intake include seasonal availability of foods, socioeconomic status, group size, sex ratio, activity patterns, household work roles, and cultural definitions of appropriate "food portions" and ideal body shape. Discussion of the impact of one or more of these factors on household food consumption can be found in DeWalt, Kelly, and Pelto (1980); Dufour (1983); Goode, Theophano, and Curtis (1984); Lane (cited in Sanjur 1982:86); Madden and Yodder (1972); and Rosenberg (1980).

Data Collection Techniques

Two useful techniques for collecting data on household food intake are food lists and food records (Sanjur 1982). These techniques can be hierarchically ordered. Food lists, a recall method, are less time intensive but rely on respondents' memory and are subject to the problems of all recall data. The food record method is more time intensive but can provide more accurate data on the quantities of food consumed. Both food lists and food records are typically used with household groups but can be used with other types of groups as well. Food records kept by an observer may be particularly appropriate in very small, nonliterate groups (such as foragers) in which food consumption of all members can be monitored visually, or in groups in which interviewing is inappropriate.

Food lists. A food list is produced by asking the person or persons responsible for household food preparation to recall the types and corresponding quantities of foods consumed by the group over a specified period of time, along with the age and sex of the persons consuming the food. Given the problems with recall data, one-day recall is recommended.

Interviews should be conducted in the home and preferably in the food preparation and consumption areas. This setting may help the respondent better to remember the foods consumed and may afford the interviewer an opportunity to observe food preparation techniques or snacking behavior. The investigator should start the interview session by asking the respondent what were the first foods eaten on the previous day by members of the household group. The interview should cover not only high-bulk and/or high-protein foods (such as the main course and side dishes) but also beverages and supplementary items (sugar, butter, honey, etc.). Once the foods consumed first in the day have been described, the investigator should continue by asking, "What was the next food eaten by any member of the household group?" One should avoid asking "What did the group eat at the next meal?" so as not to impose a "meal pattern" on a group that does not eat at set times of the day or eats small amounts continuously throughout the day.

Once all foods have been identified, the respondent is then asked to estimate total quantity of each item consumed. For mixed or composite dishes, the respondent should be asked to enumerate and quantify the individual ingredients. The investigator should ask to see the containers in which foods were cooked or from which foods were consumed and verify the level at which containers were filled prior to and after consumption. If interviewing is done outside the home, containers of varying sizes, cardboard circle cutouts of varying diameters, and pencil and paper should be available so the respondent can estimate or draw food amounts.

After the recall interview has been completed, all estimated food quantities should be converted to metric weight, or SI (see Hunt, chapter 9). Volumes can be calculated from the dimensions of the containers or measured directly using a graduated cylinder, then converted to metric weight. Weight of individual items can be estimated by weighing a duplicate sample. Appendix 6.B provides an example of a typical data collection form.

Food records. A food record is a description of the food eaten and an estimate of quantity, recorded at the time of consumption. This record can be kept by an outside observer, or a literate member of the group can learn to keep food records. If the record is maintained by an outside observer, one or more practice sessions should precede actual data collection to ensure that the group is comfortable with the observer's presence and that the observer can accurately estimate quantities of foods consumed and discarded. If the food record is kept by a literate member of the group, a training period and a practice session should precede actual data collection. During the training period, the researcher should stress that the primary objective of the recording process is to record *actual* food intake and should reassure the recorder that there are no "expected" results, no "good" or "bad" foods and no "good" or "bad" food quantities. As part of the training, both the researchers and recorder should simultaneously record household food intake over one twenty-four-hour period. Time between meals should be used to compare records, to discuss ways to improve the accuracy of the record, and to record food intake consumed between meals.

As with food lists, food quantities can be weighed directly or calculated from volume measurements. A sample data collection form is shown in Appendix 6.C. In ethnographic situations where there are likely to be variable numbers of individuals present at each meal, it will probably be necessary to use a separate data collection form for each meal or food consumption event.

Sampling Considerations

In all but the smallest villages, a sample of households should be selected. Carefully completed measurements done on a sample of the population are more valuable than poor measurements done on everyone. In selecting a sample, three important considerations are sample size, sample type, and sample of days for which data will be collected.

Sample size is limited by time, personnel, and money. To estimate manageable sample size, a rough estimate should be made of the time, personnel, and funds needed to assess food intake of one household using a selected method of data collection. For example, the collection of a one-day food list from one household may take a researcher two hours; this estimate includes fifteen minutes to travel to the home, twenty to thirty minutes to familiarize the respondent with the nature of the study and the interview procedure (and to engage in social conversation to ensure an amiable and candid interview), and twenty to forty-five minutes to collect the actual food list. Given this estimate, a single researcher could complete three to four one-day food lists in a day and fifteen to twenty-five in a week. If three one-day food lists are desired (see following section), then the total data collection time for a single household would be six hours, and a researcher could collect information from five to seven households per week.

Pelto (1989:45–46) suggests that a sample size of 100 households is needed to permit multivariate data analysis. Even if the research population consists of only 200 households, the goal of 100 cases is recommended if complex statistical analysis is planned. If economic, practical, and logistical limitations prohibit the use of such a large sample, a smaller sample (e.g., 15 to 25) can be used; the size of the sample relative to the total population should be calculated and reported, and statistical analysis should be limited to nonparametric and univariate analysis.

Although it is more manageable, a small sample can obscure intrapopulational variation. If preliminary observations and data indicate that interhousehold variation is low, a small sample may adequately represent the food habits of the entire population. However, if the population is relatively heterogeneous, then entire subgroups may be eliminated or poorly represented in a small sample. If populational variation requires the use of a large sample and the necessary resources are not available, assessment of diet should probably be limited to a description of food habits (see above) or to an investigation of the intake of one definable subgroup (female-headed households, households having the mean household size, etc.). If the latter approach is used, a principal subgroup should be selected to ensure that a significant sector of the target population is studied. For example, assessing the food intake of single-member households may be manageable, but if such households are unusual the data provide little insight into the food habits of the larger population. If the objective of the research is to compare the intake of two subsets or subsamples of a population, sample size tables, as provided by Fleiss (1981), can be used to determine adequate sample sizes for varying levels of statistical significance and power.

The sample of days for which food consumption data will be collected also must be considered. The collection of household food consumption data should be scheduled so that the information recorded is representative of usual or customary intake observed during the research period. Food intake typically shows considerable day-to-day, week-to-week, and seasonal fluctuations in both type and amount.

A random sample of days, dispersed over the research period, can be used to assess average daily consumption without regard to season. The number of days needed to assess average daily quantitative intake from nonconsecutive days will depend on the interday and intergroup variation and the number of groups or households in the sample. In general, as sample size decreases, the number of days surveyed should increase. With a sample of 100 or more households, one- to three-day food intake records may be appropriate; with a sample of less than 100 households, three- to seven-day intake records should be used.

To determine "habitual" patterns of food consumption over a particular season, a random sample of three to seven consecutive days is recommended (Acheson et al. 1980; Block 1982; Lieberman 1986). If the diet consists of a limited number of foods and quantities show little variability, a three-day survey may provide the same results as a seven-day survey; observation, interviews, and possibly food frequencies should be used to determine the sample number of days appropriate for use with a particular study group. As a rule, unless the sample is large, a minimum of three days is needed to estimate typical quantitative intake (Chavez and Huenemann 1984:137).

Sample type—for example, unrestricted random, proportionate stratified random, or opportunistic—should be chosen based on the objectives of the research and the composition and cooperativeness of the community (Reh 1962; Lieberman 1986). To implement an unrestricted random sample, a list of households in the population should be produced or obtained from a regional or local census office. Each household on the list is numbered consecutively. Using a table of random numbers or a lottery (e.g., numbers drawn from a hat), households can be picked according to their assigned number until the predetermined sample size is drawn. At this time, a few extra numbers should be drawn to serve as backups in case some households selected are not willing to cooperate or are not available at the time of the study.

A proportionate stratified random sample is useful with populations exhibiting considerable internal variation. The households are divided into homogenous groups based on economic and/or social factors (household income, head of household's occupation, etc.). Each group's relative contribution to the total number of households in the population is calculated, and a proportionate number of households is drawn from each group to produce the projected sample size. For example, in a population divided into three groups, 50 percent of the households have been assigned to group A, 25 percent to group B, and 25 percent to group C. A sample of forty households is desired. To draw a proportionate stratified random sample, twenty households will be randomly selected from group A, ten from group B, and ten from group C.

An opportunistic sample should only be used when the population is small and relatively homogenous. This sample is composed simply of those households willing to participate. To ensure that all households have an equal chance of inclusion within the sample, the project and forthcoming sample selection should be well advertised by word of mouth, written announcements posted in high-traffic areas (such as stores or the village plaza), and/or public verbal announcement. Once the population has been informed, the sample can be formed on a "first come, first serve" basis. The opportunistic sample must be used if preliminary field observations and experiences suggest that cooperation level will be low and that a truly random sample will be difficult to obtain. When an opportunistic sample is used, the representativeness of the sample should be documented.

Once a sample of households has been selected, the consumption group within each household needs to be defined in terms of number and preferably age and sex composition. The household consumption group consists of all of those individuals fed from the food supply. See Appendix 6.C for a sample data collection form.

Data Analysis

Before the food intake data of groups can be interpreted and compared, the data must be standardized to minimize the effects of variation in group size and composition. There are two basic ways to standardize the data. First, the food consumption values can be converted to average per capita consumption regardless of age or sex (Reh 1962). This calculation can be made by simply summing the total weight of each of the foods consumed and dividing by the total number of group members. An example of data standardized using this method is provided in Table 6.7. Unfortunately the table does not specify whether weights are for raw/dry or cooked foods. This is a common error that seriously limits the comparability of the data.

Table 6.7 **Average Daily per Capita[a] Consumption of Selected Foods Consumed by Sixty-Two Households**

Socioeconomic groups[b]	Corn (gm)	Beans (gm)	Meat and Poultry (gm)	Eggs	Milk (ml)
I	587	48	1.7	0.2	7
II	690	32	2.7	0.4	18
III	596	15	2.5	0.3	18
IV	423	39	7.0	0.7	28

Source: Adapted from DeWalt, Kelly, and Pelto (1980:212).
Notes: a. Daily per capita intake was calculated by dividing the total weekly household consumption by seven and again by the number of people in the household.
b. Total sample size of sixty-two households divided into quartiles based on a "material style of life" scale (MSL).

There is little theoretical justification for adjusting per capita consumption data to reflect age and sex composition or variables such as reproductive status unless within-group food distribution is known in detail. Distribution should not be assumed to be equal to need. If an objective of the research is to compare household food intake to some estimate of requirement, such as those of FAO/WHO/UNU (1985), then the mean requirement of the group should take age and sex distribution into account (see below).

A second way to standardize household data is to convert food quantities to nutrients and to present the diet in terms of the percent contribution of each food or food category to total nutrient intake. This is the preferred method of standardizing group data, as it provides an indication of the overall nutritional quality of the diet. An example of data standardized to percent of energy contributed by each food is provided in Table 6.8. Standardization can be limited to energy or expanded to include additional macronutrients (protein, fat, and carbohydrate) and/or micronutrients (specific vitamins and minerals). Energy is considered the best single indicator of dietary adequacy, but in some cases a nutrient such as iron or folic acid might be a good indicator of the quality of the diet.

The accuracy of the conversion of intake data to nutrients is dependent on the adequacy of the food composition table used in the conversion. The most appropriate food composition tables are those based on locally available foods prepared as they are commonly eaten. The International Network of Food Data Systems (INFOODS) maintains and distributes a list of food composition tables grouped by country (Rand 1986). If compositional data on locally consumed foods are not available, chemical analyses of local foods may be necessary. Data for comparable foods can sometimes be used, but these kinds of substitutions should be done in consultation

**Table 6.8 Comparison of Preharvest and Postharvest Diet Composition in
Households of Lower and Upper Socioeconomic Status in
Nuñoa, Peru**

Food Type	Preharvest		Postharvest	
	Lower SES (n = 93)	Upper SES (n = 26)	Lower SES (n = 99)	Upper SES (n = 47)
Fresh tubers	11.7	19.7	44.6	30.7
Chuno/moraya	12.9	2.0	5.5	<1.0
Flour	15.6	4.3	8.9	<1.0
Rice/oats	14.5	26.1	7.3	21.0
Oil/milk	1.0	6.8	0.7	4.2
Other	44.3	41.1	33.0	44.0

Source: Adapted from Leonard (1989:344–345).
Note: Composition is evaluated in terms of percent of energy that a given food item contributes during that season.

with people experienced in this type of analysis. If compositional data on composite dishes are not available, values can be calculated from weighed recipes, though again someone experienced in this type of analysis should be consulted. Even if data on composite dishes are available, the collection of recipes used may provide valuable insights into food use. For example, although all members of a group might eat a common dish—say, a meat-potato stew—the relative amounts of meat and potatoes may vary with the economic situation of the household.

The conversion of food intake data to nutrients is laborious. The use of dietary analysis computer software (Teufel and Teufel 1988; Nieman et al. 1992) can facilitate the task.

Data Presentation

The results of the household dietary data can be presented in table format. The investigator should report the number of households and/or individuals in the sample, the age-sex composition of the sample, the average household or group size, and the number of days for which food lists recalled or records were kept. The age-sex composition, important to presentation of per capita data, can be given by percent contribution of each age-sex group (e.g., 10 percent females over fifty, 5 percent males over fifty, etc.), or in raw numbers (e.g., three females over fifty, one male over fifty, etc.). This information can be included in a footnote accompanying the table or in the text under a discussion of sample characteristics. The investigator should identify food weights as being for raw or cooked foods or should note method of food preparation.

Examples of data presentation are shown in Tables 6.8, 6.9, and 6.10.

If dietary diversity is low, household intake of individual food items can be shown (Table 6.9) and should include taxonomic names. If dietary diversity is high, individual food items can be combined into food clusters or groups based on similar usage and energy/nutrient content (Table 6.10). If individual foods are grouped for the purpose of presentation, the items in each group should be specified.

Table 6.9 Average Food Consumption (gm/day, raw weight) for a Three-Day Period for Five Families in Koravake Village in the Purari Delta, Papua, New Guinea

Food	Mean Intake (gm)	Range (gm)
Sago	1,855	1,386–2,521
Cassava	644	417–914
Coconut	627	262–912
Banana	557	52–1,301
Fish	455	60–516
Sweet banana	246	43–992
Flour	178	0–853
Rice (dry weight)	158	0–188
Green leaves	124	72–232
Sugar	55	15–60
Taro	62	0–310
Tinned meat/fish	37	0–107
Meat	31	0–155

Source: Adapted from Ulijaszek (1982:88).

Table 6.10 Quantity of Selected Food Groups Consumed in a Week in Spring 1965 by U.S. Nonfarm Households, North-Central and South Regions

Food Group	North-central Region (n = 1,594 households)		South (n = 1,818 households)	
	Mean (kg)	Standard Deviation (kg)	Mean (kg)	Standard Deviation (kg)
Beef, pork, poultry, fish	7.0	4.5	6.5	4.5
Milk products, excluding butter	13.4	9.7	11.6	8.3
Eggs	1.2	0.9	1.3	1.0
Fats and oils[a]	1.2	0.8	1.4	1.0
Flours, cereals, bakery products	3.6	2.8	4.3	3.6
Vegetables[b]	7.9	3.0	7.1	2.7
Fruits[c]	3.4	3.9	2.8	3.8
Sugars and sweets	1.5	1.4	1.6	1.6

Source: Adapted from Burk and Pao (1976:30).
Notes: a. Includes butter.
b. Excludes dark green and yellow vegetables.
c. Includes citrus fruits.

Uses and Limitations

Household surveys should not be used to assess individual intake. However, household data can provide insight into questions of group behavior and/or adaptation to variations in the food supply. Interesting questions might include: How do households vary in their access to food? How does meal composition vary between households? How do households of a given size/composition cope with seasonal fluctuation in the food supply? How is socioeconomic status reflected in household diet? These kinds of questions may yield more interesting insights into group behavior than do records of individual behavior.

Food lists. The food list is quick and economical. Interview time for each household ranges from fifteen to forty-five minutes, equipment needs are minimal, and the interview format does not require respondents to be literate. One-day food lists can be used to compare the types and amounts of food consumed by households of varying socioeconomic status at any one point in time. For example, the data could be used to compare the relative energy contribution of dietary staples and supplementary foods or the relative weight and energy contribution of foods carried from the market, outlying fields, or kitchen gardens.

Food consumption over one day, however, does not provide a picture of habitual household intake. Day-to-day variation in food consumption prevents any one day from being representative of the typical household diet. One-day food lists can be used to assess habitual intake if repeated over three to seven days. To account for seasonal variations in intake, interviews should be conducted over several consecutive days within each season. To record annual daily intake, interviews can be conducted randomly throughout the year. Food lists are probably most effective when dietary diversity is low and sample size is large.

Food record. Collection of food records requires the cooperation of the entire social group. Whether a group is observed by one of its own members or by an outsider, the "in progress" recording method may cause household members to alter food consumption patterns—for example, by consuming less so as not to appear gluttonous or by limiting their use of certain foods, such as condiments, that are difficult to measure. They may also avoid eating food perceived to be of lower status, such as insects or wild leaves, and/or increase the consumption of high-status foods.

If a group member maintains the food record, considerable time and cooperation and a reasonable level of literacy are required from that individual. If the recorder is also the cook, meal contents may be altered to facilitate the recording process or to demonstrate that, indeed, "good" or nutritious meals are served in this household.

Food records collected over three or more days can be used to estimate the food intake of household groups and to provide a gross assessment of the adequacy of a group's diet. This can be done by comparing the total household requirement (sum of individual requirements) for energy or a given nutrient with an appropriate standard, such as the FAO/WHO/UNU (1985) recommendations. As these recommendations are defined in terms of age, sex, reproductive status, and activity level, these variables would have to be known for each household member. An example is shown in Dufour (1983).

If seasonal and/or economic information is collected, the effect of these variables on nutrient intake also can be examined. Given the relatively brief period of data collection and the daily, weekly, monthly, and yearly variations in dietary intake, it is not possible to identify individual households as being at risk of inadequate nutritional intake. Nor can this type of data provide any indication of the adequacy of the diets of individuals unless their share of the total household food supply is accurately known.

Assessing Nutritional Status

Anthropometric assessments of nutritional status are usually limited to young children. Nutritionally they are the most vulnerable members of the community because their energy and nutrient needs per unit of body weight are the highest and because they are the least able to obtain their own food or a share of the family food supply.

A large number of anthropometric measurements have been used to assess the nutritional status of children, but the most useful appear to be height-for-age and weight-for-height (Johnston 1986; Waterlow et al. 1977). Height-for-age provides a measure of growth over time and is an indicator of long-term nutritional status. Weight-for-height is a measure of relative thinness and an indicator of current nutritional status. Weight-for-age is a classic measure and is still used. For adults, weight and height are the most useful anthropometric measurements, and BMI (body mass index) is the most useful index to calculate.

Weight and height should be measured using standard techniques. Good descriptions can be found in Lohman et al. (1988) and Frisancho (1990). These techniques are not difficult, but the measurements should be carefully done, and the researcher should gain competence in their use *before* going to the field. In the field, height of children two years of age and older can be measured with an anthropometer or with measuring tape (affixed to a wall) and a flat headboard. Heights of children less than two years of age are measured as supine length and require an infant measuring board.

For measuring body weights, an accurate beam balance is preferable. A bathroom-type spring scale is easier to use in the field, but care must be taken to ensure that it is only used on a flat level surface and regularly calibrated to guarantee accuracy. Calibration can be done by weighing a series of items of known weight that span the range of body weights to be measured. Known volumes of water can be used as calibration weights if nothing else is available. Infants should be weighed on one of the specially designed infant balances or from a hanging spring scale fitted with a sling to hold the infant.

Children's ages are difficult to determine in populations without written birth records, but every effort should be made to obtain whatever documentation is available. Several techniques for estimating age in such populations have been reported, and two or more are often used in combination. One technique is to estimate the birth date of each child using a detailed calendar of historical events of significance to the local group (Jelliffe 1966). The preparation and testing of such calendars, however, is time intensive. The use of a calendar can be combined with rank ordering of age of all children in the group (Howell 1979). Failing other sources of data, approximate age range can be assessed from dental eruption. The most suitable standards are recent ones established on the population in question (Weiner and Lourie 1981). If these are not available, other standards (such as the British or U.S. ones shown in Appendix 6.D) can provide a rough indication of chronological age.

Data on children should be reported by sex and age (intervals of one year) in terms of two indices: height-for-age and weight-for-height. Values for the study population can be compared to reference values in terms of z-scores or as percentages of the median reference value.[2] Good discussions of data analysis and presentation are provided by Waterlow et al. (1977), WHO (1986), and Frisancho (1990). For comparative purposes, a minimal data set would be the percentage of children with z-scores of -2SD or less or the percentage of children of less than 80 percent of the median weight-for-height and less than 90 percent of median height-for-age. For adults the minimal data set would be mean values for weight (kilograms), height (centimeters), and BMI (weight in kilograms/height in meters squared) by sex and age (ten-year intervals).

Although height and weight are used as indicators of nutritional status, they are really nonspecific indicators of overall health status. For children, linear growth and weight gain are affected by many environmental variables (Martorell 1985; Holmes 1984). Of these, diet and disease are generally the most important, but their direct effects on body size are difficult to distinguish on the basis of anthropometric data alone. Furthermore, the interpretation of anthropometric data relies on reference values from North American children. The use of these values is based on the assumption that environmental variables, rather than genetic differences, are the primary cause of the large differences in the growth of children in different populations (Martorell 1985; Waterlow et al. 1977). However, the question of genetic differences between populations with regard to growth potential is still open (Habicht et al. 1974; Dietz et al. 1989).

Conclusions

In this chapter we have outlined some of the techniques that can be used to assess diet, food intake, and nutritional status. Each of these techniques is associated with a substantial literature that discusses them in greater detail.

The minimal data set for the assessment of diet is a good description of food habits. This description can be expanded by adding information on the frequency of foods used and still further by adding information on the amounts consumed by household groups. Food consumption data sets are necessary to answer some questions, but the collection, analysis, and interpretation of the data involve a considerable amount of time and effort that is justifiable only when such questions are central to the case study.

Nutritional status can be more easily assessed using anthropometric data than dietary data. Anthropometric data can stand alone as a measure of health of a population, but its interpretation is greatly enhanced by detailed information on diet and disease.

Appendix 6.A
Sample Food Frequency Data Collection Form
(Modified from den Hartog and van Staveren [1983]
for use with Tukanoan Indians [Amazonia])

Food Frequency

Subject/Code: _____ Sex: M/F Age: _____
Interviewer: _____ Date: _____ Repeat: _____

Origin: P = produced, B = bartered/purchased, G = gift

Code #	Food	Consumed Yesterday	Origin	Notes
25	Agouti, meat			
26	Palm grubs			
28	Peccary, meat			
29	Small rodents, meat			
30	"Shrimp"			
32	Tapir, meat			
34	Termites			
38	Turtle, meat			
39	Wasp brood			
40	Corn cakes			
41	Avocado			
42	Banana/plantain			
48	Breadfruit			
50	Caimo			
54	Casabe			
55	Cashew apple			
62	Coca leaves			

Appendix 6.B
Sample Household Food List Data Collection Form

Food List   Household # _____

Respondent code: _____ Sex: M/F Age: _____

Interview date: _____ Recall of what day: M T W Th F S S

Number of people eating in household yesterday: _____
    no. of males _____, ages _____
    no. of females _____, ages _____

Food and how prepared	Amount	Weight (grams)	Code #

Appendix 6.C
Sample Food Intake Record Form

Food Intake Record

Page _____ of _____

Group _____ Recorder _____

Group composition: total no. members _____
    no. of males _____, ages _____
    no. of females _____, ages _____

Date: _____ Day of week: _____ Record day ____ of ___

Food and how prepared	Amount	Weight (grams)	Code #

Notes for food intake record:

1. Indicate day in sequence as well as total number of days in survey (e.g., 2 of 3 days).

2. When possible, record individual food items. If a composite dish is consumed, record the name of the dish, total quantity of the dish, individual ingredients and individual quantities (e.g., tamales: 14 tamales, followed by corn meal, yellow (4.5 cups/1080 gm), lard (3 Tbs/39 gm), shredded beef, cooked (4 cups/680 gm), and green chilis, raw (1 cup/245 gm).

3. Obtain a description of or observe the preparation method. The meaning of terms can vary. "Fried" can refer to food cooked in a frying pan with no added fats as well as food cooked by completely submerging foods in hot oil. If items are added in the cooking process (such as fat), record type and quantity of item.

Appendix 6.D
Estimation of Dental Age

"Dental age" can be assessed from the number of teeth present using Table 6.D1. In using the table, Weiner and Lourie (1981) have the following cautions:

1. The investigator should be able to distinguish primary and secondary teeth with certainty.
2. As the table is based on data from European and North American children, it can only serve as a rough indicator of chronological age in other populations.
3. It is unwise to extrapolate ages between about 2 and 6 years when the primary dentition is complete but the secondary has not yet begun to emerge.

Table 6.D1 Age Levels for Specified Number of Teeth Present in European and North American Children

Number of Primary Teeth Present	Age (years) Boys	Girls	Number of Secondary Teeth Present	Age (years) Boys	Girls
1	0.55	0.60	2	6.21	5.94
2	0.65	0.70	4	6.40	6.22
4	0.82	0.86	6	6.54	6.26
6	0.97	1.03	8	7.47	7.20
8	1.12	1.18	10	7.70	7.34
10	1.27	1.33	12	8.67	8.00
12	1.43	1.50	14	10.40	9.86
14	1.62	1.70	16	10.79	10.03
16	1.85	1.97	18	10.82	10.18
18	2.13	2.35	20	11.18	10.88
			22	11.47	10.89
			24	11.69	10.98
			26	12.12	11.66
			28	12.68	12.27

Source: Adapted from Weiner and Lourie (1981).

Notes

1. We would like to thank Francis Conant, Emilio Moran, Millicent Fleming-Moran, Lisa Staten, and Carol Waslein for their helpful comments on an earlier draft.

2. Two computer programs, (for IBM-compatible systems), CASP and ANTHRO, are available from the Centers for Disease Control (Division of Nutrition, Statistics Branch, CDC, 1600 Clifton Rd., Atlanta, GA 30333) and provide both percentile ranks and z-scores and greatly facilitate the analysis of anthropometric data.

References

Acheson, K. J., I. T. Campbell, O. G. Edholm, D. S. Miller, and M. J. Stock, 1980. The measurement of food and energy intake in man—An evaluation of some techniques. *American Journal of Clinical Nutrition* 33:1147–1154.

Bernard, H. R., P. Killworth, D. Kronenfeld, and L. Sailer, 1984. The problem of informant accuracy. *Annual Review of Anthropology* 13:495–518.

Block, G., 1982. A review of validations of dietary assessment methods. *American Journal of Epidemiology* 115(4):492–505.

Block, G., F. E. Thompson, A. M. Hartman, F. A. Larkin, and K. E. Guire, 1992. Comparison of two dietary questionnaires validated against multiple dietary records collected during a one-year period. *Journal of American Dietetic Association* 92:686–693.

Burk, M. C., and E. M. Pao, 1976. *Methodology for Large-scale Surveys of Household and Individual Sets.* Washington, D.C.: United States Department of Agriculture.

Chavez, M., and R. Huenemann, 1984. Measuring impact by assessing dietary intake and food consumption. In D. S. Sohn, R. Lockwood, and N. S. Scrimshaw, eds., *Methods for the Evaluation of the Impact of Food and Nutrition Programmes,* pp. 127–141. Tokyo: United Nations University.

Delgado, L., 1991. Food aid in Peru: Refusal and acceptance in a peasant community of the Central Andes. *Food and Foodways* 5(1):57–77.

den Hartog, A. P., and W. A. van Staveren, 1983. *Manual for Social Surveys on Food Habits and Consumption in Developing Countries.* Wageningen: Centre for Agricultural Publishing and Documentation.

DeWalt, K., and G. H. Pelto, 1977. Food use and household ecology in a Mexican community. In T. K. Fitzgerald, ed., *Nutrition and Anthropology in Action,* pp. 79–93. Assen/Amsterdam: van Gorcum.

DeWalt, K. M., P. B. Kelly, and G. H. Pelto, 1980. Nutritional correlates of economic microdifferentiation in a highland Mexican community. In N. W. Jerome, R. F. Kandel, and G. H. Pelto, eds., *Nutritional Anthropology,* pp. 147–179. Pleasantville, N.Y.: Redgrave Publishing.

Dietz, W. H., B. Marino, N. R. Peacock, and R. C. Bailey, 1989. Nutritional status of Efe pygmies and Lese horticulturalists. *American Journal of Physical Anthropology* 78:509–518.

Dufour, D. L., 1981. Household variation in energy flow in a population of tropical forest horticulturists. Ph.D. diss. Binghamton: State University of New York.

———, 1983. Nutrition in the northwest Amazon: Household dietary intake and time-energy expenditure. In R. B Hames and W. T. Vickers, eds., *Adaptive Responses of Native Amazonians*, pp. 329–355. New York: Academic.

Fleiss, J. L., 1981. *Statistical Methods for Rates and Proportions,* second edition. New York: John Wiley & Sons.

Fleuret, A., 1979. Methods for evaluation of the role of fruits and wild greens in Shambaa diet: A case study. *Medical Anthropology* 3:249–269.

Food and Agriculture Organization, World Health Organization, and United Nations University, 1985. *Energy and Protein Requirements.* Technical Report Series No. 724. Geneva: World Health Organization.

Frisancho, A. R., 1990. *Anthropometric Standards for Assessment of Growth and Nutritional Status.* Ann Arbor: University of Michigan.

Goode, J., J. Theophano, and K. Curtis, 1984. A framework for the analysis of continuity and change in shared sociocultural rules for food use: The Italian-American pattern. In L. K. Brown and K. Mussell, eds., *Ethnic and Regional Foodways in the United States,* pp. 66–88. Knoxville: University of Tennessee.

Habicht, J. P., R. Martorell, C. Yarbough, R. M. Malina, and R. E. Klein, 1974. Height and weight standards for children: How relevant are ethnic differences in growth potential? *Lancet* 1:611–615.

Holmes, R., 1984. Nondietary modifiers of nutritional status in tropical forest populations in Venezuela. *Interciencia* 9(6):386–390.

Howell, N., 1979. *Demography of the Dobe !Kung.* New York: Academic.

Hunt, I. F., L. S. Luke, N. J. Murphy, V. A. Clark, and A. W. Coulson, 1979. Nutrient estimates from computerized questionnaires vs. 24-hour recall interviews. *Journal American Dietetic Association* 74:656–659.

Jelliffe, D. B., 1966. *The Assessment of Nutritional Status of the Community.* Geneva: World Health Organization.

Johnston, F. E., 1986. Reference data for physical growth in nutritional anthropology. In S. A. Quandt and C. Ritenbaugh, eds., *Training Manual in Nutritional Anthropology,* pp. 60–68. Washington, D. C.: American Anthropological Association.

Lane, S., 1975. *Food Distribution and Food Stamp Program Effects on Nutritional Achievement of Low Income Households in Kern County, California.* Unpublished paper.

Leonard, W. R., 1989. Nutritional determinants of high-altitude growth in Nuñoa, Peru. *American Journal of Physical Anthropology* 80(3):341–352.

Lieberman, L. S., 1986. Nutritional anthropology at the household level. In S. A. Quandt and C. Ritenbaugh, eds., *Training Manual in Nutritional Anthropology,* pp. 225–260. Washington, D. C.: American Anthropological Association.

Lohman, T.G., A. F. Roche, and R. Martorell, 1988. *Anthropometric Standardization Reference Manual.* Champaign, Illinois: Human Kinetics.

Madden, P., and M. Yodder, 1972. Program evaluation—food stamps and commodity distribution in rural areas of central Pennsylvania. *Pennsylvania State University Agricultural Experiment Station Bulletin* 780.

Martorell, R., 1985. Child growth retardation: A discussion of its causes and its relationship to health. In K. Blaxter and J. C. Waterlow, eds., *Nutritional Adaptation in Man,* pp. 13–30. London: John Libbey.

McLaren, D. S., 1976. Concepts and content of nutrition. In D. S. McLaren, ed., *Nutrition in the Community,* New York: John Wiley.

Mead, M., 1943. Dietary patterns and food habits. *Journal of the American Dietetic Association* 19:1–5.

Messer, E., 1977. The ecology of a vegetarian diet in a modernizing Mexican community. In T. K. Fitzgerald, ed., *Nutrition and Anthropology in Action,* pp. 117–124. Amsterdam: van Gorcum.

Messer, E., and H. Kuhnlein, 1986. Traditional foods. In S. A. Quandt and C. Ritenbaugh, eds., *Training Manual in Nutritional Anthropology,* pp. 66–81. Washington, D. C.: American Anthropological Association.

Milton, K., 1991. Comparative aspects of diet in Amazonian forest-dwellers. *Philosophical Transactions of the Royal Society of London,* Series B 334(1270):253–273.

Newman, J. L., 1980. Dimensions of Sandawe diet. In J.R.K. Robson, ed., *Food, Ecology and Culture,* New York: Gordon and Breach.

Nieman, D. C., D. E. Butterworth, C. N. Nieman, K. E. Lee, and R. D. Lee, 1992. Comparison of six microcomputer dietary analysis systems with the USDA nutrient data base for standard reference. *Journal of the American Dietetic Association* 92:48–56.

Orlove, B., 1987. Stability and change in highland Andean dietary patterns. In M. Harris and E. Ross, eds., *Food and Evolution: Toward a Theory of Human Food Habits,* pp. 481–515. Philadelphia: Temple University Press.

Pagezy, H., 1985. Anthropology of food, crossroads of biology and culture: Its proper methodology from a case study in Zaire. In T. G. Taylor and N. K. Jenkins, eds., *Proceedings of the XIII International Congress of Nutrition,* pp. 943–945. London: John Libbey.

Pelto, P., 1989. Strategies of field research in nutritional anthropology. In G. H. Pelto, P. J. Pelto, and E. Messer, eds., *Research Methods in Nutritional Anthropology,* pp. 34–56. Tokyo: United Nations University.

Quandt, S. A., 1986. Nutritional anthropology: The individual focus. In S. A. Quandt and C. Ritenbaugh, eds., *Training Manual in Nutritional Anthropology,* pp. 3–20. Washington, D.C.: American Anthropological Association.

Rand, W. M., 1986. International directory of food composition tables. In S. A. Quandt and C. Ritenbaugh, eds., *Training Manual in Nutritional Anthropology,* pp. 140–149. Washington, D.C.: American Anthropological Association.

Reh, E., 1962. *Manual on Household Food Consumption Surveys.* Rome: Food and Agriculture Organization of the United Nations.

Rosenberg, E. M., 1980. Demographic effects of sex-differential nutrition. In N. W. Jerome, R. F. Kandel, and G. H. Pelto, eds., *Nutritional Anthropology,* pp. 181–221. Pleasantville: Redgrave.

Sanjur, D., 1970. *Puerto Rican Food Habits.* Ithaca, NY: Cornell.

Sanjur, D., 1982. *Social and Cultural Perspectives in Nutrition.* Englewood Cliffs, N.J.: Prentice-Hall.

Teufel, N. I., and G. J. Teufel, 1988. Diet 123: A computerized dietary analysis program using Lotus 123[tm]. *Northwest Anthropological Research Notes* 22(2):135–143.

Ulijaszek, S. J., 1982. Nutritional status of a sago-eating community in the Purari delta, Gulf Province. *Institute of Social and Economic Research, Discussion Papers* 44:77–97.

Waterlow, C., R. Buzina, W. Keller, J. M. Lane, M. Z. Nichaman, and J. M. Tanner, 1977. The presentation and use of height and weight data for comparing the nutritional status of groups of children under the age of 10 years. *Bulletin of the World Health Organization* 55(4):489–498.

Weiner, J. S., and J. A. Lourie, 1981. *Practical Human Biology.* New York: Academic.

WHO Working Group, 1986. Use and interpretation of anthropometric indicators of nutritional status. *Bulletin of the World Health Organization* 64(6):929–941.

Willett, W. C., R. D. Reynolds, S. Cottrell-Hoehner, L. Sampson, and M. L. Brown, 1987. Validation of a semi-quantitative food frequency questionnaire: Comparison with a 1-year diet record. *Journal of the American Dietetic Association* 87:43–47.

7

Micro-Ethnodemographic
Techniques for Field Workers
Studying Small Groups

WARREN M. HERN

Scientists increasingly find it valuable and necessary to approach small scale societies—villages, colonies, settlements, clusters of villages—as ethnologists have, studying groups and their relationships to their environments. Anthropologists have traditionally used this approach to learn how an entire society works in an integrated fashion. But scientists such as anthropologists who study group behavior and the cultures of groups need objective ways of grasping characteristics of the group. In this respect, the social scientist, like any other scientist who is studying living organisms, must know something about the universe of individuals under study. Unfortunately, a key type of information often missing from otherwise valuable case studies is elementary demographic description: How many people are there? Where are they located? How are they distributed? How are they grouped? Are they increasing in numbers or are they diminishing in numbers? Are they reproducing? If so, how often? Do they survive in sufficient numbers to reproduce? How long do they live? Why do they die, and how often? How many are born, and how often?

In addition to asking these basic questions, the social scientist will want to know whether the group interactions require a certain number of people playing certain roles and whether changing the number of people changes the interactions. Are there rituals? Are there enough people to conduct them? Does the group break down if there aren't? What happens if resources are abundant or scarce relative to the number of people? How does the number of people in a group affect social relations and family structure? What is the role of the sex ratio in family formation?

The effects of growth, stability, or decline of the population have important theoretical implications that may help predict events or guide policy decisions. A classic controversy is whether growth of the population stimulates improvements in technology, including agricultural intensification (Boserup 1965), whether growth results in degradation of resources and disruption of the society, or whether improved technology results in greater population growth with variable consequences (see Netting et al., Chapter 4, and Hunt, Chapter 9). Did agriculture result from the aggregation of growing hunting-gathering groups into sedentary communities and the need for more reliable food supplies, or did the discovery of plant domestication result in the formation of communities (Cohen 1977)? What has been the demographic impact of health and disease (Omran 1971; McKeown 1976; Cohen 1989)?

No matter what the objective of study of a community, it is necessary to know how many members it has (or how many call themselves members), as well as something about its biological viability or potential. Humans are animals, and population biology is an important basis for understanding their ways of living. To what extent, an anthropologist must ask, does the biology of a human community influence its culture, and to what extent does its culture influence its biological success as a community? Before any of these questions can be answered or even posed in a manner specific to the group in question, certain data must be collected. In her discussion of the vital statistics of Melanesia, Powdermaker (1931) noted that the difficulty with most theories of population dynamics is that there is "little factual material to prove them." In particular, she referred to Rivers's classic volume, *Essays on the Depopulation of Melanesia* (1922), in which only one of the essays (the one by Rivers) contained any numerical data. Other authors in the volume, including Speiser, Durand, and Macgregor, asserted that the Melanesian population was declining ("that the natives are decreasing in numbers cannot be disputed" [Speiser 1922:25]) but no verifiable data were offered.

Firth (1957) documented the Tikopia response to population pressure and the subsequent events when cultural regulation of population growth was interrupted by Western missionaries, a sequence that had severe consequences for the indigenous culture and welfare of the Tikopia. A proper study of such processes cannot occur without the collection of at least elementary demographic data. Dumond (1976) described the difficulties of using incomplete archaeological data in deducing long-term population trends in a prehistoric Tlaxcaltecan culture and in estimating the population decimation resulting from Western contact. Population sizes interact with resource availability, and population growth may be density-dependent (Fearnside 1986:68–69). The introduction of new diseases by Western colonists had a devastating impact on native American peoples (Dumond

1976; Dobyns 1983; Thornton 1987; Myers 1988; Ramenofsky 1987). This severe depopulation resulted in disruption of indigenous cultural life, as there often were too few individuals left to conduct the society's ceremonial life or maintain kin networks (Wagley 1974a, 1974b; Chagnon and Melancon 1984). Losses of up to three-quarters of the population left the survivors of whole communities destitute and homeless (Lovell 1981). Contact profoundly changed a variety of demographic patterns, including sex ratios, death rates, and migration patterns (Early and Peters 1990; Kunitz 1983). The onslaught of epidemic disease was sometimes met with fatalistic acceptance and societal collapse that may have resulted in secondary deaths (Chagnon and Melancon 1983).

Reconstructions of the demography of prehistoric peoples can be enhanced by sophisticated techniques in archaeology and physical anthropology (Hassan 1981; Martin et al. 1984; Brewis 1989; Brewis et al. 1990), but they also can be informed by the detailed demography of living preindustrial and tribal societies (Howell 1984; Early and Peters 1990; Borgerhoff-Mulder 1989; Hern 1977, 1988). Zubrow (1976) asserted that demographic information is vital to the testing of anthropological hypotheses and relevant to many other areas of study, including economics, sociology, history, geography, health and medicine, biology, and political science. He listed thirty-four demographic and forty-eight anthropological variables that are interrelated, and he listed thirty-five anthropological variables that are correlated with average population size. There is little doubt that the collection of demographic data, no matter how primitive, is helpful in studying agrarian societies.

Basic demographic descriptions have usually been left to demographers, who are trained to approach these scientific issues in ways very different from those of anthropologists. Demographers tend to deal almost exclusively with aggregate data sets from censuses of developed countries, whose records are ostensibly accurate. However, these approaches are of little use in the settings in which anthropologists commonly work (Caldwell and Hill 1988:4). Until recently cultural anthropologists traditionally have done their fieldwork among people who do not have a written language. Among Amazonian tribes, ethnologists encounter cultures and languages in which it is only possible to count to two—1, 2, "many" (Chagnon 1974:65; Holmberg 1985:121; Early and Peters 1990:54).

Time categories are similarly imprecise by Western standards, however useful they may be. The Shipibo, for example, have one word— *vakish*—for "yesterday" and "tomorrow." Things happen "about a week ago," "during or since the last full moon," "during the last rainy season," or *moatian*—a long time ago. Personal names—not to mention their pronunciation—change as the result of changed relationships, and sometimes an individual uses multiple names depending on the context. Requests by the ethnographic interviewer for specific times, dates, or places may be cheer-fully perceived as amusing opportunities for exercise of the creative imagi-nation. What we think of as some "objective" standard of reference may have little if any meaning to the subjects of study. It is important to know where on the river and during what season it is possible to catch *shahua'n-huara' (Pez torre [Sp.]; Practocephalus hemiliopterus;* Villarejo 1979:146), but it is not particularly important to remember how long ago one's fourth child died of diarrhea or when the last one was born. Old peo-ple—older than, say, 30—may not have the faintest idea of their actual age. For the sake of amity, however, they are most eager to make up a number that sounds (to them) plausible, even if it is actually less than the stated age of one of their younger children. The conjured estimate just doesn't mean anything to the speaker. This is only one of the sources of what Hill called the "poor quality of official statistics" in her review of field data deficien-cies. Conjured numbers in official government statistics may be equally common and no less misleading (Hill 1986).

Western scientists studying a group need to know not only how peo-ple construct notions of time but also what their vital statistics are in order to understand the biology of the group and the outcomes of its interaction with the environment. We need to know how many people there are (and how many pertain to the group, not merely how many are present at that time); their birth and death rates; how fast the group is increasing or decreasing; the major causes of death; the age structure; and how fertile the group is. These are all independent but also interdependent questions. They may be asked and answered separately, and each gives us important infor-mation, but they are all related and are best understood in context. The dili-gent and sympathetic field-worker must understand the context and probe to discover the truth to the extent it can be known.

It is also necessary to have information about the larger demographic context in which the study is taking place. It is helpful in studying a tribe in the Upper Peruvian Amazon, for example, to know that population growth in the region is heavily influenced by immigration and may be as much as 8 to 10 percent per year (Aramburú 1982; personal communication). Emigration from a community, seasonal migration, and the arrival of recent immigrants must be carefully noted, as these factors can produce profound errors in the evaluation of vital statistics. For example, the Shipibo Indians, with whom I have worked in Peru for more than twenty-five years, leave their home communities for months at a time to visit relatives or work. They are often not counted in official censuses, and their absence is not considered appropriate to report to the outside observer. One only learns of these absences by observing communities over long periods of years or decades and by becoming a trusted member of the community.

The purpose of this chapter is to identify those minimum demographic characteristics of small human communities that should routinely be reported in any ethnography, to suggest how scientists not trained as demographers can collect these data, to specify the kinds of demographic measures that can be derived from such data, and to identify the significance of such measures. Levels of intensity and depth from minimum to intensive will be described so that field-workers can adapt their methods to local conditions and to their research goals. It is assumed that the reader will apply these methods to the study of groups ranging from a few dozen to a few thousand in different communities, although they may be applied through probabilistic sampling techniques to larger communities.

Demographic Minima

The minimum information to report on a group would be the total population and its age-sex composition, which is obtained by conducting a community census. This count should be taken household by household, using a structured interview technique if possible. If a formal census is not possible, the observer should unobtrusively and informally inquire or observe how many people live in each household, noting or estimating the age and recording the sex of each individual. Wherever birth records are available, they should be requested and their contents noted, but these may be unreliable. When dates or years are not known, it is possible to gain approximate dates by referring to some widely known natural or community event—for example, "Was this child born since the last *fiestas patrias* (or rice harvest, or dry season, or measles epidemic)?" "Did this individual die before you moved the village to the new site or after?"

The total population is needed in order to have the most elementary concept of the size of the community. It is also necessary in order to calculate sex ratios and vital trends such as birth and death rates. It is necessary to the calculation of migration rates over time. Ages are necessary in order to study age distribution, and gender is necessary in order to determine sex ratios, vital rates by sex, and a population pyramid. I recommend here a "community-based" study (that is to say, one involving everyone) rather than a "sample" study. In a small community, the apparently inexplicable choice of some individuals or families for study instead of others could arouse hostility, suspicion, or lack of cooperation. If a large population is being studied, almost any random sampling scheme (Slonim 1960) can be used.

A census should obtain the following minimum information about each individual: name, sex, age and date of birth with accuracy to the extent possible; length of residence in the community; place of birth; and number of deaths and births in the household during the past year, including sex and ages of the deceased. A census is a "cross-sectional" study—it is a snapshot in time that may not be accurate. This is especially true if it is a de facto census, in which only those who are present on the day of the census are counted. Because human groups are often highly mobile, even seminomadic, it is preferable to conduct a de jure census, meaning that all those who legally or formally pertain to a locality are counted as being present. Information about each individual so enumerated must be obtained at some point.

Even a de jure census may not be totally accurate, as the census on a given day reflects the results of the sum total of all births, deaths, immigration, and emigration that has occurred in the community up to that point. Most vital rates and demographic indices relate to the number of events per annum, so the census should reflect all that has happened during the year prior to the census. If it is possible to take two completely accurate censuses exactly one year or various years apart, some of these difficulties are minimized, but that is not always feasible. It is therefore necessary to obtain a history of events that occurred during the past year: Were there any births in the household? Were there any deaths? Who died, how old were they at the time of death, what was the sex of the deceased, and what was the probable cause of death? It may not be possible to know the (etic) cause of death by Western reference, but it should always be possible to know the (emic) cause of death by local cultural definitions. These may coincide, but they may not. Sex and age at time of death are critical to know in order to determine patterns of disease incidence and causes of death as well as the demographic impact of mortality.

It is also necessary to know, as much as possible, the extent of migration in and out of the community. In addition to affecting population size, migration influences susceptibility to disease (Coimbra 1988). Length of residence can indicate if a new family or individual has moved to the community within the last year. The absence of emigrants who left during the census year, however, may be more difficult to determine, especially if a family or individual left as the result of social conflict or stigma; in such cases, a code of silence may prevail.

Mid-year population is the first population parameter or statistic to be determined. It tells us the actual size of the community and is necessary for most other calculations. This figure may be obtained by performing the following arithmetic on the number of individuals enumerated in the de jure census: add the number of individuals born alive; subtract the number of individuals who died; add the number of individuals who have immigrated into the community; subtract the number of individuals who emigrated from the community; and divide by two.

Basic Demographic Measures

The most fundamental features of any biologic community are the birth and death rates and rate of growth. To what extent is a community renewing itself, growing, or declining? The mid-year population should be used for the determination of community size and the calculation of all vital rates. Crude birth rate equals the number of live births divided by the mid-year population, per 1,000 people; crude death rate is the number of deaths divided by the mid-year population, per 1,000 people.

From these simple observations and calculations, several other extremely important observations can be derived. For example, the crude rate of natural increase (RONI) can be calculated by subtracting the crude death rate from the crude birth rate. In my 1969 study of the Shipibo, for example, I calculated a crude RONI of 48.9 (CBR=69.3 - CDR=20.4), or 4.89 percent per year (48.9 per 1,000 population) (Hern 1977). Using the general rule that 70 divided by RONI equals doubling time, I concluded that the Shipibo population at that time, in that village, was doubling every 14.3 years.

Though the Shipibo in this instance displayed the highest documented fertility of any human group, it is important to remember that the fertility and growth rates of small groups are volatile and vary widely from year to year (Kunstadter 1972; Black et al. 1978; Early and Peters 1990). The numbers given above are the result of a cohort (longitudinal) calculation taken over five years (1964–1969, n=549) of a specific group of individuals enumerated in two censuses. Even so, they may not be taken as a wholly reliable measure of the group's fertility. More communities, more individuals, or a longer period of observation are required for better reliability. For example, an extremely high birth rate in one year is almost certain to be followed the ensuing year by a low rate even if every recently delivered woman is pregnant, as there is a period of postpartum infecundability (inability to become pregnant) followed by the nine months of gestation. Small numbers and short observation times, however, should not discourage the investigator from making the observations. High fertility rates should alert the investigator to the possibility of a compensatory or "rebound" phenomenon of high fertility to make up for high population losses due to disease, war, or natural calamities (Teitelbaum and Winter 1985:79; Johnston and Kensinger 1971; Thornton et al. 1990).

From these data it is also possible to construct a table of age distribution by sex and a population pyramid, as well as to calculate the age-specific sex ratio. Figure 7.1 shows the population pyramid from my study of eight Shipibo villages conducted in 1983–1984 (Hern 1992b); raw figures are presented in Table 7.1 (Hern 1992a). One of the remarkable things I have continuously observed in the Shipibo population since 1964 is that

Figure 7.1 Age-Sex Pyramid for the Shipibo

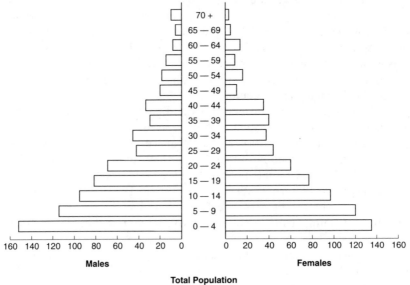

Source: Based on Hern 1992b.

Table 7.1 Age Structure of Population by Sex

	Males		Females		Total	
Age	Number	Percent	Number	Percent	Number	Percent
0–4	152	20.6	136	19.2	288	19.9
5–9	114	15.5	120	16.9	234	16.2
10–14	94	12.8	97	13.7	191	13.2
15–19	82	11.1	77	10.9	159	11.0
20–24	68	9.2	61	8.6	129	8.9
25–29	43	5.8	45	6.4	88	6.1
30–34	46	6.2	38	5.4	84	5.8
35–39	30	4.1	42	5.9	72	5.0
40–44	33	4.5	36	5.1	69	4.8
45–49	21	2.8	11	1.6	32	2.2
50–54	19	2.6	16	2.3	35	2.4
55–59	14	1.9	9	1.3	23	1.6
60–64	7	0.9	13	1.8	20	1.4
65–69	6	0.8	4	0.6	10	0.7
70+	8	1.1	3	0.4	11	0.8
Total	737	100.0	708	100.0	1,445	100.0

Source: Based on Hern 1992a.

more than 50 percent of the population is under the age of 15. This fact is consistent with the observation of rates of natural increase exceeding 4.5 percent per year, in which generation times are around fifteen years; it is characteristic of a young, healthy, rapidly growing, high-fertility population.

The shape of the population pyramid indicates the age structure of the population; in the case of the Shipibo, it is an extremely young population, as indicated by the preponderance of individuals of both sexes in the young age groups. The shape may also indicate a skewed sex ratio resulting from, say, female infanticide, high homicide rates among young males, a high maternal mortality rate among young women in the childbearing age groups, high death rates among the very young or very old, or considerable longevity. Any of these factors may be differentially distributed by sex, and such differences pose questions for social scientists: Why are ratios different, and why at different age groups?

Ordinarily, individuals should be grouped by age ranges, with the customary groupings being 0–4 years, 5–9 years, 10–14, and so on. The advantages of this scheme are that it makes community phenomena such as high infant or maternal mortality rates easily visible and that it is an efficient use of data. Males should be placed on the left side of the population pyramid for the sake of convention in order to facilitate comparison of age-sex distributions with other studies.

Basic Health Indices

Following the elementary demographic descriptions just reviewed, the next level of intensity for the collection of data includes basic health indices (see Fleming-Moran, Chapter 8, for a more detailed discussion of health minima). These are intrinsically valuable for each group described, but they also, as in the cases of infant and maternal mortality rates, tell us much about the community.

Two other areas of observation may be conducted or derived from minima. Knowledge of the sex and age of the deceased permits the calculation of age-specific mortality rates by sex. Most important, it permits calculation of the infant mortality rate, the single most important indicator of child health and overall community health. An infant is defined as a live-born child who is less than one full year old (up to 11 months, 30 days). The infant mortality rate is calculated as the number of deaths of infants under age one year divided by the the number of live births during census year, per 1,000 people.

For those who wish to concentrate on this area of research, two other public health measures can be calculated: neonatal mortality rate and post-neonatal mortality rate. A neonate is defined as an infant of 28 days of age or less. Therefore, neonatal mortality rate equals the number of deaths of infants under the age of 28 completed days divided by the number of live births during census year, per 1,000 people; postneonatal mortality rate equals the number of deaths of infants above 28 days of age, but less than one year divided by the number of live births during census year. To be recorded, the infant death does not have to be experienced by an infant born *that* year: An infant dying early during the census year at the age of 11 months and 15 days is recorded as an infant death. A more complicated way to study infant mortality is to do a longitudinal cohort study over time and measure the survival, adjusted for age, of all individuals born during the time of observation. However, this is a lengthy and costly procedure that has its own shortcomings and is mainly used for intense research concerning a particular health or disease problem.

The most important measure of maternal health is the maternal mortality rate. In the absence of modern medical care, women are likely to die from the complications of pregnancy or delivery at the rate of about 0.7 percent. For example, the maternal mortality rate in the United States in 1920 was about 680 per 100,000 live births (Lerner and Anderson 1963:32). It is currently 10–11 per 100,000 live births (Sachs et al. 1983). The maternal mortality rate, however, is more truly a ratio than a rate—a *rate* customarily denotes how fast something is happening, although a *ratio* is usually expressed for a given period of time (such as a year) rather than a given number of occurrences. The maternal mortality ratio includes "deaths due to pregnancy and the puerperium," which includes the delivery and postpartum period of approximately six weeks (Last 1983). Death can occur from various complications of pregnancy, such as ectopic (tubal) pregnancy (usually during the early weeks of pregnancy), placental abruption, uterine rupture, amniotic fluid embolism, eclampsia, dystocia, hemorrhage, sepsis, coagulopathy, infection, and other complications (see the glossary at the end of this chapter for definitions of these medical terms). Classically, the maternal mortality ratio has also included deaths due to illegal septic abortion, although these now tend to be considered separately (they are, fortunately, rare in the United States). Deaths due to illegal abortion may not be included in maternal mortality rates in countries where abortion is still illegal. The calculation of the maternal mortality ratio is performed by dividing the number of deaths of women due to pregnancy, delivery, or the puerperium during census year by the number of live births in the census year, per 1,000 people. The maternal mortality ratio is a sensitive indicator of both general maternal health and the availability of competent obstetrical care for pregnant women.

Fertility Indices

The third level of intensity for demographic data is the study of fertility, which can be done with the data already collected. In order to have a firm grasp on the population dynamics of a small group (or any group, for that matter), it is necessary to calculate certain standard fertility indices. Some of these are quite elementary. The most widely used basic index is the general fertility rate (GFR), which is an expression of the approximate number of live births per woman of reproductive age per year. To calculate it, take the number of live births during the census year and divide by the number of females aged 15 to 49.

The general fertility rate for the 1964–1969 five-year cohort of the Shipibo was 0.305 (Hern 1977). There was a little less than one live birth per year for every three women of reproductive age for that period. By comparison, Eaton and Mayer's (1953) study of the Hutterites, who are commonly regarded as having the world's highest fertility, found that group to have a GFR of 0.198, or one live birth per year for each five women of reproductive age.

Another basic fertility index is the child-woman ratio (CWR), or "effective fertility ratio." It is calculated by taking the number of children under age five and dividing by the number of females aged 15 to 49.

A fundamental problem with both the general fertility rate and the child-woman ratio is that neither is adjusted for age distributions, which can be quite skewed. Demographers and epidemiologists tend to prefer age-adjusted measures (measures taking into account the uneven distributions among age groups within the society). The advantage of these measures for scientists studying small societies is that they permit some analysis of data that are deficient; just knowing or estimating that a child is younger than age five permits use of the CWR. Although Palmore and Gardner (1983:104) have shown that the CWR is highly correlated with crude birth rate, general fertility rate, and total fertility rate (r = 0.961, 0.975, and 0.970, respectively), Coimbra (1989:119) notes that the CWR underestimates fertility since it includes only those children surviving during the past five years. The correlations also can be misleading because they depend on variations in both numerators and denominators and are partially the result of autocorrelation.

The building block of an age-adjusted fertility measure is the age-specific birth rate. Age-specific birth rates can be shown graphically, as in Figure 7.2, which is taken from my 1983–1984 study of the Shipibo (Hern 1988). This graph shows a young, high-fertility, noncontracepting "natural fertility" population, with fertility extending into the late reproductive years. In calculating age-specific birth rates, the number of births occurring among the women in each age group is counted, as shown in Table 7.2. The sum of age-specific birth rates, shown at the bottom of the table, is called the total fertility rate (TFR). The gross reproduction rate (GRR), generally considered one of the most accurate and reliable indicators of group fertility, is the sum of the age-specific *female* birth rates.

Figure 7.2 Age-Specific Birth Rates, All Women

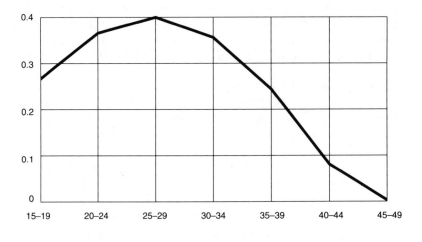

Source: Hern 1988:155.

Table 7.2 Age-Specific Birth Rates and Female Birth Rates, All Villages, for Census Year

Group	Women	Live Births Male	Live Births Female	Total Births	Birth Rate	Female Birth Rate
15-19	76	9	11	20	.263	.145
20-24	60	9	13	22	.367	.217
25-29	45	11	7	18	.400	.156
30-34	38	5	8	13	.342	.211
35-39	42	5	5	10	.238	.119
40-44	36	2	1	3	.083	.028
45-49	18	0	0	0	.000	.000
					1.693	.876
					x5 =	x5 =
					TFR =	8.467
					GRR =	4.379

Source: Hern 1988:164.

Though the total fertility rate and gross reproduction rate are considered standard and are among the most reliable measures of group fertility, the amount of information needed to calculate them may be beyond the scope of many studies, and attempts to calculate them on the basis of insufficient information may be misleading.

A new measure I constructed for evaluating Shipibo fertility is the individual fertility rate (IFR), which is especially helpful for work in preliterate societies (Hern 1990). A reproductive span (RS) is determined for each woman by calculating the number of months from the first birth to the last. The woman's parity (number of term births) is then divided by the reproductive span in years (RS divided by twelve) and the total multiplied by 100. The result, which is a whole number with a common range from about 30 to 100, allows comparison of individual fertility experience within communities as well as, when individual results are summed, for the community as a whole. Among the Shipibo, I was able to determine that polygynous women had 1.3 fewer term births (i.e., lower fertility) than monogamous women (Hern 1992b).

Beyond these measures, it is possible to construct life tables in order to obtain measures such as life expectancy and the net reproduction rate, which is the sum of age-specific female survival rates.

Reconstructive demography can be considered a specialized field technique. It requires considerable pre-fieldwork demographic training and long interviews during which an extensive reproductive history is taken for each woman aged 13 or older. In this research, it is often necessary to conduct interviews with many family members present so that the timing of events such as the births and deaths of children, causes of death, and approximate dates of events such as menarche and menopause can be ascertained or estimated as a joint family effort. This exercise requires a more extensive knowledge of the language and culture than is necessary for the collection of elementary demographic data, but it can give a more accurate historical perspective of fertility and population dynamics. Although it diminishes the hazards of cross-sectional studies by taking a historical prospective approach to fertility, it runs the risk of losing important information through selection bias—namely, selective survival and loss due to emigration. Without decades of close observation, however, it is the only way to construct a cohort study of fertility. Table 7.3 shows a relative ranking of demographic measures and analyses by complexity, ranging from the minimum data to be collected to more difficult and complex tasks that can be undertaken if demographic variables are of greater interest to the case study.

Conclusions

The most rapid and fundamental changes—social, cultural, demographic, and economic—are occurring in the tribal and peasant societies studied by anthropological and other field workers. Patterns that have been maintained for thousands of years are disappearing within a few generations. Some of the most dramatic of these changes are taking place in the areas of fertility and population growth, and these in turn are leading to other important

Table 7.3 Demographic Indices and Analysis by Complexity of Task

Index Level	Data Needed	Classification of Complexity
Population no.	Total count	I
Age-sex distribution	Age and sex	I
	Date of birth	II
Midyear population (MYP)	Number of births, deaths, migrations	I
Crude birth rate (CBR)	Number of births, MYP	I
Crude death rate (CDR)	Number of deaths, MYP	I
Rate of natural increase	CBR - CDR	I
Infant mortality rate	Number of infant deaths (under 1 year)	II
Neonatal, post- neonatal MR	Number of infant deaths by exact age in months	II
Maternal mortality rate	Number of maternal deaths	II
General fertility rate	Number of live births, number of women aged 15–49	III
Effective fertility ratio	Number of children under 5, number of women aged 15–49	III
Total fertility rate	Age-specific birth rates	III
Gross reproduction rate	Age-specific female birth rates	III
Net reproduction rate	Life table	IV
Life table	Age-specific mortality rates	IV

Some High And Low Boundaries For Demographic Variables

	High	Low	World 1985-1990[a]
Sex ratio (males/females)	1.4	0.8	
Crude birth rate	60/1,000	5/1,000	26.9
Crude death rate	30/1,000	3/1,000	9.8
Rate of natural increase	49/1,000 (4.9%)	1/1,000 (0.1%)	17.9
Infant mortality rate	500/1,000	10/1,000	71.0
Neonatal mortality rate	100/1,000	1/1,000	
Post-neonatal mortality rate	400/1,000	9/1,000	
Maternal mortality rate	750/1,000	8/1,000	
General fertility rate[b]	0.305	0.088	
Effective fertility rate	1.30		
Total fertility rate	9.935	2.573	3.417
Gross reproduction rate	4.933	1.255	(1.70)[c]
Net reproduction rate[d]	3.66		1.441

Notes: a. Zachariah and Vu (1988).
b. Hern (1977).
c. Approximation based on world TFR.
d. Eaton and Mayer (1953).

changes. Those who study human societies have a special opportunity to learn how these changes are occurring and to document their impacts on people. Methods described in this chapter are essential to this task.

"Micro-ethnodemographic" field techniques refer to the application of standard demographic methods to small groups in the context of ethnographic fieldwork or similar activities. The application of these methods can be relatively straightforward and simple, but they must be adjusted for societies with few or no vital records or with limited ability to estimate the time and details of vital events. The collection of such data is, however, necessary to the accurate scientific understanding of such groups in terms of both their function and their well-being.

Appendix 7.A
Glossary of Medical Terms

Amniotic Fluid Embolism. Escape of the amniotic fluid from the amniotic sac into the bloodstream where it is carried to heart and lungs. It can be fatal.

Coagulopathy. A failure of the blood-clotting mechanisms that can develop as the result of several conditions. These include placental abruption, fetal death, retained placenta and infection, infected incomplete abortion, and other conditions.

Dystocia. "Difficult labor or delivery." It can result from inability of the woman to deliver the baby because either bony or soft tissue is obstructing the birth canal.

Eclampsia. A condition of pregnancy resulting in high blood pressure; can end in convulsions and death.

Ectopic Pregnancy. A pregnancy that develops outside the uterine cavity, such as in the fallopian tube or abdominal cavity. This can result in death from internal bleeding.

Hemorrhage. Bleeding that is life threatening. Can result during pregnancy and delivery from a variety of conditions, such as failure of the uterus to contract after delivery, retained placenta or membranes, or lack of clotting.

Historical prospective study. A study that prospectively follows the health and/or fertility experience of a cohort of individuals by means of a reconstructed history through existing records or interviews.

Placental abruption. In this case, the placenta separates from the wall of the uterus. A blood clot develops behind the placenta that absorbs all the fibrinogen and clotting factors so that they are unavailable elsewhere, leading to coagulopathy, or failure of the blood-clotting mechanisms.

Sepsis. Development of infection with the kinds of organisms that can grow in the uterus. Infection may spread to adjacent organs and to the blood stream. Once this happens, the entire body is affected, and various organ systems, such as the kidneys and adrenal glands, fail, and the infection is quickly fatal.

References

Aramburú, C. E., 1982. Expansión de la frontera agraria y demográfica de la selva alta Peruana. In C. E. Aramburú, ed., *Colonización en la Amazonía,* pp. 1–39. Lima: Ediciones CIPA.

Black, F. L., et al., 1978. Birth and survival patterns in numerically unstable proto agricultural societies in the Brazilian Amazon. *Medical Anthropology* 2(3):95–127.

Borgerhoff-Mulder, M., 1989. Marital status and reproductive performance in Kipsigis women: Re-evaluating the polygyny-fertility hypothesis. *Population Studies* 43:285–304.

Boserup, E., 1965. *The Conditions of Agricultural Growth.* Chicago: Aldine.

Brewis, A., 1989. Reconstructions of prehistoric fertility: The Maori case. *Man and Culture in Oceania* 5:21–36.

Brewis, A. A., M. A. Mulloy, and D. G. Sutton, 1990. Modeling the prehistoric Maori population. *American Journal of Physical Anthropology* 81:343–356.

Caldwell, J. C., and A. G. Hill, 1988. Recent developments using micro-approaches to demographic research. In John C. Caldwell, Allan G. Hill, and Valerie J. Hull, eds., *Micro-Approaches to Demographic Research,* pp. 1–9. London: Kegan Paul.

Chagnon, N., 1974. *Studying the Yanomamo.* New York: Holt, Rinehart, and Winston.

———, 1977. *Yanomamo: The Fierce People,* second edition. New York: Holt, Rinehart, and Winston.

———, 1983. *Yanomamo: The Fierce People,* third edition. New York: Holt, Rinehart, and Winston.

Chagnon, N. A., and T. F. Melancon, 1983. Epidemics in a tribal population. In *The Impact of Contact: Two Yanomamo Case Studies,* pp. 53–78. Working Papers on South American Indians #6/Cultural Survival Occasional Paper #11.

Chagnon, N. A., and T. F. Melancon, 1984. Reproduction, numbers of kin and epidemics in tribal populations: A case study. In N. Keyfitz, ed., *Population and Biology: A Bridge Between Disciplines.* Liege, Belgium: Ordina Editions.

Cohen, M. N., 1977. Population pressure and the origins of agriculture: An archaeological example from the coast of Peru. In C. A. Reed, ed., *The Origins of Agriculture,* pp. 135–177. The Hague: Mouton.

Cohen, M. N., 1989. *Health and the Rise of Civilization.* New Haven: Yale University Press.

Coimbra, C.E.A. Jr., 1988. Human settlements, demographic pattern, and epidemiology in lowland Amazonia: The case of Chagas' disease. *American Anthropologist* 90(1):82–97.

———, 1989. From shifting cultivation to coffee farming: The impact of change on the health and ecology of the Surui Indians in the Brazilian Amazon. Ph.D. dissertation, Indiana University.

Denevan, W. M., 1976. Epilogue. In William M. Denevan, ed., *The Native Population of the Americas in 1492,* pp. 289–292. Madison: University of Wisconsin Press.

Dewar, R. E., 1984. Environmental productivity, population regulation, and carrying capacity. *American Anthropologist* 86(3):601–614.

Dobyns, Henry F., 1983. *Their Numbers Became Thinned: Native American Population Dynamics In Eastern North America.* Knoxville: University of Tennessee Press.

Dumond, D. E., 1976. An outline of the demographic history of Tlaxcala. In Michael H. Crawford, ed., *The Tlaxcaltecans: Prehistory, Demography, Morphology & Genetics,* pp. 13–23. Lawrence, KS: University of Kansas, Publications in Anthropology #7.

Early, J. D., and J. F. Peters, 1990. *The Population Dynamics of the Mucajai Yanomama.* New York: Academic Press.

Eaton, J. W., and A. J. Mayer, 1953. The social biology of very high fertility among the Hutterites. *Human Biology* 25:206–264.

Fearnside, P. M., 1986. *Human Carrying Capacity of the Brazilian Rainforest.* New York: Columbia University Press.

Firth, R., 1957. *We, The Tikopia.* Boston: Beacon Press.

Hassan, F. A., 1981. *Demographic Archaeology.* New York: Academic Press.

Hern, W. M., 1977. High fertility in a Peruvian Amazon Indian village. *Human Ecology* 5(4):355–368.

———, 1988. Polygyny and fertility among the Shipibo: An epidemiologic test of an ethnographic hypothesis. Unpublished Ph.D. dissertation. University of North Carolina School of Public Health.

———, 1990. Individual fertility rate: A new measure for small populations. *Social Biology* 37:102–109.

———, 1992a. Polygyny and fertility among the Shipibo of the Peruvian Amazon. *Population Studies* 46:53–67.

———, 1992b. Shipibo polygyny and patrilocality. *American Ethnologist* 19(3):501–522.

Hill, Polly, 1986. *Development Economics on Trial.* Cambridge: Cambridge University Press.

Holmberg, A. R., 1985. *Nomads of the Long Bow: The Siriono of Eastern Bolivia.* Prospect Heights, IL: Waveland Press.

Howell, N., 1984. *Demography of the Dobe !Kung.* New York: Academic Press.

Johnston, F. E., and K. M. Kensinger, 1971. Fertility and mortality differentials and their implications for microevolutionary change among the Cashinahua. *Human Biology* 43:356–364.

Kunitz, S. J., 1983. *Disease Change and the Role of Medicine: The Navajo Experience.* Berkeley: University of California.

Kunstadter, P., 1972. Demography, ecology, social structure, and settlement patterns. In G. A. Harrison and A. J. Boyce, eds., *The Structure of Human Populations,* pp. 313–351. Oxford: Clarendon Press.

Last, J. M., ed., 1983. *A Dictionary of Epidemiology.* New York: Oxford University Press.

Lerner, M., and O. W. Anderson, 1963. *Health Progress in the United States: 1900–1960.* Chicago: University of Chicago Press.

Lovell, W. G., 1981. The historical demography of the Cuchumatan Highlands of Guatemala, 1500–1821. In David J. Robinson, ed., *Studies in Spanish American Population History,* pp. 195–216. Boulder: Westview Press.

Martin, D. L., G. J. Armelagos, A. H. Goodman, and D. P. Van Gerven, 1984. The effects of socioeconomic change in prehistoric Africa: Sudanese Nubia as a case study. In Mark Nathan Cohen and George J. Armelagos, eds., *Paleopathology at the Origins of Agriculture,* pp. 193–214. Orlando: Academic Press.

McKeown, T., 1976. *The Modern Rise of Population.* New York: Academic Press.

Myers, T. P., 1988. El efecto de pestilencia sobre las poblaciones de la Amazonia superior. *Amazonia Peruana* 8:61–81.

Omran, A. R., 1971. The epidemiologic transition. *Milbank Memorial Fund Quarterly* 49:509–538.

Palmore, J. A., and R. W. Gardner, 1983. *Measuring Mortality, Fertility and Natural Increase.* Honolulu: East-West Center.

Powdermaker, H., 1931. Vital statistics of New Ireland (Bismark Archipelago) as revealed in genealogies. *Human Biology* 3(3):351–375.

Ramenofsky, Ann F., 1987. *Vectors of Death: The Archaeology of European Contact.* Albuquerque: University of New Mexico Press.

Rivers. W.H.R., ed., 1922. *Essays On the Depopulation of Melanesia.* Cambridge, England: University Press.

Sachs, B. P., P. M. Layde, G. L. Rubin, et al., 1982. Reproductive mortality in the United States. *Journal of the American Medical Association* 247:27–89.

Slonim, M. J., 1960. *Sampling.* New York: Simon and Schuster.

Speiser, F., 1922. Decadence and preservation in the New Hebrides. In W.H.R. Rivers, ed., *Essays on the Depopulation of Melanesia,* pp. 25–61. Cambridge: University Press.

Teitelbaum, M. S., and J. M. Winter, 1985. *The Fear of Population Decline.* San Diego: Academic Press.

Thornton, R., 1987. *American Indian Holocaust and Survival: A Population History Since 1492.* Norman: University of Oklahoma Press.

Thornton, R., T. Miller, and J. Warren, 1990. American Indian population recovery following smallpox epidemics. *American Anthropologist* 93:28–45.

Villarejo, A., 1979. *Asi Es La Selva.* Iquitos, Peru: CETA.

Wagley, C., 1974a. Cultural influences on population: A comparison of two Tupi tribes. In P. J. Lyon, ed., *Native South Americans: Ethnology of the Least Known Continent,* pp. 377–384. Boston: Little, Brown.

———, 1974b. The effects of depopulation upon social organization as illustrated by the Tapirape' Indians. In P. J. Lyon, ed., *Native South Americans: Ethnology of the Least Known Continent,* pp. 373–376. Boston: Little, Brown.

Zachariah, K. C., and M. T. Vu, 1988. *World Population Projections, 1987–88 Edition: Short- and Long-Term Estimates.* Baltimore: Johns Hopkins Press.

Zubrow, E.B.W., 1976. Demographic anthropology: An introductory analysis. In E.B.W. Zubrow, ed., *Demographic Anthropology: Quantitative Approaches,* pp. 1–25. Albuquerque: University of New Mexico Press.

8

Health Status Indicators for Rural Societies in Transition: Estimating Morbidity and Mortality Using National and Community Data

MILLICENT FLEMING-MORAN

In studies of socioeconomic change, the role of family health must be recognized in household productivity, social adaptation, and economic decisionmaking. These interrelations are also central in interpreting both positive and negative outcomes of national development programs, demographic changes, or specific innovations adopted by communities (Cumper 1984:64). The epidemiologic perspective emphasizes the distribution of cases of disease, the analysis of which identifies causative and preventative factors within populations. Thus, case-to-population ratios or rates of cases per unit of time are basic to the description of the societal impact of disease and of possible barriers or behaviors that promote it.

Although definitions of individual health indicators are debated, population-level indicators are more consistently accepted by the World Health Organization (WHO) and U.S. Public Health Service. These include indicators of *health status* (such as infant mortality or incidence of preventable diseases), indicators of *health service access and utilization,* and broad socioeconomic indicators of *well-being,* such as freedom from disability or lost productivity (WHO 1981a). The health status and well-being indicators are usually thought of as "outcome" variables, whereas service access and utilization are considered process, or dependent, variables in modeling health status.

These three types of data, as well as cultural and financial variables, are needed in comparing two populations or in assessing change over time (Institute of Medicine 1993; WHO 1981a). Single health-status measures highlight inequities in health services but not the barriers that limit access to and/or effective use of such services. For example, some 70 to 80 percent of rural persons in less developed nations have no access to modern health care (Johnson and Clark 1982:120). In "late developing countries," 60 percent of the labor force is rural and low-income, and this segment continues to grow at rapid rates (Johnson and Clark 1982:44). In these countries, the "demographic transition" of declining fertility and infant mortality rates (IMRs) is not as apparent as in other developing countries where the IMR has been reduced through improvements in maternal and infant nutrition (Johnson and Clark 1982:52–58; Delgado et al. 1986) or in the role of women in rural development (Johnson and Clark 1982:101–105). Thus, although health-status outcome variables are important in their own right, process and access variables help define where and how improvements can be made.

Vital event, census, and health surveillance data normally form the basis for health-status indicators. In the absence of adequate census and vital statistics systems in many developing nations, however, WHO now advocates the use of household surveys to assess general health conditions in monitoring progress toward its "Health for All" goals for the year 2000 (1981). WHO also proposed morbidity and vital event estimation procedures in those member nations with severe under- or biased reporting to improve the accuracy in reported magnitude and causes of death (WHO 1978a).

The World Bank, the U.S. Agency for International Development, the UN Statistical Office, and the UN Department of Economic and Social Affairs exemplify international agents that now incorporate basic fertility, health status, and, to some degree, health cost data as part of household level surveys of local socioeconomic conditions (UN Department of International Economic and Social Affairs 1984; Grootaert 1986; Freedman and Mueller 1977; UN Department of Technical Co-operation for Development 1982). The international development community is slowly reducing emphasis on goals of expanded production or increased GNP, moving toward a view that education and health programs are "public goods" that also increase consumption and thus help achieve the goals of socioeconomic development (Johnson and Clark 1982:117). For example, demonstration projects emphasizing specific health and nutritional goals and active local participation (Hilsum 1983) have achieved greater reductions in infant mortality rates than projects where health care was viewed as a "welfare" program or health initiatives that were limited to family planning assistance (Johnson and Clark 1982:117, 126–128).

In this chapter I outline health status and access indicators accepted by the World Health Organization for feasible collection in locales where public records are not collected or reliable. Such minimal health data address the variable levels of analysis that must be addressed in setting national- versus community-level priorities in development or in measuring the impact of health status upon agricultural, social, and demographic transitions in rural areas. The following objectives have been adopted for this review: 1) assess major health issues in a region using existing national and unpublished data to outline leading causes of morbidity and mortality; 2) identify national and private health resources in the research area of interest; and 3) glean available local information on community health status and use of health services.

Health Status Indicators

Murnaghan defines health indicators as "those statistics which have the power to summarize a larger body of statistics, or serve as efficient proxy measures to represent health status less reliably reflected in other data" (1981:303). They generally represent measures of mortality or morbidity and are expressed as rates or percentages. Though biased reporting or underreporting of vital events and cases of specific diseases is always a problem, the value of these proposed data lies in their ready comparability, versatility in their research applications, and simplicity; they are less value-laden than complex "quality of life" indices that combine educational, economic, *and* health indicators (Murnaghan 1981:81). A range of data, however, is needed to place vital event measures in context. These data and their sources are outlined in Table 8.1.

Health and demographic data all begin with reliable crude birth and death rates and a current population census that includes significant age, sex, and residential categories (1981:317) (see Hern, Chapter 7, and Netting et al, Chapter 4). However, the Pan American Health Organization's (PAHO) study of infant and child mortality found deaths that should appear in civil registries as well as medical records, and yet were reported in neither (Puffer 1984). The extent to which such omissions occur varies tremendously from nation to nation (Puffer 1984; PAHO 1982). Reasons for underreporting include limited public access to medical services and civil offices, unenforceable requirements to record deaths and/or causes of death, and, in the case of neonatal mortality, the cultural view of the social status (or lack thereof) of infants (PAHO 1982).

Through UN efforts, emphasis is shifting from fragmentary coverage of vital events and national registry systems to focused local reporting by trained, nongovernmental lay observers of their community's mortality and morbidity events (WHO 1978a). During the 1980s the UN Statistical Office and Department of Technical Co-operation for Development initiated

Table 8.1 Health Data by Source

National Data, per Region of Interest:

Health Care Access:
   Number of primary health care workers/10,000 population
   Number of hospital beds/10,000 population
Utilization of services:
   Percent of preschool children with full immunizations
   Percent of attended births/total births
Health status (for interregional comparisons):
   National/regional infant mortality rates (or alternatively child mortality ratios; births to
     women < 18).
   Child mortality rates (ages 0–4) due to malaria, pneumonia, diarrhea
   Three leading causes of mortality for ages 0–4, 5–15, 16–45, and 45+
   Percent of children < 10 falling below WHO 80th percentile growth measures
   Children 5–15 and adults over 15 with permanent disabilities per 1,000 age-specific popu-
     lation

Community level data:
Health Care Access (if infeasible by household survey):
   Coverage/ continuity of potable water, sanitation, endemic disease control, immunizations,
     and emergency food
   Local health hazards: flooding, drought, wastewater use, irrigation, immigration, endemic
     warfare
   Coverage by primary care, pharmaceuticals, and inpatient services
Health Status:
   Official consensus of ten most common health problems and underserved populations

Household-survey data:
Health Care Access:
   Proximity of potable water, sanitation
   Travel time to nearest pharmacy, first aid, hospital
   Youngest child's immunization contacts
   Percent of total expenditures for health care, previous month
Health status.
   Total days/person lost to normal activity in previous fourteen days (with seasonal sam-
     ples); itemized costs
   Total births and surviving children per woman aged 15+

household surveys in eighty-five developing countries, an effort endorsed by the World Bank, UNICEF, UN Population Fund, and other UN organizations (UN Department of Technical Co-operation, 1982). The goal was not only to achieve a better quality of social health data but also to provide mutually supportive and integrated data sources to further both health and development objectives. In India, Kenya, Iran, and other UN member states, household surveys of vital events, morbidity, and the impact of disability are far more effective and less expensive than civil registries (UN Department of International Economic and Social Affairs 1984).[1] In the United States, too, the 1956 National Health Survey Act established annual household samples to be drawn for in-home surveys of nutrition status, specific conditions, and health of targeted groups (Basch 1990).

The infant mortality rate (IMR) is one of the most widely accepted and internationally available health indicators (Murnaghan 1981; Institute of Medicine 1993). IMR is defined as the number of deaths of children aged younger than 12 months per 1,000 live births in a year for a given population (Cumper 1984). Infant mortality rates are affected not only by the nutritional status, age, prior fertility experience, and literacy status of the mother but also by sanitary conditions, infant feeding, enteric and other infectious disease exposure, and pre- and postnatal access to health care (Basch 1990:139–140; Wallace and Tahir Taha 1988). As such, this measure reflects those barriers to improved health status that are most amenable to changes in primary health care, literacy, and household income levels— problems most critical in developing countries (PAHO 1982; UNICEF 1989).

As high IMRs are particularly attributable to preventable respiratory and enteric infectious and nutritional causes (Basch 1990)—factors that also contribute heavily to adult mortality—IMRs are appropriate population indicators of health status for developing areas. Moreover, unlike life expectancy, which reflects cumulative health effects and changes, IMRs are more sensitive to current health conditions (Cumper 1984:15). As an indicator of "development," McGranahan's analysis for 115 countries shows a strongly negative correlation (−.70 or better) of IMRs with household access to electricity and water, per capita calorie and protein consumption, and levels of adult literacy (1970). In developing nations with a per capita GNP of $1,000 or more, IMRs range between 25 and 95 (per thousand live births), but many countries with much lower per capita GNPs had IMRs within this range as well (Wallace and Tahir Taha 1988). The need for region-specific data on health status and access to care is once more emphasized by Wallace and Tahir Taha.

Though IMRs may be reasonably accurate for countries with a high percentage of registered births, it must be recalled that the percentage of recorded infant births and deaths may vary widely by country, for rural versus urban areas, or between minority populations (Puffer 1984; PAHO 1982). According to the United Nations, of fifty African countries, over half lack estimates of life expectancy at birth, 28 percent lack infant mortality statistics, and in one-third, estimates of IMR are based on data from the 1960s (United Nations 1985).

Many factors limit efforts to collect vital statistics. Infant naming and burial practices that preclude official registration of events (Puffer and Serrano 1973), surreptitious infanticide, unattended births, and cultural prohibitions concerning discussion of deceased individuals (see Coimbra 1989 and Cassidy 1987 for illustrations) increase underreporting of deaths of persons not yet considered full social beings. One PAHO study site in Chile found that a large urban maternity hospital routinely failed to file either birth or death certificates in cases of neonatal deaths if the family did not claim the infant's body for burial (Puffer 1984). In several countries of Latin America, infants must survive twenty-four hours to be registered as a live birth (Basch 1990:52).[2]

Estimates of both crude birth and death rates may necessitate reliance on indirect evidence of fertility and mortality (Preston 1984). Births are less subject to recall bias than infant deaths (Adlakha and Nizamuddin 1984). However, crude birth rate is sometimes difficult to elicit when total pregnancies, mother's age, and even pregnancy status are ill-defined or not easily reported to strangers (Coimbra 1989). When birth and death registers are not available, the ratio of children under 5 years of age per woman (CWR) is highly correlated with actual crude birth rates (r=.96) and may be used as a substitute for birth rate (Palmore and Gardner 1983). However, as the CWR includes only surviving children, it underestimates total fertility (Palmore and Gardner 1983).

In cases where birth reporting is less culturally influenced, an alternative measure is to report total children ever born to each of a household's women over age 15. Women of all age groups are thus sampled, giving retrospective information on past as well as current fertility patterns. Similarly, indirect estimation of child mortality is also suggested for household-level surveys, specifically matching the total children ever born with the reported household census of living children and the total number of surviving children (some of whom may reside elsewhere) for the same sample of household women over 15 (National Academy of Science/ National Research Council 1983).

These methods are suggested because deaths of named, baptized, or weaned children are more likely to be recalled than neonatal deaths, biasing reports of total infant mortality (cf. Cassidy 1987). Although these estimated birth and mortality measures are less accurate than fully detailed fecundity histories per woman for birth and infant mortality rates, they have proved equally useful for describing levels and trends in fertility and mortality and regional differences in these measures (Cassidy 1987). The CWR or total parity estimates for fertility and child mortality are suggested as minimal data where: 1) community size prohibits full maternity histories by household; 2) vital event reports for infants and children are limited by severe cultural restrictions; and/or 3) the investigator cannot obtain reliable, region-specific infant mortality and birth rate data. Finally, as in any household survey, it should be noted whether birth data are provided by a head of household or, more accurately, are reported by the mother herself (Adlakha and Nizamuddin 1984).

Where national household demographic survey programs use retrospective reporting of deaths for a defined period as well as detailed maternity histories, a viable alternative exists to large-scale household survey estimates of infant mortality (cf. Adlakha and Nizamuddin 1984:104 for examples). Surveys of selected households repeated over one or more periods of time improved the coverage, accuracy, and age-specific estimation of mortality, especially of infant mortality, when interviewers followed up on pregnancies reported in earlier rounds. Similar success was achieved during the World Fertility Survey, which included child mortality data within maternal-reported birth histories (Hobcraft 1984).

Given additional time, and for areas where most births are attended by trained personnel but not uniformly registered, the researcher may opt to collect the community proportion of attended births as an indicator of access to health care (Puffer 1984). Additionally, if birth weights are recorded routinely in attended births, the percentage of low-weight births per year (live births under 2,500 grams per total live births per year) serves as a good proxy for size of the infant population *at risk* of mortality in these populations (WHO 1981a). The percentage of low-birth-weight infants, particularly in urbanized settings, can also serve to indicate maternal nutritional status.

Some national data are required to provide a context for local birth and mortality estimates generated from household surveys.[3] In countries with severe underreporting of vital events for infants and children, national figures of child mortality rates for ages 1 through 4 can be used to infer relative levels of child mortality between countries. These figures, like IMR, directly reflect environmental and nutritional influences on the health of the young (WHO 1981a). Another useful alternative for underreporting countries is the ratio of deaths of children under 5 years of age to total mortality (UNICEF 1989:82) In this approach, a country's age structure is taken into account and is useful when cross-national comparisons of health status are desired (UNICEF 1989:98–99). A final option is the proportion of total births to mothers under the age of 18, taken from national age-specific birth data (WHO 1981a:27). Here, well-described relationships between young maternal age, lower maternal nutritional status and physical development, and lower socioeconomic and educational achievement of young mothers are used to infer the rates of low-birth-weight infants and poorer infant survival (Puffer 1984; Martorell 1982).[4]

For researchers interested in women's role in developing nations, the proportion of total births to women under age 18 also acts as an indicator of the population at highest risk of maternal mortality (WHO 1981a:63). In developed countries only 5 to 30 maternal deaths occur per 100,000 births; in developing countries this rate ranges from 50 to 800 maternal deaths. The lifetime risk of maternal mortality may be as high as 1 in 14 (Mahler 1987). Similar insight is gained from the proportion of mothers who fall below mean stature figures for females (see Martorell et al. 1975) or those with highest parity rates (WHO 1981a:91). All these measures share factors associated with greater risk of both maternal[5] and infant deaths.

UNICEF and other health surveillance organizations such as the U.S. Centers for Disease Control use certain *sentinel conditions* to mark critical problems in primary health care and nutritional status in preschool children. These include the estimated child mortality rates due to pneumococcal pneumonia, diarrhea, and malaria, in children under 5 years of age. Here we suggest that the researcher merely obtain these data from published national or WHO sources, taking into account the expected underreporting. The preventable but ubiquitous high incidence of diarrhea in developing regions exacts a toll of of 7.4 million child deaths and is a chief contributor to malnutrition as well as to vitamin A deficiency and the latter's associated 250,000 annual cases of blindness (UNICEF 1989:37, 64). UN efforts to improve access to successful oral rehydration therapy for diarrhea found that only 6 percent of rural health workers were adequately trained in this simple but effective treatment (UNICEF 1989:8; Rohde 1986). (Unsuccessful efforts have been reported in the introduction of this low-cost measure in the care of dehydrated U.S. children [Institute of Medicine 1993].)

The Pan American Health Organization's findings on child mortality in Central and South America found that nutritional deficiency was an underlying or associated cause of death in 52 percent of all mortality in children under the age of 5 in some thirteen countries (Puffer and Serrano 1973:167) and was an associated cause in 60 percent of deaths due to infectious disease in the same age group (Puffer 1984). Malaria is among the leading causes of death in children under age 5 (UNICEF 1989:37) and globally contributes to the 20 percent of births that are low-weight/high risk (WHO 1981:32).

Only half of the world's children are fully immunized against infectious childhood diseases, which together with malaria account for 80 percent of mortality in those under 5 years of age (WHO 1981a:37). WHO has set a goal of universal child immunization by the end of the 1990s for pertussis, diptheria, measles, tetanus, and poliomyelitis to prevent an estimated 25 percent of deaths among children under age 5 (Basch 1990). The U.S. Centers for Disease Control (CDC) also sets standard target values for cases of immunization-preventable diseases (Chorba et al. 1990) and targets low-income U.S. children, who are 50 percent more likely than higher-income peers to have incomplete immunization (Wood et al. 1990). Even in wealthy countries, lack of immunization signals financial barriers and fragmented delivery of these services (Institute of Medicine 1993). Measures of access to immunization are addressed in a later section.

Although high child mortality may explain the fatalism concerning infant deaths seen in some developing regions (Cassidy 1987; Good 1987), certain developing countries are now experiencing a "health transition" in addition to a demographic transition (Findley 1989). Vaccination, clean water, nutrition programs, and educational opportunities for women (Delgado et al. 1986; Chandler 1984) are reducing infectious disease and more specifically infant mortality in some developing areas (PAHO 1982; UNICEF 1989; Walsh and Warren 1986).

A greater range of available health interventions also leads to greater variability in disease outcome. For example, lower IMRs may be accompanied by increasing rates of undernutrition (Basch 1990:188; Johnson and Clark 1982; Coimbra 1989) and disability caused by childhood disease when the food and health care needs of a growing dependent population cannot be met (see Rohde 1986). WHO thus recommends collection of household data on the percentage of children under 10 who do not meet 80th percentiles in three growth standards (WHO 1978b; see also Dufour and Teufel, Chapter 6). As height and weight-for-age are useful indicators of both long-term and current health and nutritional status, they serve to identify the proportion of the young population at highest risk of infectious disease mortality (UNICEF 1989). As Dufour and Teufel note, the applicability of these growth standards to differing ethnic and genetically distinct populations has been debated. National data on children below established growth standards are recommended to allow comparison of long-term patterns of undernutrition between countries.

Despite their inadequacies, published national and international sources are suggested as minimal data. They cost little to collect, and they establish officially recognized causes of death and morbidity, which in turn lend impetus to existing health programs and policy. Nationally published IMRs are useful in providing a relative ranking of the healthfulness of life in a region and provide a broad context for IMR estimates from local communities. Contrasting household-reported and national systems of lay-reported vital statistics can be useful in highlighting the magnitude of reporting bias in civil registries or in identifying specific events or groups most likely to be underrepresented or inequitably served by health services. National estimates of child mortality attributed to preventable diseases, rates of malnutrition, and prevalence of debilitating parasitic disease provide a rapid snapshot of health problems of likely concern to local communities.

Morbidity Indicators

The toll of chronic and acute conditions greatly reduces total household productivity. In the early 1970s, Ghana found that rural workers on average lost one month per year of normal activity to disabling disease (Walsh 1985), and rural Sri Lanka workers reported as many as sixty days lost (Findley 1989), a pattern seen in many developing nations (Chandler 1984;

Corbett 1989; Renker 1982). In comparison, U.S. citizens annually lost nine days from their normal activity to disability (U.S. National Center for Health Statistics 1985).

Childhood disability bears an even higher long-term cost than adult disability and is most frequent in the poorest social strata (Werner 1986). For example, 45 percent of the poorest rural Bangladesh families had at least one disabled child, compared to 8 percent for wealthier rural families (Renker 1982:172). Zimbabwe recorded 52 percent of the population as being disabled to some degree by the age of 15 (Davies 1983). In areas where life expectancy is 50 to 55 years, some 24 percent of the life span may be hampered by disability, leaving an effective, productive life of only 37 years (Manton et al. 1989).

Household surveys are an efficient way to ask each member, including school-aged children, to report the total days of normal level of work, school, or household duties, lost for *any* health reason or chronic disability. A short, easily recalled time frame—usually the previous fourteen days—is the most frequently used referent period (U.S. National Center for Health Statistics 1972). This normative concept of "usual" activity is broader than scales used to assess actual capacity for work or self-care (McDowell and Newell 1987). In areas with marked seasonality in disease incidence, these surveys should be repeated in the relevant periods for an accurate annual estimate of days lost. The advantage of this measure is that it does not require skilled diagnoses nor official reporting. However, it allows an estimate of lost productivity, by age and sex groups, including time involved in seeking and obtaining treatment (Walsh 1985). This measure is also suggested by Netting et al. in Chapter 4.

As permanent disability is one of the primary causes of lifetime low productivity in the developing world (Findley 1989; Kalimo and Rabin 1976; WHO 1981a:18; Lowenson 1988), minimal health data should also include nationally reported figures for permanently disabled but noninstitutionalized children aged 5 to 15 and adults over age 15 per 1,000 population (WHO 1981a). These data are regularly published by PAHO, UNICEF, and health ministries for most countries[6] and should be qualified with available methodological information concerning screening programs, reporting requirements, and estimate of bias, particularly for age-eligible persons missed in such surveys.

Again, depending on research constraints, an optional addition to the household survey could be a record of the age and sex of any household member over 15 whose chronic impairment(s), for whatever cause, permanently limits their normal (i.e., socially characteristic for their age and sex) role. The data might be pertinent in any research region where prevalence of permanently impaired adults exceeds 100 per 1,000 persons over age 15.

This definition follows that used in the U.S. Health Interview Survey (U.S. National Center for Health Statistics 1985, 1972). Though WHO recommends inclusion of school-age children in household surveys of chronic disability (1981), defining "usual" role or "permanence" of impairment for younger persons can be difficult.

National morbidity patterns should be couched in local context. Prefield data collection should list the nationally reported three leading causes of death for four major age groups: children 0–4 years and 5–15 years, adults 16–45 years, and persons over age 45. Then local health and civil leaders should be asked to list the ten most common health problems in the community as part of any minimal health data collection. Midwives or endemic-disease control teams are good informants,[7] particularly for pinpointing medically underserved groups. This "focus group" approach should identify common reasons for the disability days and health care expenditures reported by households. In lieu of (usually unreliable) data on prevalence and incidence of major diseases, the list is useful in defining the relative burdens of high mortality and high morbidity diseases, endemic versus seasonally acute diseases, perceived impact on working versus dependent segments of the population, and relative losses due to nonfatal but chronic debilitating ailments.

For example, in many developing countries accidents (often motor vehicle accidents) are the leading cause of death in adolescents and adults under 45 (PAHO 1982). Eight diseases—malaria, onchocerciasis, schistosomiasis, tuberculosis, leprosy, polio, leishmaniasis, and filariasis—are frequently reported in developing regions. Productivity may not be drastically affected in initial stages, but untreated and/or recurrent infections can result in long-term and nearly complete disability (Walsh 1985; Evans 1989; Tropical Disease Research 1985). As noted by Netting et. al in Chapter 4, a household survey of labor and productivity must take into account health constraints. Malaria is one of the most frequently reported noninfectious diseases (6–11 million cases annually), contributing to high maternal mortality losses (McGregor 1984). Malaria may have a high case-fatality rate of 5–15 percent in areas with poor nutritional status, low prior immunity, and high rates of *Plasmodium falciparum* infections (Ruebush et al. 1986).

National mortality figures may *not* reflect major *local* causes of mortality. These include adult tuberculosis fatalities, which generally occur at home; acute causes such as seasonal diseases; and injuries that do not allow time for hinterland populations to reach care. The researcher may design household sampling to cover several periods of a year, fourteen-day morbidity trends, and access to primary care services (covered in the following section).

Access Indicators

Early stages of development and the health transition may generate additional demands for care (Findley 1989). These include revised attitudes and expectations regarding normal standards of health, growth, and development, as well as new awareness of environmental and social conditions that lead to disease (ibid.). Attitudes toward health and health care prompt demands for services apart from those created by changes in health, population, and environmental conditions. Thus, estimates of community disease prevalence, mortality loss, and health costs optimally should be coupled with indicators of service utilization. The latter not only allow estimation of the cost of illness to a community but also serve as proxies for measuring the acceptability of, and equity of access to, care for various subpopulations.

"Primary health care" was defined at the Alma-Ata conference as services that should be integrated with any development effort, including health education and training of local health workers; basic sanitation; maternal and child health programs; endemic disease prevention; provision of essential acute care, nutritional support, and pharmaceuticals; and use of traditional medicines (Basch 1990).

One group of indicators measures the potential or "structural" accessibility of health services—that is, whether such services exist and are in reasonable proximity. Four questions are used to ascertain each surveyed household's access to sanitation, basic primary care and supplies, and hospitalization services, on a year-round basis. The first asks whether each household has daily access to safe, potable water either at a household spigot or within a fifteen-minute walk. Investigators also should ask whether households have access to WHO-defined "essential" pharmaceuticals (1977), first aid for common injuries, and oral rehydration therapy for acute diarrhea within an hour's travel time. Distribution of medications often occurs apart from regular care delivery and is therefore noted as a separate indicator. Household surveys provide the most reliable indication of whether primary care is hampered by the lack of medications and personnel, especially in isolated settings (Coimbra 1989). They are equally important as part of the assessment of labor required to secure daily water and of noncash resources expended for health care.

Proximity to medicines and health care is defined by travel time, not distance. It serves as a proxy for other social and financial barriers to care such as time expended in seeking care, level of inconvenience, or other economic barriers (cf. Stock 1983). Travel time to the nearest care (primary or first aid; pharmaceuticals; hospital care) is recommended in a minimum-data household survey as an indicator of equitable service distribution and potential utilization, including seasonal disruption of services. Travel time allows comparison of communities or households with widely differing means of transportation or terrain to cover. There is little firm agreement as to a standard unit of time to be used in household interviews (Murnaghan 1981). One hour is used as a frequent standard for primary-level care, one day's travel for inpatient hospital services, when normal means and conditions of travel are considered.

Where research constraints preclude household surveys concerning available services and alternatives, it may be necessary to implement a community-expert survey of the preventative care system to provide broad information on health infrastructure. Within this framework, local authorities can outline the availability of trained physicians, hospital facilities, and government or private health initiatives. Each of the following areas should be addressed by local civil and health officials in the researcher's checklist of basic preventive services: 1) water and sanitation systems, and the proportion of households covered; 2) endemic disease control program to eliminate vectors in households; and 3) the availability of emergency or supplementary food programs, where applicable. Each of these may not exist, but local informants should be able to identify the responsible agency and/or deliverer(s) of service and whether these are regularly offered or available (see Aday et al. 1981). Major seasonal variations in supply and demand, such as wet-season increases in infectious or parasitic diseases and/or lack of required medications, can also be addressed (Chambers et al. 1979).

For example, where basic services are generally available, community officials should be able to provide an estimated percentage of households with regular outlets to potable water, or outlets within a fifteen-minute walk, in lieu of including such items in household surveys (WHO 1981b; Murnaghan 1981; O'Kern 1988). Though some authors debate the real impact of "modernized" water and sanitation systems in reducing diarrheal disease in developing countries (O'Kern 1988; Rohde 1986), other success stories appear in the literature (WHO 1981b). A community water program may entail water storage and treatment, a responsible local agent, and/or a network of access pipes to households or community spigots, any of which may be subject to failure (Rohde 1986; Jordan 1985). This indicator's greatest value is in providing a relative measure of the extent of primary health infrastructure, rather than an absolute criterion of accessible safe water, when multiple sites or economic strata are being compared.

A similar socioeconomic measure involves human fecal waste disposal from the domicile (WHO 1981b). Again, a scaled item for a focus group might include public waste treatment; garbage collection; construction, inspection, and/or instruction concerning latrines; or individual disposal or treatment of nightsoil to describe the relative extent of community involvement in preventive services. In the developing world, 23 percent of urban areas are without safe water supplies, and 42 percent have no sewage system; up to 85 percent of rural areas may lack these services (UNICEF 1989:48).

Where human and animal wastes are regularly used for agricultural or aquacultural production, an important link between common human infectious and parasitic enteric diseases may exist. Though the subject is too extensive to explore here, the practice is widespread and not at all limited to the developing world. The reader is directed to Shuval and colleagues' (1986) excellent review, which outlines the economic importance and health implications of the use of nightsoil as fertilizer. In brief, the health implications depend on 1) the current prevalence of enteric and parasitic disease, 2) the infectivity of endemic pathogens and parasites, 3) available treatment, composting, and/or holding of wastes before handling or use in the fields, 4) whether the crop or fish product is eaten raw or is processed in contaminated water, 5) the length of time between nightsoil application and harvesting, 6) the method of application, soil conditions, and rainfall or flooding patterns, and 7) the use of protective footgear by field workers (Shuval et al. 1986).[8]

If the use of nightsoil fails one or more of these criteria, adult disability often results from the pararasitic loads (Walsh and Warren 1979). Child morbidity and mortality are affected by enteric diseases' contribution to nutritional deficiencies (Chen and Scrimshaw 1983). Control of parasitic disease through wide, careful dispersal of wastes, habitations, and/or village locations may also be relevant to environmental health (Lee 1985; Last 1987). Under conditions of development, periurban populations often face dire health consequences when traditional waste disposal or village migration are replaced with fixed settlement patterns and dysfunctional "modern" water, housing, and sewage (cf. Coimbra 1989; Patterson 1979; Scofield and White 1984; WHO 1984). Rates of village relocation and proximity of human waste disposal to drinking and bathing water sources are alternative data to be gathered from consensus interviews, if these are more pertinent in isolated settings (Lee 1985).

Service Utilization

Surveys may be the only way to estimate primary care access in some countries (Lee 1985). An additional advantage to household surveys is that, unlike clinic-based utilization data, they cover both users and nonusers of services. Child immunization programs address some of the major forces of mortality in the very young—tetanus and the secondary infections that follow childhood diseases. At the household level, the number of preschool immunization contacts for the youngest child in the household should be included in the minimal household database. Although WHO advocates household survey coverage of all children, this compromise allows a quick grasp of local effectiveness in delivering primary care. If time permits, investigators may ask each resident under age 15 if the WHO standard—at least three immunization contacts per child before the age of 6—has been met, illustrating the completeness of childhood immunization (UNICEF 1989). Use of health care services at the household level may be queried to reflect visits for specific services (prenatal visits; immunizations) or, alternatively, for the latest illness episode in the previous two weeks (Ho 1982).

In most developing countries, the proportion of household income devoted to health care services and medications far exceeds that expended in developed countries (WHO 1978c). This disparity exists because of poorer health status, the absence of third-party payers, high costs of transportation and drugs, and because low-literacy populations tend to use multiple curing resources for the same illness episode (Kroeger 1983). High out-of-pocket expenditures have traditionally been considered an access barrier. Health care expenditures have traditionally been a part of most household economic surveys (cf. Scott et al. 1980). Minimal data should be obtained on the portion of the generalized monthly household budget expended for seeking and using health care, as well as on any actual expenditures within the fourteen-day morbidity reporting frame. These estimates provide a gauge of the relative drain of poor health on the household. Expenditures may include transportation costs, food for hospitalized relatives, pharmacy purchases, and, in many regions, gifts or prescribed purchases for ritual healings. The investigator may optionally probe for items secured on credit (such as pharmaceuticals) or received through reciprocity (herbal cures, for example).

An optional item may be a request to local health officials for annual data on hospital deaths by major age and mortality grouping (infectious disease, cardiovascular, perinatal, trauma, etc.), along with the nearest hospital's latest available annual summary of admissions, births, and discharges. These data often require time-consuming authorizations from higher-level officials and may not reflect the same time frame as the field visit. Nonetheless, local hospitalization data can be extremely useful. They serve to confirm (or question) the published leading causes of mortality and, if timely, help in interviewing local officials about health problems in their community.

National-level service and utilization data are routinely generated by institutional care providers and ministries of health. Data on household-level indicators of health care use and access should be complemented with minimal data for the national ratios of primary health workers (physicians, nurses, midwives, health visitors, etc.) per 10,000 population and of in-patient hospital beds per 10,000 population (Murnaghan 1981). These indicators should be disaggregated by region if possible to show the relative distribution of health services around the country. International health reporting has accepted varying definitions of "primary care" personnel—the main criterion is that they must represent a community's entry point to modern medical care. Hospital beds often reflect the bulk of national health expenditures and, in many instances, the extent of maldistribution of resources in the system, particularly in developing countries.

National data on immunization levels—such as WHO's estimates of 90 percent immunization coverage of the preschool population in Argentina and Singapore, 60 percent in Brazil and Algeria, and 20 percent or less in Haiti, Guatemala, and Yemen (UNICEF 1989:38)—should be obtained as *pre-fieldwork* minimal data to measure the reach of primary health services to rural communities. Finally, the national rate of hospital attended births per 1,000 births is a more feasible indicator of primary care accessibility for adults than less easily defined visits (for prenatal care, for example).

The gains achieved through massive health delivery efforts are frequently offset by regional economic downturns (UNICEF 1989:31; PAHO 1982). Regional development programs also have reversed health gains through migration-related crowding and undernutrition (Patterson 1979). There may be a reintroduction of diseases such as malaria into previously controlled areas (Marques and Pinheiro 1982; WHO 1984), even where governments attempt to meet these challenges through, for example, increased spraying for insect vectors (Costa Chagas et al. 1982). Migrants' acceptance of such health services may in turn depend on factors such as their own willingness to "health shop" between known and untested modes of treatment (Fleming-Moran 1992; Kroeger 1983) and to incur debt for such services (Nabarro et al. 1989; Vaa et al. 1989), as well as the degree to which community-based health services address the multiple causes of disease in a developing area (Walt 1988). In other words, the existence of health infrastructure per se is not enough to ensure that services are accessible to or accepted by potential users.

Conclusions

Although the list of minimal health indicators for an agrarian community study appears extensive, the majority are obtainable from published sources, and several replicate household-level indicators suggested by other authors in this volume. Rural and poor segments of society bear the greatest burden of disability and death (Corbett 1989; Evans 1989; Renker 1982; Manton et al. 1989), which in turn is a major barrier to their development. Several facets of this burden have thus been addressed: The national and local measures of mortality and morbidity, resource accessibility measures, and household health expenditures are included as minima. These minima allow scholars to relate community health and mortality patterns to observed economic, social, and ritual behaviors.

Cumper has noted three major questions that demand local as well as national information (1984). First, national differences in broad health indicators are often a result of very specific health problems within specific subpopulations. How can else can these be identified except through local-level studies? Second, what are the processes by which changes in other social factors (such as income or educational achievement) get translated into improved health status? And last, macrolevel international comparisons often note health status effects that appear to be independent of economic growth or input measures. How do we identify the pertinent variables and their relative roles for setting development policy or evaluating health change? Demographic and to a great degree health transitions in industrialized Europe have attracted much scholarly attention. To date, limitations in both demographic and basic health data have thwarted similar attention to the history of demographic and social change in developing nations (1984:5). Perhaps the issues addressed in this volume will help to resolve these deficiencies.

Notes

1. Field experience with vital-event registrars and household reporting of vital events has now been evaluated concerning health service utilization, cost and duration of morbidity, and use of a streamlined International Classification of Disease (ICD) for reporting cause of mortality (WHO 1978a).

2. Civil and religious authorities are able to address legal requirements for registering vital events and areas of recognized underreporting, such as accidental or violent deaths, infant or other nonreligious burials, or the relative prevalence of unattended births. They may identify secondary clues to these events, such as requests for ritual purifications or sacraments related to illness, death, or childbirth (Kleinman 1988), unusual periods of clinic or police activity, or segments of the population that do not participate in mainstream religious or civil practices.

3. Country- or age-specific summaries of morbidity and mortality (often specifying recognized limitations of these data) are available, as well as data on health resources (see PAHO 1982; Puffer 1984; Saltman 1988 as examples). Information for other regions can be found in the UN Population Studies series, the World Fertility Survey occasional papers, UNICEF and Statistical Office publications, country-specific reports on experience with household-survey data systems, and recent World Bank publications.

4. Other socioeconomic indicators that are highly correlated with morbidity and mortality present alternatives to descriptors of preventive health services per se. Examples include literacy rates for adult women and men, the proportion of the population with less than some minimum annual income (see Murnaghan 1981). These variables are often used to explain divergent IMRs in international comparisons, where other measurements of social status—particularly those associated

with vital event records—are unreliable or unavailable (Cumper 1984; Wallace and Tahir Taha 1988).

5. Maternal mortality rates have been widely used as a more sensitive indicator of the effectiveness, quality, and coverage of the primary health care than, for example, rates of neonatal tetanus (UNICEF 1989:91). However, maternal death is not always documented as such, nor is the leading cause of death in women aged 15–45, even for countries with very high birth and infant mortality rates (Murnaghan 1981). Conversely, the coverage and quality of primary care may be equally reflected in the aforementioned indicators of child and infant mortality, especially that attributable to preventable diseases. For these reasons the suggested minimal indicator for primary care to adults is national data on the proportion of total annual births attended by trained health personnel.

6. For international measures of long-term disability and loss of productivity, see the OECD Working Party on Social Indicators, which published reviews, field-tested questionnaires, and made available data from member countries in an attempt to standardize concepts and measurements of chronic disability (Murnaghan 1981).

7. Vector-control workers, water services, or visiting nurse services can be helpful in mapping and enumerating remote and even temporary households. For example, in some countries with WHO malaria control programs, each house is individually enumerated, mapped, and sprayed on a regular cycle to control mosquitos. In Brazil, for example, malaria-control efforts include temporary shelters in "boom" areas of gold-prospecting and agricultural expansion (Tropical Disease Research 1985; Costa Chagas et al. 1982). Similarly, World Bank projects with focused health initiatives or urban areas with public sanitation services may also map and enumerate households. If so, a sampling base for household interviews can be readily drawn if such registers are updated (Abramson 1984).

8. The latter is of special concern in highly endemic schistosomiasis areas, where chemotheraputic treatment of the disease or elimination of the host snail are not yet effective (Jordan 1985). In such cases, ethnographic data on use of streams for bathing and washing (Jordan 1985), cultural values regarding hand-washing (Black et al. 1981, in Rohde 1986), may provide insight as to the modes of transmission of parasitic and infectious disease. If the pre-field investigation of mortality rates indicates high infant mortality rates resulting from diarrheal diseases, the investigator may opt to add household-level information on the prevalence and duration of breast-feeding (Jelliffe and Jelliffe 1982, in Rohde 1986; Butz et al. 1984; Esrey 1988) as well as the suggested community experts' estimates of the available oral rehydration therapy (ORT) for childhood diarrhea (see Rohde 1986; WHO/UNICEF 1989; Griffin et al. 1988). Diarrheal episodes inflict highest mortality, morbidity, and nutritional decimation in the period following weaning (Jelliffe and Jelliffe 1982; Butz et al. 1984), and contaminated water supplies appear to have a disproportional impact on this age child.

References

Abramson, J. H., 1984. *Survey Methods in Community Medicine: An Introduction to Epidemiological and Evaluative Studies,* third edition. London: Churchill Livingstone.

Aday, L. A., C. Sellers, and R. M. Anderson, 1981. Community health surveys. *American Journal of Public Health* 71:835.

Adlakha, A., and M. Nizamuddin, 1984. Mortality data collections: A review of integrated multi-purpose household surveys and multi-round demographic surveys. In UN Department of International Economics and Social Affairs, *Data Bases for Mortality Measurement,* Population Studies No. 84, pp. 104–114. New York: UN/ST/ESA/SER/84.

Basch, Paul F., 1990. *Textbook of International Health.* New York: Oxford University Press.

Black, R. E., A. C. Dykes, and K. E. Anderson, 1981. Handwashing to prevent diarrhea in day-care centers. *American Journal of Epidemiology* 113:445–451.

Burke, May, 1979. An inter-American investigation of mortality in childhood: Report on a household sample. In M. Burke, M. York, and I. Sande, eds., *Inter-American Investigation of Mortality in Childhood.* Washington, D.C.: WHO/Pan American Health Organization. PAHO Scientific Publication No. 386.

Butz, W. P., J. Habicht, et al., 1984. Environmental factors and the relation of breast feeding and infant mortality: The roles of sanitation and water supply in Malaysia. *American Journal Epidemiology* 19:516–525.

Cassidy, Claire M., 1987. World view conflict and toddler malnutrition: Change against the elements. In N. Scheper-Hughes, ed., *Child Survival,* pp. 293–324. Dordrecht, Holland: Reidel.

Chambers, R., R. Longhurst, D. Bradley, and R. Feachem, 1979. *Seasonal Dimensions to Rural Poverty: Analysis and Political Implications.* Brighton, U.K.: University of Sussex, Institute of Development Studies, Paper No. 142.

Chandler, William U., 1984. *Improving World Health: A Least Cost Strategy.* Washington D.C.: Worldwatch Institute, Paper No. 59.

Chen, L. C., 1986. Primary health care in developing countries: Overcoming operational, technical and social barriers. *Lancet* 2:1260–1265.

Chen, L. C., and N. S. Scrimshaw, eds., 1983. *Diarrhea and Malnutrition: Interactions, Mechanisms and Interventions.* New York: Plenum Press.

Chorba, T. L., R. L. Berkelman, S. K. Stafford, et al., 1990. Mandatory reporting of infectious disease by clinicians. *Morbidity and Mortality Weekly Report* 39:1–17.

Coimbra, Carlos E. A. Jr., 1989. From shifting cultivation to coffee farming: The impact of change on the health and ecology of the Suruí Indians in the Brazilian Amazon. Ph.D. Dissertation, Anthropology Department, Indiana University, Bloomington, Indiana.

Corbett, Janet, 1989. Poverty and sickness: The high cost of ill health. *IDS Bulletin* 20(2):58–62.

Costa Chagas, José Alberto, M.A.B. Barroso, R.D.S. Amorim, and C.R.Q. Robles, 1982. Contrôle da malaria em projecto hidrelétrico no estado do Amazonas. *Revista Brasileira da Malariologia e Doenças Tropicais* 34:68–81.

Cumper, G. E., 1984. *Determinants of Health Levels in Developing Countries.* Letchworth, England: Research Studies Press.

Davies, M. P., 1983. The Zimbabwe national disability survey. *African Rehabilitation Journal* 1(1):18–21.

Delgado, H. L., V. Valverde, and E. Hustado, 1986. Effects of health and nutrition interventions on infant and child mortality in rural Guatemala. In *Determinants of Mortality Change and Differentials in Developing Countries,* UN Population Studies No. 94. New York: UN/ST/ESA/SER/84.

Esrey, S. A., 1988. Drinking water source, child growth and diarrheal morbidity. *American Journal of Public Health* 78:1451–1455.

Evans, J., 1989. The impact of permanent disability on rural households: River blindness in Guinea. *IDS Bulletin* 20(2):41–48.

Fassin, Didier, and I. Badji, 1986. Ritual buffoonery: A social preventative measure against childhood mortality in Senegal. *The Lancet* 1:142–143.

Findley, Sally, 1989. Social reflections of changing morbidity during health transitions. Paper presented at the Health Transition Workshop, "Cultural, social and behavioral determinants of three health transitions: What is the evidence?" National Center for Epidemiology and Population Health, Australian National University, Canberra, May 15–19.

Fleming-Moran, Millicent, 1992. The folk view of natural causation and disease in Brazil and its relation to traditional curing practices. *Boletim do Museu Emilío Goeldi (Antropología)* 8(1):65–156.

Freedman, Deborah, and E. Mueller, 1977. *A multi-purpose household questionnaire: Basic economic and demographic modules.* Washington D.C: World Bank.

Good, Charles, 1987. *Ethnomedical Systems in Africa.* New York: Guilford Press.

Griffin, P. A., C. A. Ryan, et al., 1988. Risk factors for fatal diarrhea: A case-control study of African children. *American Journal of Epidemiology.* 128:1322–1329.

Grootaert, Christiaan, 1986. *Measuring and Analyzing Levels of Living in Developing Countries: An Annotated Questionnaire.* The Living Standards Measurement Study, Working Paper No. 24. Washington D.C.: World Bank.

Hewson, D., and A. Bennett, 1987. Childbirth research data: Medical records or women's reports? *American Journal of Epidemiology.* 125:484–491.

Hilsum, Lindsey, 1983. Nutrition education and social change: A women's movement in the Dominican Republic. In David Morley, J. E. Rohde, and G. Williams, eds., *Practicing Health for All.* Oxford, UK: Oxford University Press, pp. 114–132.

Ho, Teresa J., 1982. *Measuring Health as a Component of Living Standards.* The Living Standards Measurement Study, Working Paper No. 15. Washington, D.C.: World Bank.

Hobcraft, John, 1984. Use of special mortality questions in fertility surveys: The World Fertility Survey experience. In UN Department of International Economic and Social Affairs, *Data Bases for Mortality Measurement,* pp. 93–103, Population Studies No. 84. New York: United Nations.

Institute of Medicine, 1993. *Access to Health Care in America.* Washington, D.C.: National Academy Press.

Janzen, John M., 1988. *Ngoma: Discourses of Healing in Central and Southern Africa.* Berkley, CA: University of California Press.

Jelliffe, D. B., and E.F.P. Jelliffe, 1982. *Human Milk in the Modern World: Psychosocial, Nutritional, and Economic Significance.* Oxford: Oxford University Press.

Johnson, Bruce F., and William C. Clark, 1982. *Redesigning Rural Development: A Strategic Perspective.* Baltimore, MD: Johns Hopkins University Press.

Jordan, Peter, 1985. *Schistosomiasis: The St. Lucia Project.* New York: Cambridge University Press.

Kalimo, A., and D. L. Rabin, 1976. Relationships among indicators of morbidity: Cross-national comparisons. *Journal of Chronic Disease* 29:1–4.

Katz, J., et al., 1989. The importance of age in evaluating anthropometric indices for predicting mortality. *American Journal of Epidemiology* 130:12, 19–26.

Kleinman, Arthur, 1988. *The Illness Narratives.* New York: Basic Books.

Kramer, Joyce, and A. Thomas, 1982. The modes of maintaining health in Ukambani, Kenya. In P. Stanley Yoder, ed., *African Health and Healing Systems: Proceedings of a Symposium,* pp. 159–198. Los Angeles: UCLA African Studies and African Studies Association Publications.

Kroeger, Axel, 1983. Health interview surveys: Review of methods and results. *International Journal of Epidemiology* 12:465–481.

Last, J. M., 1987. *Public Health and Human Ecology.* East Norwalk, CT: Appleton and Lange.

Lee, James P., 1985. *The Environment, Public Health, and Human Ecology: Considerations for Economic Development.* Baltimore: Johns Hopkins University Press.

Lowenson, R., 1988. Labour insecurity and health: An epidemiological study in Zimbabwe. *Social Science and Medicine* 27(7):733–741.

Mahler, H., 1987. The safe motherhood initiative: A call to action. *Lancet* 1:668–670.

Manton, Kenneth, M. Woodbury, and J. Dowd, 1989. Methods of identifying geographic and social clustering of disability and disease burden. Paper presented at the Health Transition Workshop, London, England, June 8–10, 1989. National Center of Epidemiology and Population Health, Australian National University, Canberra, May 15–19.

Marques, Agostinho C., and E. A. Pinheiro, 1982. Fluxos de casos de malaria no Brasil em 1980. *Revista Brasileira de Malariologia e Doenças Tropicais* 34:1–31.

Martorell, Reynaldo, 1982. *Nutrition and Health Status Indicators: Suggestions for Surveys of the Standard of Living in Developing Countries.* Living Standards Measurement Study, Working Paper No. 13. Washington, D.C.: World Bank.

Martorell, Reynaldo, J. P. Habicht, C. Yarbrough, et al., 1975. Acute morbidity and physical growth in rural Guatemalan children. *American Journal of Diseases in Children* 129:1296–1301.

Martorell, Reynaldo, J. P. Habicht, C. Yarbrough, et al., 1976. Under-reporting in fortnightly recall morbidity surveys. *Journal of Tropical Pediatrics* 22:129–134.

McCormick, M. C., 1985. The contribution of low-birth weight to infant mortality and childhood morbidity. *New England Journal of Medicine* 312:82–90.

McDowell, I. W., and C. Newell, 1987. *Measuring Health.* New York: Oxford University Press.

McGregor, I. A., 1984. Epidemiology, malaria and pregnancy. *American Journal of Tropical Medicine and Hygiene* 33:517–525.

McGranahan, D. V., C. Richard-Proust, N. V. Sovani, et al., 1970. *Contents and Measurement of Socio-economic Development: An Empirical Inquiry.* Geneva: UN Institute for Social Development, Report No. 70.10.

Murnaghan, Jane H., 1978. Uniform basic data sets for health statistical systems. *International Journal of Epidemiology* 7(3):263–269.

———, 1981. Health indicators and information systems for the year 2000. *Annual Review of Public Health* 2:299–361.

Nabarro, David, C. Cassels, and M. Pant, 1989. Coping strategies of households in the hills of Nepal: Can development initiatives help? *IDS Bulletin* 20(2):68–74.

National Academy of Sciences/National Research Council, Panel on Brazil, 1983. *Levels and Recent Trends in Fertility and Mortality in Brazil.* Committee on

Population and Demography Report No. 21. Washington, D.C.: National Academy Press.

O'Kern, D. A., 1988. Water supply and sanitation in development: An assessment. *American Journal of Public Health* 78:1463–1467.

Palmore, J. A., and R. W. Gardner, 1983. *Measuring Mortality, Fertility, and Natural Increase: A Self-teaching Guide to Elementary Measures.* Honolulu: The East-West Population Institute.

Pan American Health Organization (PAHO), 1982. *Health Conditions in the Americas, 1977–80.* Publication No. 427. Washington D.C.: WHO/PAHO.

Patterson, K. David, 1979. Health in urban Ghana: The case of Accra, 1900–1940. *Social Science and Medicine* 13:251–268.

Preston, Samuel H., 1984. Use of direct and indirect techniques of estimating the completeness of death registration systems. In UN Department of International Economic and Social Affairs, *Data Bases for Mortality Measurement,* Population Studies No. 84, New York: UN/ST/ESA/SER/84.

Pryer, Jane, 1989. When breadwinners fall ill: Preliminary findings from a case study in Bangladesh. *IDS Bulletin* 20(2):49–57.

Puffer, Ruth R., 1984. Experience of the Pan American Health Organization in using death certificates for intensive studies of mortality. In UN Department of International Economic and Social Affairs, *Data Bases for Mortality Measurement,* Population Studies No. 84, pp. 127–145. New York: UN/ST/ESA/SER/84.

Puffer, Ruth, and Carlos V. Serrano, 1973. *Patterns of Mortality in Childhood: Report of the Inter-American Investigation of Mortality in Childhood.* Pan American Health Organization Scientific Publication No. 262. Washington, D.C.: WHO/PAHO.

Renker, K., 1982. World statistics on disabled persons. *International Journal of Rehabilitation Research* 5(2):167–177.

Rohde, J. E., 1986. Acute diarrhea. In J. A. Walsh and K. S. Warren, eds., *Strategies for Primary Health Care,* pp. 14–28. Chicago: University of Chicago Press.

Ruebush, T. K., J. G. Breman, R. L. Kaiser, and M. Warren, 1986. Malaria. In J. A. Walsh and K. S. Warren, eds., *Strategies for Primary Health Care,* pp. 47–59. Chicago: University of Chicago Press.

Saltman, R. B., 1988. *The International Handbook of Health Care Systems.* New York: Greenwood Press.

Scofield, C .J,. and G. B. White, 1984. House design and domestic vectors of disease. *Transactions of the Royal Society of Tropical Medicine* 78:285–292.

Scott, C., P.T.A. de Andrade, and R. Chandler, 1980. *Conducting Surveys in Developing Countries: Practical Problems and Experience in Brazil, Malaysia and the Philippines.* Living Standards Measurement Study Working Paper No. 5. Washington, D.C.: World Bank.

Shuval, H .I., A. Adin, B. Fattal, et al., 1986. Wastewater irrigation in developing countries: Health effects and technical solutions. World Bank Technical Paper No. 51, pp. 104–114.

Starfield, B., 1985. Postneonatal mortality. *Annual Review of Public Health* 6:21–40.

Stock, Robert, 1983. Distance and the utilization of health facilities in rural Nigeria. *Social Science and Medicine* 17(9): 563–570.

Tropical Disease Research Program/WHO, 1985. *Tropical Disease Research 1985.* Washington, D.C.: World Bank.

UNICEF, 1989. *The State of the World's Children, 1989.* New York: UNICEF.

United Nations, 1985. *World Population Trends. Population and Development Interrelations and Population Policies.* 1983 Monitoring Report. Vol. 1. Population Trends. New York: UN/ST/SER/SER.A/93.

UN Department of International Economic and Social Affairs, 1984. *Data bases for mortality measurement.* Population Studies No. 84. U.N. Department of International Economics and Social Affairs. New York: UN/ST/ESA/SER/84.

UN Department of Technical Co-operation for Development and Statistical Office, 1982. *National Household Survey Capability Programme.* New York: Department of Technical Cooperation for Development, DP/UN/INT-81-041/2.

U.S. National Center for Health Statistics (NCHS), 1972. *Interviewing Methods in the Health Interview Survey.* DHEW Pub. #(HSM) 72-1048. Washington, D.C.: Government Printing Office.

————, 1985. Current Estimates from the National Health Interview Survey, U.S. 1982, *Vital and Health Statistics.* Series 10(150), DHHS (PHS 85-1578). Washington, D.C.: Government Printing Office.

————, 1986. *Data from the National Health Interview Survey: Health Promotion and Disease Prevention.* Advance Data No. 1, 19. Rockville, MD: NCHS.

U.S. Public Health Service, 1991. *Healthy People: National Health Promotion and Disease Prevention Objectives.* DHHS Pub. No. (PHS) 91-50212. Washington, D.C.: Government Printing Office.

Vaa, Marikan, S. Findley, and A. Diallo, 1989. The gift of economy: A study of women migrants' survival strategies in a low-income Bamako neighborhood. *Labor, Capital, and Society* 22(2):234–261.

Wallace, Helen M., and T. El Tahir Taha, 1988. Indicators for monitoring progress in maternal and child health care in Africa. *Journal of Tropical Pediatrics* 34: 158–164.

Walsh, Julia A., 1985. Estimating the burden of illness in the tropics. In Kenneth Warren and A.A.F. Mahmoud, eds., *Tropical and Geographic Medicine,* pp. 1073-1085. Singapore: McGraw Hill Book Co..

————, 1986. Measles. In J. A. Walsh and K. S. Warren, eds., *Strategies for Primary Health Care,* pp. 60–70. Chicago: University of Chicago Press.

Walsh, Julia A., and Kenneth Warren, 1979. Selective primary health care: An interim strategy for disease control in developing countries. *New England Journal of Medicine* 301:967–974.

————, eds., 1986. *Strategies for Primary Health Care.* Chicago: University of Chicago Press.

Walt, Gill, 1988. Child-health workers: Are national programmes in crises? *Health Policy and Planning* 3(1):1–21.

Werner, D., 1986. Disabled village children: A part of primary health care. *Contact* 91:1–8.

Wood, D. L., R. A. Hayward, C. R. Corey, et al., 1990. Access to medical care for children and adolescents in the United States. *Pediatrics* 86:666–673.

World Health Organization (WHO), 1977. *Report of a Select WHO Committee: The Selection of Essential Drugs.* WHO Technical Report Series No. 614. Geneva: WHO.

————, 1978a. *Lay Reporting of Health Information.* Geneva: WHO.

————, 1978b. *Growth Chart for International Use in Maternal and Child Health: Guidelines for Primary Health Care Personnel.* Geneva: WHO.

————, 1978c. *The Financing of Health Services.* Report of a WHO Study Group. WHO Technical Report Series #625. Geneva: WHO.

————, 1981a. *Development of Indicators for Monitoring Progress Toward Health for All by the Year 2000.* Health for All Series. No. 4. Geneva: WHO.

————, 1981b. *Drinking Water and Sanitation, 1981–1990, A Way to Health.* A WHO Contribution to International Drinking Water Supply and Sanitation Decade. Geneva: WHO.

————, 1984. *Migration and Health: Population Distribution, Migration and Development.* Proceedings of the Expert Committee in Population Distribution, Migration and Development, UN International Conference on Population, Tunisia, March 1983.

————, 1986a. Analysis of data on the global indicators. *WHO Statistics Annual* 1986:33–46.

9

Agrarian Data Sets:
The Comparativist's View

ROBERT C. HUNT

The essays in this book concentrate on the production of data sets during fieldwork and on the reporting of those data sets. One of the uses for these data sets is in comparative studies, where each case supplies one set of data points. In this chapter I discuss the problems and constraints that face a comparativist who would use these case-study data. The purpose is to explore how the construction of case studies might make the comparative effort more successful.

There is a voluminous literature on comparison in virtually all the social sciences and in philosophy as well (see Marsh 1967; Naroll and Cohen 1970; Smelser 1976). There are many different purposes for doing comparative studies and many different ways of constructing them (see Lewis 1956). It has been argued that there is no knowledge without some sort of comparison (Kaplan and Manners 1972), a position I accept. Great variation may be discerned in the comparative studies that have been published. The number of cases used can vary from two to the thousands. The territorial coverage can vary from two neighboring villages (Epstein 1962) to a region or social type (Brookfield 1972) to the entire cultural world (Textor 1967). The purpose of the study can vary from heuristic exploration to illustration to a formal test of a hypothesis.

The species of comparison that I refer to in this chapter systematically probes the relationships among variables, uses more than a few cases, and attempts to confirm a finding. The comparative efforts that attempt to confirm a finding typically occur in a series.[1] Although the first efforts may well be heuristic explorations, the ultimate goal of such efforts is to test hypotheses about cause and effect, often in a diachronic design (Ember and

Levinson 1991; see also Naroll 1970 and Levinson and Malone 1980 for surveys of results).

A number of interesting and productive questions about relationships between variables for agrarian systems cannot be settled without comparative studies. The relationships between population and development, between labor productivity and development, between a cultural orientation (such as the Protestant work ethic) and development, can usefully be investigated in a detailed and diachronic case study. However, when such a case is completed and digested, we still have only one case. No single case study can confirm or disconfirm a probabilistic generalization. The case studies are necessary for the confirmation process, but they are not sufficient. The comparative studies, examining many different cases simultaneously, are equally necessary for getting the job done.

There are a number of conditions for the success of such comparative studies. Some are not relevant for the construction of case studies and will be only briefly mentioned here. The research design is of prime importance (see Campbell and Stanley 1963), as is the sampling strategy (see Ember and Otterbein 1991). Neither affects the construction of the case study. Once the data from the cases are assembled, they must be analyzed with the appropriate techniques (see Bradley 1989). This step poses a complex set of questions of its own, with its own literature. The decisions made in this part of the comparative effort depend upon information contained in the case study but do not constrain or drive how that case study is conducted.

Case Studies

If a case study is to be useful for a systematic comparative effort, a number of requirements must be met. First, we want each case to present a complete set of the critical variables. Missing data pose very difficult problems for a comparative study. Second, the comparativist has to solve for equivalence, so the case has to present information that will help provide the solution. Finally, comparativists need to estimate the uncertainty in the results; detailed reporting of measuring procedures in the case study is a necessary part of that process.

Case studies and comparative studies have different purposes and different conditions for success and are designed for largely different audiences. The purpose of any given comparative study is quite clear. The question being asked is discrete and specific, and the results add some specific knowledge of the subject. Furthermore, comparative studies based on literature searches can be replicated at any time, as the data to be used are already in existence. The comparative study is tightly focused, limited in time, and is not a unique opportunity to observe life. Much time and effort are needed to complete one—time and effort spent in the library and at the computer, not in the field.

The standard case study, by contrast, is usually subject to many different and shifting purposes and constraints. Anthropological case studies, especially first trips to field sites, are the product of extended fieldwork and often exact a considerable cost in time, money, and effort.

We are all taught that fieldwork is preceded by a tight and specific research design that spells out the questions to be asked and how to get the answers. In fact, very few field trips actually work out this way. Once we get there, things rarely evolve the way we assumed they would. We find that the questions prepared beforehand somehow do not mean very much or distort the local reality. We find that other questions are much more interesting. And the local reality rarely yields the kinds of information that we so confidently predicted before we arrived. Upon our return home we set out to analyze and publish our results. If the fieldwork lasted eighteen months or more, we have large amounts of data on a large number of subjects. The ideal reporting strategy is to utilize subsets of these data for a substantial number of different topics. The inevitable result of all this shifting and multiple interests is that reports of fieldwork may lose sight of the requirements of comparative study, especially one being conducted by someone else.

There are, of course, exceptions. Some field studies were designed to fit into a comparative study. One of the best-known of these in the United States was the Whiting Six-Culture Series (B. Whiting 1963; B. and J. Whiting 1975; Minturn and Lambert 1964). The comparative study came first in the design. Young anthropologists were recruited to collectively design and then carry out the field studies. Each produced a monograph on the field site in which certain predetermined topics were addressed. Finally, comparative study was performed based on the data systematically collected by the six field teams. This was a tremendous effort for anthropology, involving many years from beginning to end, many person-years of endeavor, and many dollars. In the end we had a comparative study with a sample size of only six, focusing on the relationships of dozens of variables. There have been a few other such projects, including the Cultural Ecology Study of East Africa (Edgerton 1971; see Munroe and Munroe 1991 for a review).

Cultural anthropology has not been receptive to this type of study. It is very expensive in terms of money and management effort. The payoff is usually not very large. And there is something in the cultural anthropologist that does not take very well to being part of a large team effort for fieldwork, with the necessary discipline that goes with a high degree of division of labor. Rather, the usual way to organize comparative efforts is for a single person to pull together and systematically compare a large amount of previous literature that was prepared for a multitude of reasons. Most systematic comparative studies are organized by a single investigator using multiple independent case studies.

The first time that a question is posed and answered—for example, that labor productivity declines with evolution—it results in a very small and not very well done comparative study (Carneiro 1961; Boserup 1965; Dumond 1961; Sahlins 1972). Subsequent rigorous comparative efforts are a major way to test the general claims that have been made. These large-sample systematic comparative studies will rarely produce new questions; rather, they assess answers to *old* questions. Insofar as we are a discipline that is interested in the empirical world, all claims to empirical knowledge must be testable. And the systematic comparative empirical study is one of the major ways for testing those claims.

In the rest of this chapter I will discuss how the case study can be constructed so as to meet the needs of the comparativist. I will address what is to be measured, how it is to be measured, and how it should be reported as these affect the systematic research design, the problem of equivalence, and the problem of estimating uncertainty.

What Is to Be Measured?

The comparative test of a proposition is most productive when all the cases have measured all the relevant variables. If measures or variables are missing, it causes serious problems for the analysis, and weakens the results. The issue, then, is which variables should be measured in each case study. These can only be chosen in the context of some wider substantive questions.

The substantive questions determine which variables are relevant. As substantive questions are potentially almost infinite in number, how can it be possible to offer those who will be constructing case studies general advice on which variables to measure? With limited resources for fieldwork and shifting multiple purposes of the case study, it would seem unlikely that any specific variables could be named that would be generally useful for comparative efforts. However, there are three major substantive questions that have been interesting for centuries and that continue to intrigue and puzzle. If there are major substantive questions and a core set of variables relevant for investigating them, then a solution to the dilemma of which variables should be measured in every field study is fairly clear.

One question is the relationship of population, environment, food supply, technology, and productivity. Does food supply constrain population? How do levels of population affect agrarian technology? What is the relationship of technology and productivity to food surplus? We have here a knot of questions that have been worried over since the time of Adam Smith and addressed by Malthus, Marx, Boserup, Sahlins, and others (see also Hayami and Ruttan 1985; Netting 1993).

A second major substantive question flows from the first: the course of evolution. Humans have not always had agriculture, cities, and civilization. These phenomena must have evolved. Population, food supply, and technology must have been deeply implicated in that evolution. How these variables relate to each other in the evolutionary context is a major unresolved question. Some argue that rising population drives development, with technology changing in consequence. Others argue that technological change drives development, with population changing in consequence.

The third major substantive question is the structure of rational decisionmaking in humans. For a long time it was thought that European monetarized capitalists made decisions based on economic rationality, whereas the decisions of others were based on "custom." T. W. Schultz in 1964 argued that there was evidence that Third World peasants (actually, Indian peasants in Guatemala and in India) made many decisions based on economic rationality. Economic rationality meant that in conditions of a scarcity of means, and multiple uses of the means, the decisions about how to allocate those scarce means were based on a calculus of individual gain. There are those who argue that some (many) peasants live in an economy where group interests override individual interests, that there is a moral rather than a rational economy (Scott 1976). Others argue that most of the decisions on the part of peasants are driven by self-interest and are therefore economically rational (Popkin 1979).[2]

The rationality problem has engaged scholars in virtually every discipline (including biologist Garret Hardin [1968] in his discussions of the "tragedy of the commons") and remains a central question. Part of the struggle has been over theoretical issues such as the definitions of rationality, scarcity, and decision. But part of the struggle has been over the correlation of various kinds of decisionmaking with the degree of development of the society, an inherently comparative question. And the kinds of decisions in focus have been concerned with production, consumption, and exchange in agrarian systems. Any comparative study of this issue demands measures of variables of consumption, production, and so on. We are therefore back to the major purpose of this volume.

I suggest that there is a core set of variables that most analysts of any of these three substantive questions want to have measured. It follows that if the scholar producing the case study is alert to the major substantive questions, s/he will want to make some effort to measure the relevant variables, even if they are not central to the purpose of the case study. The variables are:

Population. For any time period of analysis we want to know what the total population is (see Hern, Chapter 7, for detailed discussion of the variable). Sometimes counting people is rather easy (the host society may do it rather accurately itself). What is not so easy is to determine with exactitude the territorial unit that contains this population. Anthropologists usually study some sort of settlement, which usually has a name. This unit needs to be specified rather exactly. Then there are often fringe categories relevant for considerations of labor, consumption, surplus, and so forth. These include itinerant shepherds, members of the society who are away for extended periods of time, outcasts who live outside the settlement but who are dependent upon the settlement for substantial provisioning, and so on.

Units. In many parts of the agrarian world the household is the primary unit of production and consumption (Netting 1989 and Netting et al., Chapter 4). The households in the sample should be measured for size and activities. If there are substantial agrarian activities that are not connected to households but instead are performed by other units (such as temples or age grades), these should be specified and measured as well.

Consumption. The major items of food consumption, housing, clothing, tools, and capital items (boats, draft animals) should be measured. Consumption levels are an integral factor determining surplus or scarcity and are linked with health levels.

Agricultural Inputs. Land is a prime input, and the land available to a unit of production should be measured. Tenure variations should be noted as well (how much owned, how much leased in, how much leased out, conditions of leasing).

Labor is another prime input. Here the unit of measure is a problem: Ecologists like to measure it in energy terms, but economists prefer money. Most field workers are limited to measuring the labor in terms of time, and most of the case and comparative literature uses time units. Most case studies report time in terms of man-days; a few report it in hours. If the report is in days, it would be very useful to include an estimate of the number of hours in a working day for each task in a given case study.

A usually ignored but important aspect of labor measurement is the question of how much labor time is available. This consideration involves the question of underemployment and of labor constraints on production. All agricultural systems have rhythms, with periods of intensive labor and periods of slack labor. The most intensive periods are often field preparation and/or harvest. If a settlement is homogeneous with respect to crops and cropping patterns, then all households are likely to be intensely involved at the same time. That agricultural task is likely to set a constraint on levels of production because of a scarcity of labor for that task. Thus, it is productive if the case study measures the labor time available for the task as well as the labor invested.

Labor is often exchanged by and between households. There are several forms of this exchange, including reciprocal exchange, market exchange, and redistributive exchange. A household may send labor out and may take labor in. How much of this exchange occurs and in what form should be measured (see Netting et al., Chapter 4, for additional discussion of labor; also Trager, Chapter 5).

Infrastructure. There is extrahousehold infrastructure involved in almost every system. Irrigation and/or drainage systems will need construction and maintenance, roads and paths need work, and there may be communal facilities such as an assembly hall, a shrine, or a school that need labor. These tasks absorb some portion of household labor (or cash) and should be included.

Genetic Material. The aspect of agrarian systems most neglected by anthropologists is the genetic material available. Selection, storage, and propagation of genetic materials, and how these issues relate to productivity and surplus, are virtually never studied or reported in publication. It is, I suspect, a prime subject of local systematic knowledge, one that probably has profound impacts on levels of productivity and is deeply involved in decisionmaking. If so, it should bear heavily on the question of rationality, evolution, and the relations among population, technology, and food supply.

Technology. I prefer a broad definition of technology, including knowledge and practice as well as object. Detailed studies of technology are desirable. For most studies of agrarian systems, the barest fundamentals will do. Do they irrigate? Do they use traction animals? Do they add nutrients to a field? Do they rotate crops in fields? Do they interplant? These are easy to observe and report and do not need detailed investigations.

Information. There are probably many deep natural culture information systems having to do with agriculture. Soils, weather, behavior characteristics of genetic variation, pest behavior, properties of beasts of burden, and labor supervision are just some of the topics that are probably deeply developed in local culture. These have only begun to be explored and would be a very rich source of knowledge if plumbed in depth. Of major import for our purposes here are local systems of measurement in their agricultural systems. If these exist they should be noted.

Environment. The latitude, longitude, altitude, and topography of the study site should be reported. The climate is also of intense interest. From these factors one can usually deduce the natural vegetation if necessary. The difference between the natural and the actual vegetation cover is therefore of great interest, for it will tell us something about the degree of exploitation by man. In addition, it is always important to specify the main weather features for the years of the study. Freeman reported that 1949 was an exceptionally wet year for his Iban study and that in consequence there were several problems, including a bad burn (the slash was too wet) and the worst harvest in years, according to local opinion (1955). In consequence rice production and productivity were unusually low. Evaluating Iban agricultural productivity comparatively is improved with this opinion of that particular year's conditions. It would be best, of course, if the field report contained a measured account of the conditions for that year, combined with thirty-year averages. Wilken's chapter in this volume (Chapter 2) details what data are useful minima and how to derive other useful climatic indicators.

Equivalence

One of the major epistemological dilemmas of social science is the problem of conceptual equivalence across cultural boundaries. The dilemma goes under a variety of names, including relativism and comparability (cf. Hunt 1979, n.d.). Briefly, it is the problem of achieving comparability of concepts across cultural boundaries. The problem arises for several reasons, including translation from one language to another and contextualization of events, leading to the conclusion that things do not have the same meaning in different cultures.

Because a science requires identical meaning of concepts across boundaries, it follows that there cannot be a social science that depends upon such arbitrarily varying meanings. There is a great deal of literature that presents this point of view, from Winch (1958) to Leach (1968), Needham (1975), and Geertz (1984).

Conceptual equivalence is one of the most fundamental challenges to the idea of a social science, and if it cannot be resolved there is no point in trying to do systematic comparative work. In point of fact, a large number of people have argued for the other side, including notably Gellner (1985), Goodenough (1970) and Spiro (1984, 1986). Those of us who believe the struggle for social science is worthwhile deny that "cultural meanings" are the only human phenomena worth studying. For many, behavior is equally structured, equally produced by society and culture and observable with little reference to native meanings. The observation of the calories and grams of protein that a household consumes is not dependent upon native meanings (although what is defined as food, and when it may be eaten and with whom, is certainly strongly affected by native meanings).

The success of a comparative effort is dependent upon the creation of an unambiguous language of scientific observation, one that applies with equal validity to all the cases in the sample (Hunt n.d.). The problem for the comparativist, then, is to translate the measures in the several case studies to a common standard. A detailed example should make this clear. Derek

Freeman published an account of inputs and outputs for swidden rice agriculture among the Iban of Borneo (1955). He measured household consumption, household labor input, and household rice output. His account is still one of the most detailed in the literature and has appeared as a case in virtually every comparative study of agriculture since it appeared. Freeman reported his seed and crop results with the terms "gallon," "bushel," and "acre." Some comparative efforts have used bushels, pounds, and acres (e.g., Hanks 1972), but most have used the metric, or SI (Système International d'Unités), system of liters, kilograms, and hectares. Case study results that are not reported in SI terms must be transformed into this common measurement language if the purpose is comparison.

There is a source of error in the use of the Iban case (he measured with pints). Most have transformed Freeman's gallon and bushel measures into the SI system (kg/ha). However, the fact that gallon and bushel are polysemic, meaning one thing in England and another in the United States, has been ignored. The secondary analysts have for the most part been Americans and have used the American meanings of the terms. But Freeman assures me that he could not have been using American pints, gallons, and bushels (personal communication). He could only have been using Imperial dry measures, which are about 3 percent larger than the American ones. Therefore, past presentations of the Iban yields must be corrected to correspond with the Imperial measures in the original field report. It is absolutely essential that both case studies and comparative studies be very explicit about measurement procedures. If procedures and calculations are not presented in detail, it is very difficult to assess whether conceptual equivalence has been achieved.

The units of measure for a case study are a critical factor. Many case studies report in the local, native measures (*mou, rai, tang, almud,* etc.). If data are reported in local measures, the investigator must show how these relate to some universal standard, preferably SI. There are severe difficulties with native units of measure. As the discussion of measuring productivity in *Culture and Agriculture* has so clearly shown, native measures of length and area are not necessarily stable (cf. Moran 1986 and Chapter 1, this volume). Often the measure is for a day's work, and the area a farmer expects to be covered in one day's work varies with the task—a day's worth of clearing, planting, weeding, and harvesting may each represent different areas.

Some case studies use a native measure (cases from Thailand usually report in *rai* of land and *tang* of rice). The relation of the native measure to SI is usually stated in a footnote, and it is usually stated as an absolute (for example, a *tang* contains 20 liters of rice). If native measures are used, it is important to report how they were calibrated with some other (preferably SI) standard. Most researchers assume homogeneity of native measures of things; one or two cases are measured and reported as "typical." The case study should report *exactly* how many measures were used in the calibration and the results (that is, the variance).

In a systematic comparison, the only solution is to use a scientific measurement language (such as SI). The natural culture categories may need to be understood, but in no case will they be sufficient. Measurement in some universal framework is absolutely necessary.

In comparing measures of work, the comparative work is strengthened by great detail in the reporting of the individual case. Travel time from house to field and back should be measured if possible, and in any event the case study should specify whether or not travel time is included in work time. Swidden systems require a great deal of travel, whereas permanent field systems perhaps require less of it. Fragmented fields probably require more travel than consolidated fields. The only way the question can be settled is if the case studies present the details. If tool repair work is included in one case study and not in another, it makes a difference for the analysis of labor productivity, and the case studies should report in detail on what is measured and what is not. Otherwise distortions are introduced into the results because of the problem of comparability. No case study will be much affected by the choice of a particular standard. The comparative studies using data from several case studies, by contrast, are profoundly affected, and in the comparative context the problem must be addressed and resolved.

One dimension of measurement—the number of observations necessary to make an assertion—needs to be emphasized. The number of observations necessary to properly measure the phenomenon vary from very few (even one will do to establish the presence of irrigation) to very many. Some critical data require very large numbers of observations spread over many years (for example, climate) and therefore require that host country institutions make those observations. Some data are local in nature (such as presence of irrigation), and a single observation by the field-worker will suffice. Other variables require a single observation of each of the units (such as land per household, crop per household, animals per household), and a single-visit household survey will do the job admirably. If one is present at the appropriate time, that measure may be quick, easy, and unobtrusive. The local society may even measure it, accurately, in the everyday course of events.

Two critically important variables demand a very different strategy. Food consumption and work input occur in small bits on an everyday basis at the household level. These will vary enormously and possibly systematically over the course of a year, and memory recall is notoriously unreliable. They should be measured frequently (weekly is probably minimal) and usually directly.[3] Because these efforts are spread out over the whole year, the task is a daunting one, and these two are the least often measured, and the least well measured, of all of the centrally important variables. Special measuring procedures need to be set up for them. We do not always do a good job of preparing students for the effort needed to investigate and measure these two variables. Important as they are, they frequently are not researched or presented. But such ratios as labor productivity and surplus/scarcity depend absolutely upon one or both of them. (In Chapter 6, Dufour and Teufel review a range of ways to get at consumption issues.)

No field study has the perfect sampling procedure with perfect response rates; all field studies are incomplete. But any data brought back from the field and reported are of *some* use. It is far more productive for the growth of knowledge if the case report is explicit about what was done and what was left undone. With these details, the comparativist can make an informed judgment about the utility of a data point. As part of the effort to produce good social science, the procedures used for gathering data should be reported in the fullest possible way. This will have several effects. It will help the comparativist solve for equivalence. It will make the pre-field-work training of graduate students more informed about what has actually happened in the past. And it should spur discussion, and adoption, of improved methods in the future.

Estimating Uncertainty

Because no case study is perfect, no comparative study can be perfect, either. There is always some uncertainty associated with case or comparative results.[4] In evaluating any findings, it is essential to estimate the uncertainties. Case studies involve two sources of uncertainty: procedures in the field, and the reporting of procedures used in the field. It is frequently the case that full field procedures are not reported, and this is a major barrier to an evaluation of the uncertainties in the case.

The amount of measuring that takes place may vary considerably from one case to another. I will use as an example the amount of work effort that goes into rice agriculture. This is a subject of great interest and is central to the argument over how labor productivity relates to technology and development. The position taken by Carneiro, Boserup, and Sahlins is that the return to labor declines with development when one compares swidden with permanent field agriculture.

A precise count of labor inputs under various development conditions is necessary for resolution of the dispute. One way to test the Carneiro/Boserup position is to confine our analysis to the production of rice in Southeast Asia (to hold the crop and the macroregion constant) and then to compare how labor input varies with degree of development. There are case studies that specify whether the rice is grown under shifting, irrigation, transplanting, animal traction, water lifting, or other technology. These are easy to observe and are almost always reported. Measuring degree of development is thus easily done.

Measuring labor input, however, is much more difficult. Only a few studies present data on labor inputs, and they contain great variation in how the measures were taken and how they were reported. Komol Janlekha, an agricultural economist, studied the Thai village of Bang Chan for five years (1949–1953). He had some output measures on all 206 households, with more complete output measures on a sample of 104 households for four years, and his data on yields of rice were remarkably full and detailed (1955). His data on labor inputs, by contrast, were derived from one household for one year. He measured labor in half-hour increments and carefully separated the tasks, specifying whether it was household or other labor that performed them. The data were very detailed and very useful. He also specified the land area under rice cultivation and the rice output of that household. His labor sample was very small (one household, one year), but the details were so abundant that we can place that household in Bang Chan context. This was the household of a super farmer, cultivating 59 percent more land than the mean and achieving a yield 49 percent higher than the Bang Chan mean (1955:106). We are able to judge, then, that Janlekha's figures on labor input have a high internal validity but have a very uncertain relationship to the mean for Bang Chan. Further, we have no idea what the measure of dispersion of labor hours around the mean would look like. These data are useful to the comparativist, but only with several kinds of caution.

Derek Freeman wrote on Iban agriculture (1955). The Iban numbered several hundred thousand at the time of the study, scattered over many thousands of square kilometers. Freeman worked in one small area and intensively studied one longhouse of twenty-five households for nearly two years. He reported that the Iban were adamant about not allowing him to measure yields or fields; he also reported why and what he did about it. His sample for intensive study of labor, consumption, and yields included four of the households. Their yields were 14 percent higher than the mean he reported for the longhouse, so they were better farmers than the average. Their labor was measured in days (hours per day not specified), and Freeman kept track of it by agricultural task and by when it was performed. He did not tell us how he managed the task of measuring labor. Freeman's labor data come from a larger sample than those of Janlekha but are less detailed in a number of ways. The internal validity of his labor data is inferior to that of Janlekha's data.

Conklin reported summary labor figures for each task for both his swidden case (Hanunóo) and his study of a terraced irrigated system (Ifugao) in the Philippines (1957, 1980). He did not, however, tell us what his sample size was, how he measured the work inputs, or over what time period they were measured. His data may have been of very high quality, but he presented none of the details needed for estimates of uncertainty.

Moerman reported on labor inputs for a community in northern Thailand, where the technology included irrigation, water buffalo, and tractors (1968). He gave details on how he measured labor inputs. His village contained 114 residential units at the beginning of fieldwork, 121 at the end. At the beginning he chose, by means of a random sample, forty household units for detailed measuring (1968:198). Most labor tasks were estimated on a per-household basis by the author, based on observation and interview. Two tasks, transplanting and harvesting, were more directly measured. Transplanting labor data were gathered by an adolescent girl living in the Moerman household who went to the home fields of each residential unit in the sample each day, counting the number of workers and asking about varieties planted and the amount of seed. For harvesting data, an adolescent boy went each night to the household of each farmer who had completed harvesting that day and administered an interview (1968:200). Labor was measured in days (hours per day not specified). Households in the community had access to four different fields, each of which had a different crop mix and used different technologies, and Moerman kept track of much of this. His data are less uncertain than either Freeman's or Janleka's because of a larger sample size and greater specification of how the data were collected.

Durrenberger's presentation of data on labor inputs resulted in the least uncertainty (1978). He studied a Shan village in northern Thailand containing thirty-five households. Of those, seven cultivated only swidden, seven cultivated only irrigated rice, and nineteen cultivated with both techniques (two of the villages did not farm) (Durrenberger 1978:118). He kept track of the labor inputs for every kind of rice field for every household over a period of fifty-two weeks, with the data collected once a week. He specified how he collected data on each of his variables (1978:9–14). Internal validity and external validity were both very high. The amount of work Durrenberger did is truly monumental. The data were presented in tabular form in great detail, permitting reanalysis. This is the ideal way to publish the data from the comparativist's point of view.

The major purpose of the systematic comparative study is to confirm claims to knowledge. A major objective of such studies is to reduce the uncertainty associated with the claim. The fuller the reporting of the case study, the more legitimate is the comparativist's claim to reduced uncertainty.

Conclusions

In this chapter I have approached the problem of data sets from the point of view of a comparativist. The comparative approach differs significantly from the ethnographic one, and the differences should be kept in mind. Yet there are substantial areas of common interest. Most ethnographies are put in the context of some generalization, either past or potential. A systematic comparison is necessary for testing and confirming those generalizations and must use case studies in that test. How then can the case study be constructed so as to facilitate the subsequent comparative efforts?

Comparative studies are weakened by case studies that lack data on one or more critical variables, by case studies whose measures cannot be related to SI units, and by case studies whose measures and measurement procedures are not fully reported.

I have suggested that there is a core set of variables for three central and enduring intellectual issues and that every case study bearing on any of these major issues should be concerned with measuring the entirety of the minimal data set.

Conceptual equivalence is the central dilemma for social science. A case study can report in any measurement language, but for that case to be useful for comparative purposes there must be a way to transform the language of reporting into SI. Again, full reporting of field procedures is highly important.

Finally, it is important for the comparativist to estimate the uncertainty of the field reports in order to estimate the uncertainty in the comparative analysis. Full reporting of procedures and of results greatly enhances our ability to make that estimate and thereby to plan future work.

Notes

Several granting agencies have supported the theoretical, methodical, and substantive work that made this chapter possible. I hereby gratefully acknowledge support from NIMH for two small grants from 1968 to 1971 and ACLS for a fellowship in 1975–1976 and NSF Grant BNS 9011704 for 1990 to 1993. In addition, Emilio Moran's editorial hand has been light but sure.

1. Such a series can be seen in Carneiro (1961), Boserup (1965), Hanks (1972), Bronson (1972), Pimentel and Pimentel (1979), Bayliss-Smith (1982), Ellen (1982), and Netting (1993). A major issue in all of these studies has been the relationship of level of intensification of agriculture, agricultural productivity, and level of development. Another and much briefer series exists for the topic of irrigation social organization, where a central issue has been size and centralization: Wittfogel (1957), Millon (1962), Kappel (1974), Hunt and Hunt (1976), Uphoff (1986) and Hunt (1988).

2. Little (1989) is a thorough and stimulating review of much of this literature.

3. Stuart (1990) is an elegant argument and solution.

4. A significant part of work in science is finding and removing uncertainty. Discovery work is unroutinized and cannot be directed or planned very well. Confirmation work is just as important as discovery but can be routinized and planned. It is in the confirmation work that the uncertainty *must* be identified and reduced.

References

Bayliss-Smith, T. P., 1982. Energy use, food production and welfare: Perspectives on the efficiency of agricultural systems. In G. A. Harrison, ed., *Energy and Effort*, pp. 283–303. Basingstoke: Taylor and Francis.

Boserup, Ester, 1965. *The Conditions of Agricultural Growth*. Chicago: Aldine.

Bradley, Candace, 1989. Reliability and inference in the cross-cultural coding process. *Journal of Quantitative Anthropology* 1:353–371.

Bronson, Bennet, 1972. Farm labor and the evolution of food production. In B. Spooner, ed., *Population Growth*, pp. 190–218. Cambridge: MIT Press.

Brookfield, H.C., 1972. Intensification and disintensification in Pacific agriculture. *Pacific Viewpoint* 13:30–48.

Campbell, Donald T., and Julian Stanley, 1963. *Experimental and Quasi-Experimental Designs for Research*. Boston: Houghton Mifflin.

Carneiro, Robert, 1961. Slash-and-burn cultivation among the Kuikuru and its implications for cultural development in the Amazon. In J. Wilbert, ed., *The Evolution of Horticultural Systems in Native North America*, pp. 47–67.

Conklin, Harold, 1957. *Hanunóo Agriculture*. Rome: FAO.

———, 1980. *Ethnographic Atlas of Ifugao*. New Haven: Yale University Press.

Dumond, Don, 1961. Swidden agriculture and the rise of Maya civilization. *Southwestern Journal of Anthropology* 17:301–316.

Durrenberger, E. Paul, 1978. *Agricultural Production and Household Budgets in a Shan Peasant Village in Northwestern Thailand: A Quantitative Description*. Southeast Asia Studies No. 49. Athens, OH: Ohio University Center for International Studies, Southeast Asia Program.

Edgerton, Robert, 1971. *The Individual in Cultural Adaptation: A Study of Four East African Peoples*. Berkeley: University of California Press.

Ellen, Roy, 1982. *Environment, Subsistence and Systems. The Ecology of Small-Scale Social Formations*. Cambridge: Cambridge University Press.

Ember, Carol R., and David Levinson, 1991. The substantive contributions of worldwide cross-cultural studies using secondary data. *Cross-Cultural and Comparative Research: Theory and Method*. Special Issue, *Behavior Science Research* 25:79–140.

Ember, Melvin, and Keith F. Otterbein, 1991. Sampling in cross-cultural research. *Cross-Cultural and Comparative Research: Theory and Method*. Special Issue, *Behavior Science Research* 25:217–233.

Epstein, T. Scarlett, 1962. *Economic Development and Social Change in South India*. Manchester: Manchester University Press.

Freeman, J. Derek, 1955. *Iban Agriculture*. London: Her Majesty's Stationary Office. Reprinted by AMS.

Geertz, Clifford, 1984. Anti-anti-relativism. *American Anthropologist* 86:263–278.

Gellner, Ernest, 1985. *Relativism and the Social Sciences.* Cambridge: Cambridge University Press.

Goodenough, Ward H., 1970. *Description and Comparison.* Chicago: Aldine.

Hanks, Lucien, 1972. *Rice and Man.* Chicago: Aldine.

Hardin, Garret, 1968. The tragedy of the commons. *Science* 162:1243–1248.

Hayami, Yujiro, and Vernon W. Ruttan, 1985. *Agricultural Development,* second edition. Baltimore: Johns Hopkins University Press.

Hunt, Robert C., 1979. *The Comparative Study of Irrigation Social Organization.* Cornell Rural Sociology Monographs No. 98. Ithaca: Cornell University.

———, 1988. Size and the organization of authority. *Journal of Anthropological Research* 44:335–356.

———, n.d. Apples and oranges. Unpublished manuscript.

Hunt, Robert C., and Eva V. Hunt, 1976. Canal irrigation and local social organization. *Current Anthropology* 17:389–411.

Janlekha, Kamol Odd, 1955. *A Study of the Economy of a Rice Growing Village in Central Thailand.* Bangkok: Ministry of Agriculture, Division of Agricultural Economics.

Kaplan, David, and Robert Manners, 1972. *Culture Theory.* Englewood Cliffs, NJ: Prentice-Hall.

Kappel, William, 1974. Irrigation development and population pressure. In T. Downing and M. Gibson, eds., *Irrigation's Impact on Society,* pp. 159–168. Tucson: University of Arizona Press.

Leach, Edmund, 1968. The comparative method in anthropology. In E. Shills, ed., *International Encyclopaedia of the Social Sciences,* vol. 1:339–345. London: Macmillan.

Levinson, David, and Martin J. Malone, 1980. *Toward Explaining Human Culture.* New Haven: HRAF Press.

Lewis, Oscar, 1956. Comparisons in cultural anthropology. In W. L. Thomas, ed., *Current Anthropology: A Supplement to Anthropology Today,* pp. 259–292. Chicago: University of Chicago Press.

Little, Daniel, 1989. *Understanding Peasant China: Case Studies in the Philosophy of Science.* New Haven: Yale University Press.

Malthus, Thomas Robert, 1798. *An Essay on Population,* G. Himelfarb, ed. New York: Random House (Modern Library, 1960).

Marsh, Robert, 1967. *Comparative Sociology.* New York: Harcourt Brace and World.

Millon, Rene, 1962. Variations in social response to the practice of irrigated agriculture. In R. W. Woodbury, ed., *Civilizations in Desert Lands,* pp. 56–88. Salt Lake City: University of Utah, Papers in Anthropology 62.

Minturn, Leigh, and William Lambert, eds., 1964. *Mothers in Six Cultures.* New York: John Wiley.

Moerman, Michael, 1968. *Agricultural Change and Peasant Choice in a Thai Village.* Berkeley: University of California Press.

Moran, Emilio, 1986. Comment on "Weights and measures and swiddens." *Culture and Agriculture* 29.

Munroe, Robert L., and Ruth H. Munroe, 1991. Results of comparative field studies. *Cross-Cultural and Comparative Research: Theory and Method.* Special Issue, *Behavior Science Research* 25:23–54.

Naroll, Raoul, 1970. What have we learned from cross-cultural surveys? *American Anthropologist* 72:1227–1288.

Naroll, Raoul, and Ronald Cohen, eds., 1970. *A Handbook for the Study of Cultural Anthropology.* New York: Columbia University Press.

Needham, Rodney, 1975. Polythetic classification: Convergence and consequences. *Man* 10:349–369.

Netting, Robert McC., 1989. Smallholders, householders, freeholders: Why the family farm works well worldwide. In R. Wilk, ed., *The Household Economy: The Domestic Mode of Production Reconsidered*, pp. 221–244. Boulder, CO: Westview Press.

———, 1993. *Smallholders, Householders: Farm Families and the Ecology of Intensive, Sustainable Agriculture.* Berkeley: University of California Press.

Pimentel, David, and Marcia Pimentel, 1979. *Food Energy and Society.* London: Edward Arnold.

Popkin, Samuel L., 1979. *The Rational Peasant.* Berkeley: University of California Press.

Sahlins, Marshall, 1972. *Stone Age Economics.* Chicago: Aldine.

Schultz, Theodore, 1964. *Transforming Traditional Agriculture.* New Haven: Yale University Press.

Scott, James C., 1976. *The Moral Economy of the Peasant.* New Haven: Yale University Press.

Smelser, Neil, 1976. *Comparative Methods in the Social Sciences.* Englewood Cliffs, NJ: Prentice-Hall.

Smith, Adam, 1776. *An Inquiry into the Nature and Causes of the Wealth of Nations*, E. Cannan, ed. Chicago: University of Chicago Press.

Spiro, Melford, 1984. Some reflections on cultural determinism and relativism with special reference to meaning and emotion. In R. Shweder and R. LeVine, eds., *Culture Theory*, pp. 323–346. Cambridge: Cambridge University Press.

———, 1986. Cultural anthropology and the future of anthropology. *American Anthropologist* 1:259–286.

Stuart, James W., 1990. Maize use by rural Mesoamerican households. *Human Organization* 49:135–139.

Textor, Robert B., 1967. *A Cross-Cultural Summary.* New Haven: HRAF Press.

Uphoff, Norman, 1986. *Getting the Process Right.* Boulder, CO: Westview Press.

Whiting, Bea, ed., 1963. *Six Cultures: Studies of Child Rearing.* New York: John Wiley and Sons.

Whiting, Bea, and John W. M. Whiting, 1975. *Children of Six Cultures: A Psycho-Cultural Analysis.* Cambridge: Harvard University Press.

Winch, Peter, 1958. *The Idea of a Social Science.* London: Routledge and Kegan Paul.

Wittfogel, Karl, 1957. *Oriental Despotism.* New Haven: Yale University Press.

Index

About the Contributors

Darna L. Dufour is associate professor in the Department of Anthropology at the University of Colorado at Boulder. Her research interests focus on the biological and behavioral responses of human populations to nutritional problems, with special emphasis on responses to food shortages and the presence of toxins in foods. She is currently conducting research on the diet of economically disadvantaged urban women in Latin America. Among her recent publications are "People and the Tropical Rainforest of Amazonia," *BioScience* and "The Bitter Is Sweet: A Case Study of Bitter Cassava (*Manihot Esculenta*) Use in Amazonia" in *Food and Nutrition in the Tropical Rainforest: Biocultural Interactions,* edited by M. Hladik et al.

Millicent Fleming-Moran is an epidemiologist with the Regenstrief Institute for Health Care in Indianapolis. She has carried out field research in Brazil and the United States. Among her recent publications are "Blood Pressure Studies Among Amazonian Native Populations: A Review from an Epidemiological Perspective," *Social Science and Medicine* and "The Folk View of Natural Causation and Disease in Brazil," *Boletim do Museu Goeldi.*

Warren M. Hern is a physician and epidemiologist and adjunct associate professor in the Department of Anthropology, University of Colorado at Boulder. He has conducted epidemiologic, demographic, and anthropologic research among the Shipibo Indians of the Peruvian Amazon since 1964. His numerous articles have appeared in *Human Organization, American Ethnologist,* and population journals.

Robert C. Hunt has taught anthropology at Northwestern, the University of Illinois at Chicago, and at Brandeis University, where he is currently professor. He has been president of the Society for Economic Anthropology (1993–1994). He has conducted field research in Mexico (the Cuicatec area) and has been studying irrigation and agricultural productivity comparison since 1976. He is currently interested in irrigation, agricultural development, and the methodology of comparison.

Emilio F. Moran is professor of anthropology, professor in the School for Public and Environmental Affairs, and director of the Anthropological Center for Training and Research on Global Environmental Change (ACT) at Indiana University, Bloomington. He is a specialist in ecological anthropology, resource management, and agricultural systems in the humid and dry tropics. He is the author of *Human Adaptability: An Introduction to Ecological Anthropology, Developing the Amazon,* and *Through Amazonian Eyes: The Human Ecology of Amazonian Populations.*

Robert McC. Netting is Regents' Professor of Anthropology at the University of Arizona at Tucson and an elected member of the National Academy of Science. He is a specialist in cultural ecology, social organization, and historical demography. His most recent book is *Smallholders, Householders: Farm Families and the Ecology of Intensive, Sustainable Agriculture.*

John J. Nicholaides III has served, since 1985, as director of international agriculture, associate dean of the College of Agriculture, and assistant vice chancellor for research at the University of Illinois at Urbana-Champaign. From 1988 through 1989 he was chairman of the U.S. National Joint Committee for Agricultural Research and Development of the presidentially appointed Board of International Food and Agriculture Development. He is chairman of the board of the Agronomic Science Foundation. Previous research, published in *Science* and other major journals, with his colleagues and graduate students at North Carolina State University, focused on making previously cleared land in the Amazon rainforest continually agriculturally productive.

Glenn D. Stone is associate professor of anthropology at Columbia University. His principal research interests are in agricultural systems, both past and present, and their spatial and social organization. He has done archaeological work in North America and ethnoarchaeological work in Nigeria with the Kofyar and recently with the Tiv. His book *Settlement Ecology: The Spatial and Social Organization of Kofyar Agriculture* is forthcoming. His recent publications include "Agricultural Abandonment: A Comparative Study in Historical Ecology" in *Abandonment of Settlements and Regions: Ethnoarchaeological and Archaeological Approaches,* edited by C. Cameron and S. Tomka and "Social Distance, Spatial Relations, and Agricultural Production Among the Kofyar of Namu District, Plateau State, Nigeria," *Journal of Anthropological Archaeology.*

M. Priscilla Stone is currently director, Program on African Studies at the Social Science Research Council. Her principal research interests include processes of economic and agrarian change in Africa with a more specific focus on the organization of labor, especially the sexual division of labor, in farming systems. Her most recent publications include a volume she edited with Lourdes Arizpe and David Major entitled *Population and Environment: Rethinking the Debate.* A forthcoming article in *American Ethnologist* co-authored with Glenn Stone and Robert Netting is entitled "The Sexual Division of Labor in Kofyar Agriculture."

Nicolette I. Teufel is assistant research professor in the Department of Family and Community Medicine at the University of Arizona. Her research interests focus on the relationship between diet, activity, and health among Native American populations of the Southwest. Currently she is involved in the development and validation of culturally competent dietary assessment tools for use with the Zuni Indians of New Mexico and the Hopi and White Mountain Apache Indians of Arizona. Among her publications are "Patterns of Food Use and Nutrient Intake of Obese and Non-Obese Hualapai Women of Arizona," *Journal of the American Dietetic Association* with D. Dufour and "Diet and Activity Patterns of Male and Female Co-Workers: Should Worksite Health Promotion Program Assume Homogeneity?" *Women and Health.*

Lillian Trager is professor of anthropology and director of the Center for International Studies at the University of Wisconsin–Parkside. Her research in Nigeria and the Philippines has focused on markets and market traders, the informal economy, migration, and rural-urban linkages. From 1985–1987 she was program officer and assistant representative in the Ford Foundation's West African office. In recent work she has been increasingly interested in local-level and indigenous approaches to development. Recent publications include *The City Connection: Migration and Family Interdependence in the Philippines;* "A Re-examination of the Urban Informal Sector in West Africa," *Canadian Journal of African Studies;* and "New Women's Organization in Nigeria: One Response to Structural Adjustment" in *Structural Adjustment and African Women Farmers,* edited by Christina H. Gladwin.

Gene C. Wilken has been professor of geography at Colorado State University and served as AID officer in Barbados until 1993. He is the author of *Good Farmers: Traditional Agricultural Resource Management in Mexico and Central America* and numerous journal articles on land use, climate, and environmental geography.

About the Book and Editor

In this era of globalization, the social sciences—including anthropology—are severely limited by a lack of agreement on methods and, particularly, on commonly accepted standards for data collection and presentation. This book addresses questions central to the problem: What units are most useful in explaining a social system's structure and function? How does a particular study relate to other studies on a given region, or country, or ecosystem? What is the relationship between ecological/physical and social variables? How do we choose from among alternative measures and protocols?

Each chapter evaluates a group of alternative measures that have been used and then proposes canons, or standards, that could apply. The authors have worked to ensure that these standards facilitate a return by both qualitative and quantitative researchers to the comparative analysis of human societies.

Emilio F. Moran is professor of anthropology, professor in the School for Public and Environmental Affairs, and director of the Anthropological Center for Training and Research on Global Environmental Change (ACT) at Indiana University, Bloomington. He is a specialist in ecological anthropology, resource management, and agricultural systems in the humid and dry tropics. He is the author of *Human Adaptability: An Introduction to Ecological Anthropology, Developing the Amazon,* and *Through Amazonian Eyes: The Human Ecology of Amazonian Populations.*